A treasured gift
from Robert & Deb
on my 91st Birthday
Grandad Lew.
x x

19th 11th 1992

WORCESTERSHIRE'S HIDDEN PAST

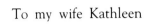

To my wife Kathleen

Worcestershire's Hidden Past

by

Bill Gwilliam

Halfshire Books

HALFSHIRE BOOKS
6 High Street, Bromsgrove
Worcestershire B61 8HQ

First published in Great Britain
by Halfshire Books 1991

ISBN 0 9513525 5 5

Typeset in Great Britain by Action Typesetting Ltd,
Gloucester, and printed in Great Britain by
Billing & Sons Limited, Worcester

Contents

Foreword
by Henry Sandon

WHEN I CAME to Worcestershire in 1953 it seemed such a peaceful and pleasant area compared to London and I rushed around looking for the places that I had read about in A E Housman's poems. So I climbed up Bredon Hill and looked across Worcestershire, which seemed transparently easy to comprehend after the packed history of London, where every street, every house seemed to have been the place where some famous person had lived or some dirty deed done. Nothing like that could have happened in these new idyllic surroundings, surely?

I was wrong, of course, and it was my dear friend Bill Gwilliam who opened my eyes. Every village, every corner of a field had a story to tell, and tell it Bill did, in his inimitable way that made you feel that he had known the perpetrators and been present at the actual event. I realised that he could not have been, of course, but like the great story tellers of folk legends he has that ability to make you believe and feel that you were really there.

Like so many people, I have devoured his stories about the City of Worcester and its fascinating characters and history. Now Bill has turned his attention to the wider County of Worcestershire and you will be able to read about some of the more unusual aspects of the county's rich and varied history — England's greatest tragic actress, the fate of the eighteenth-century hedgehog, the publican who sold ale by weight and the yard, the screaming women of Bewdley, the old lampern industry, the flying pear trees, the fall of the house of Foley. Do you know what 'lambswool' and 'wobble' were? Ever wondered what a 'fogger' did? You will wonder no longer when you have read this book and it is so nice to have been invited to write this foreword.

Henry Sandon

CHAPTER ONE

Places

Shout, oh ye winds, across the Severn plain,
Shout, for a son comes home to you again!
Long wandered I, I sought the Sussex weald,
And marked what crops the Devon red-land yield,
In Surrey lanes I found the primrose shy,
From Cornish coast I watched the ships go by;
And Kentish cherry trees I saw o'er-snowed,
And trod the broad outsketched East Anglia road.
From Lincoln fens and Yorkshire moors I sped
To see the English lakes encircled,
By brooding hills, and in the Midland drear,
I sought for truant beauty half the year;
And now, and now, my own familiar hill
Shows green above my morning window sill;
And Malvern hides in shadows blue and deep,
And Cotswold lies in sunshine half asleep.
Shout, oh ye winds, across the Severn plain,
Shout, for my heart comes home to you again!
(Dorothy Thody)

Introduction

THROUGHOUT THE CENTURIES writers from William Langland to Francis Brett Young have sung the praises of Worcestershire, seeking to express through the written word their feelings for this Severn country and its strong turbulent streams; for the land owes its richness, its towns, its very history to the great River Severn.

Yet it was not a poet but a politician who sang most the praises of Worcestershire. Stanley Baldwin, though three times Prime Minister, remained a Worcestershire countryman. 'There is something in the light on the hills, something in the transparent light of the hills themselves, something of the colour of the river at home, the colour and smell of the soil, that calls men and women as they grow older back to their native homes. One knows in one's bones that one is a Worcestershire man, and there is nothing like it. One came out of this red soil, and one will return to it and lay one's bones in it, and there is no soil like it in this country.'

Such adoration of the soil is not uncommon in this county. M I Tiltman wrote: 'A farmer with whom I was staying in Worcestershire picked up a handful of red earth. It was, I could see, very good earth indeed (the old Worcestershire sandstone crumbled into easy friable loam), but I was somewhat surprised when he held it to his lips before tossing it in the air, crying rapturously as he did so: "Ah, that soil would give an angel wings, let alone fruit to a plum tree!"'

The River Severn

THREE SISTERS

> Many years ago, when the world was much younger than it is today, three sisters, all water sprites, met on the water-logged summit of Plynlimmon. They were anxious to reach the sea, and discussed the best course to take to reach their goal. Said the first, 'I shall take the shortest road', and, facing west towards the waves which gleamed in the distance, she raced downwards at headlong speed. That was the Ystwith. The second said, 'I shall take my course through the finest scenes', and so saying she turned south-east, flowing between the purple hills and through golden valleys. That was the Wye. The third sister watched her sisters and smiled. 'My way', she said, 'shall be past the fairest cities of the kingdom', and, facing the rising sun, she wandered to and fro seeking, never far from the haunts of men, and beautifying and adorning all his works. That was the Severn.

Such is the ancient folk tale, but like most fables it holds more than a grain of truth as all who know the Severn must acknowledge. Her love for Shrewsbury is such that she is loathe to tear herself away. Almost she has made an island of the age-old city. Then circling the Wrekin, and making her way past Buildwas Abbey and the mighty furnaces of Coalbrookdale, she reaches Bridgnorth. Onwards she goes, past Bewdley's quays, under Telford's bridges to where Wulstan's great cathedral stands sentinel above Worcester's cricket field, and before she reaches Gloucester she has seen Tewkesbury and Deerhurst and a hundred waterside villages, each of which is the more beautiful for her passing.

Thomas Habington considered the Severn to be 'the greatest water ornament and prodigal benefactor of our County'. F W Harvey, a Gloucester man, described it more lovingly in a poem called 'Near Midsummer'. He wrote it when home on leave from the trenches in the First World War:

> *Severn's most fair today!*
> *See what a tide of blue*
> *She pours, and flecked always*
> *With gold, and what a crew*
> *Of seagulls, snowy white,*
> *Float round her to delight*
> *Villagers, travellers.*

A brown thick flood is hers
In winter when the rains
Wash down from Midland plains
Halting wayfarers.
Low meadows flooding deep
With torrents from the steep
Mountains of Wales and small
Hillocks of no degree —
Streams jostling to the sea;
(Wrangling yet brotherly).

Blue June has altered all
The river makes its fall
With murmurous still sound . . .
Strong Severn, all aglow,
But tideless running slow:
Far Cotswolds all a-shimmer,
Blue Bredon leagues away —
Huge Malverns, farther, dimmer . . .
Then you would feel the fire
Of the first days inspire,
There would flood through again
The old faith, the old prides
Wherein our fathers died,
Whereby our land was builded and dignified.

THE SEVERN AND WORCESTER

Worcester, like all the towns on the Severn, owes its beginnings and development to the river. The river's famous tidal bore allowed the city to become a flourishing inland port and only after the coming of the railway did Worcester's life and prosperity cease to be tied to the waterway, once known as 'The King's High Stream of Severn', along which all vessels could pass freely. Today the Severn is deserted of all commercial traffic. Yet a hundred and fifty years ago it was one of the greatest commercial highways in the world, for upstream it had cradled the Industrial Revolution. For centuries the Severn had led the Roman, Saxon, Dane and Norman into the very heart of England. The Romans have left their great field of iron slag from nearly three hundred years of bloomery workings stretching from Broad Street to Pitchcroft. The Saxons used Bevere Island as a sanctuary from Hathacanute. The Danes raided, looted and destroyed the city, and at least one left his skin nailed to the cathedral door. The Normans carried their Caen stone for the cathedral up with the tide. The river was the direct route for pestilence, too, for the Black Death and the 1637 plague were brought to the city by Bristol trowmen. Press gangs and smugglers roamed the city quays and watermen's taverns.

From the late sixteenth century the Severn was the great iron and coal river: every tributary had its forges and furnaces, and Worcester became a centre for the arms trade in the Civil War period. The first iron bridge at Ironbridge encouraged the employment of Telford to build iron bridges at Holt and at the Mythe, and the plans and finances were laid at Worcester. Down the river came the great cylinders for Watt's Cornish steam engines; cannon in large numbers for use in the French and American wars was carried down; and Trevithick's locomotive 'Catch-me-who-can' floated down under Worcester Bridge twenty years before 'The Rocket' was built. Some idea of the relative importance of Worcester in the distribution of coal can be gathered from the fact that out of the government's eighteen river coal-tax collectors in the eighteenth century seven were stationed at Worcester — by far the largest number anywhere. River traffic in pottery from the kilns of Worcester, Broseley and Coalport was considerable, much of the latter coming down river for decorating at Worcester.

Great changes have taken place since the mid-nineteenth century. The trade has gone from the river, but the pleasure craft have taken over for the beauty of the Severn remains.

The S S Atalanta unloading at the South Quay, Worcester, in 1900, the last vessel to dock direct from the coast.

A VIEW OF WORCESTER IN 1673

The river featured prominently in Thomas Baskerville's description of Worcester from his travels in 1673:

> The way to this city is a reddish earth, and very bad for travellers in winter, so that for the benefit of horsemen in dirty weather, they have made a causeway extending some miles from the town. As touching the city of Worcester, I think 'tis bigger than Oxford, and very full of people, but the streets, excepting that running through the city to the bridge, and another thwarting the upper end of this street, are narrow, and of old decayed buildings.
>
> Here are twelve or thirteen churches, with that on the other side of the Severn to which a fair bridge, with six large arches big enough for hoys to pass under, gives passage. This river is navigable for these kinds of vessels to Shrewsbury and further, and from those parts they bring down abundance of coal to serve the city and other places beneath it, and from Bristol they bring merchantable goods up stream again to serve these parts. Along the banks of the Severn here, which is well-nigh a bow-shot over, running with a nimble clear current, are large fertile meadows, but that which is most remarkable as touching ingenuity, on the shore of the town side, is a waterwork, which, . . . having a wheel which gives motion to suckers and forcers, (it) pumps the water so high into a leaden cistern, that it serves any part of the city. Nevertheless, that water may be more plentiful, they have horses also at work to force up the water, and here also, which I have nowhere else seen, save in the city of Ely, they fetch water from the river upon horses in leathern bags, to sell.

The Malverns

Worcestershire's most conspicuous physical features — the Severn, the Malvern Hills and Bredon Hill — have all been subjects for the poet's pen, none more so than the Malverns, that nine-mile chain of bold and shapely peaks that rises straight out of the Severn plain. Those hills and the land around them have been sung about ever since there were poets to sing. It was here that in the fourteenth century William Langland dreamed his dream of Piers the Plowman; where six hundred years later John Masefield, a Ledbury man, sang of 'the hearty land where I was bred, my land of heart's desire':

> *Then, hey for the covert and woodland, and ash, and elm, and oak,*
> *Tewkesbury inns, and Malvern roofs, and Worcester's chimney smoke,*
> *The apple tree in the orchard, the cattle in the byre*
> *And all the land from Ludlow town to Bredon church's spire.*

In between these two writers there have been many more eulogists. 'I esteem it', said John Evelyn, the seventeenth-century diarist, 'one of the goodliest vistas in England', and even the bluff Cobbett was struck by 'these curious bubblings up! No foothills, mark you, such as you find in the Chilterns, but a sudden heave upwards.'

Lord Byron saw them when a boy of fourteen and later recalled: 'I can never forget the effect, a few years afterwards in England, of the only thing I had seen, even in miniature, of a mountain, in the Malvern Hills. After I returned to Cheltenham, I used to watch them every afternoon, at sunset, with a sensation which I cannot describe.'

It was here, on the west side of the hills, at Colwall, that Elizabeth Barrett Browning lived most of her young life in a house, Hope End, which her father had converted into an exotic 'turkish house'. In 1832 she wrote in her diary: 'We walked thro' the rocky passage and sate down upon the Worcestershire side of the hills. Such a sight, such a sea of land; the sunshine throwing its light and the clouds their shadows upon it. I looked on each side of the elevated place where I sate. Herefordshire all hill and wood – undulating and broken – Worcestershire throwing out a grand unbroken prospect, and more than Worcestershire to the horizon. One prospect attracting the eye by picturesqueness; the other the mind, the sublimity.'

Getting over the Malverns: a group of 'donkey women' at Malvern c1870 (A Bedford stereo photograph).

She was three when she arrived at Hope End and twenty-six when the house was sold; and, despite the fall from her pony that crippled her for so long, afterwards declared that the years spent there were amongst the happiest of her life. She never wished to return however – it would be like putting a dead flower back on its stem, she said, and expecting it to grow again. Sadly, Hope End was allowed to fall into ruinous disrepair earlier in this century.

'The scenery of those beautiful hills', wrote a visitor in 1860, 'laid a strong hand upon me, whether in snow, mist or sunshine, the views to the west over Herefordshire to the hills of Radnor and Brecon, or east over the rich vale of Severn to Bredon Hill, or on to where Cheltenham stood, a glittering row of white . . . filled my heart with delight, and stored it with impressions never to be forgotten.' Much later Hilaire Belloc wrote: 'I do not know what it is but the view of the jagged Malverns seen above the happy mists of autumn, when these mists lie like a warm fleece upon the orchards of the vale, preserving them of a morning until the strengthening of the sun, the sudden aspect, I say, of those jagged peaks strikes one like a vision of a new world. How many men have thought it! How often it ought to be written down! It hangs in the memory of the traveller like a permanent benediction, and remains in his mind a standing symbol of peace.'

From the Malvern top the valleys of the Severn and Wye unfold their huge flat expanses of meadow, wood and ploughland, fat and pleasant; and it was the splendour of the view, not so greatly changed since Langland, Evelyn and Byron stood and marvelled at its beauty, that inspired John Drinkwater's Malvern lyrics:

> *Cool where the clean winds travel*
> *Along the solemn hills,*
> *We watch the flowering splendour*
> *That summer brews and spills,*
> *From Malvern down to Bredon*
> *Across the mellow plain,*
> *Transfiguring the lowlands*
> *Of shining leaves and grain.*
>
> *Above the black pine-shadows*
> *We dream beneath the sky,*
> *And watch the far-off valleys*
> *Of Severn and of Wye,*
> *And see the white clouds walking*
> *The great blue road that spans*
> *The world from Wales to Cotswold,*
> *Like ghostly caravans.*

It is a land that calls its sons back from afar, that set F W Harvey looking for his homeland during the dark days of the First World War:

> *I'm homesick for my hills again —*
>   *My hills again!*
> *To see above the Severn plain*
> *Unscabarded against the sky*
> *The blue, high blade of Cotswold lie,*
> *The giant clouds go royally*
> *By jagged Malvern with a train*
> *Of shadows. Where the land is low*
> *Like a huge imprisoning O,*

I hear a heart that's sound and high,
I hear the heart within me cry:
I'm homesick for my hills again —
My hills again!
Cotswold or Malvern, sun or rain!
My hills again!

The same call brought Edward Elgar back to write his sweetest songs, and something of the grandeur and beauty of the hills has found its way into his music which forever speaks of Worcestershire.

Sketch of Rev S P Lockett's Sunday and Day School teachers ascending the Worcestershire Beacon c1870.

The Red Earl's Dyke

On the Malvern Hills are two ancient Iron-Age hill forts: the Herefordshire Beacon, a triple entrenchment usually called British Camp, and Midsummer Hill; and ranging the whole length of the hills are the remains of the Red Earl's Dyke which marks the boundary between the two counties that are now one. This resulted from a great lawsuit about forest rights brought by Thomas de Cantelupe, Bishop of Hereford, in March 1278, against Gilbert de Clare, feudal lord of Upton and the Chase and Earl of Gloucester — the Red Earl. The bishop won the lawsuit, but the earl avenged himself by digging a ditch and building a palisade along the top of the hills to mark the boundary between the two chases, his own on the east and the bishop's (smaller) on the west. So artfully was the fence contrived that the bishop's deer could — and did — leap down into the earl's chase, but not back into the bishop's. Time has, however, changed this. The earl's deer have long disappeared, but the descendants of the bishop's deer still wander peacefully in the deer park of Eastnor Castle.

Bredon on a January morning

In January 1924 the *Times* carried an article of rare charm, of the picturesque scene from the top of Bredon Hill on a typical January morning:

> To one who climbs through the clustering underwoods of its lower slopes — stout-timbered chestnuts, unconquerable oaks, and spangled birches — to the brow of some lofty promontory like that of Bredon Hill, and looks down from its turfed ramparts, there must instinctively and inevitably come some sense of aerial, almost divine detachment.
>
> Here, some thousand feet or so above sea level, near the old 'Roman' earthworks and the mystic monolith of the Bambury Stone, the stimulant of the climb and the cold refreshing winter wind clear the brain from all lesser pre-occupations, which merely seemed typified by the dull stagnant smoke which rises like an exhalation from the towns and hamlets huddled here and there below, revealed for a moment by the pallid finger of a sunbeam, and then obscured by the sad, sudden veiling of a distant shower.
>
> Behind rolls the wide plateau of the grassy hill, quiet but for the piping wind, and noiseless but for the scutter of rabbits in the broad gashes of a crumbling quarry and the bicker of crows on the swarded summit levels. The amazing scope of visibility, the all-pervading peace, the solidity of the immediate foreground in contrast with the impalpable remoteness of the distance, exaggerate the aloofness of the altitude and suggest the illusion of some gigantic georama.
>
> Beneath the ashen canopy of a fretful January sky, the carpet of A E Housman's 'coloured counties' lies unrolled round the hill, its pattern of frosty grey woodland, rimed tilth and emerald meadow shot through with the broad silver arabesque of the encompassing Avon. The drifting sunshine, governed by the capricious movement of great mournful clouds, lights up successively, like the torch of some celestial guide, the winding and twisting ribbons of road and river, the puny activity of diminutive railway traffic, and the old storied towns and cities of the vale where fights and sieges made the sad history of England's two calamitous civil wars. . . .
>
> Tiny half-timbered villages cluster round its foot like frightened children round their mothers' skirts — Great Comberton, whose parson in 1622 was Shakespeare's friend and legatee of £5 in his will; ghost-haunted Ashton, where walked the wraith of Benedict the robber-monk, and the banshee-like 'White Lady' who flitted keening through its winding street and round its fifteenth-century village cross, and where the spectre of its hard-riding, harder-drinking Georgian squire used to spur his grizzly hunter across the fields on stormy winter nights like Wotan in the Schwarzwald; much painted Elmley Castle, where Moore the Yeoman lived, who saved King Charles from the Ironsides after Worcester fight; and Bredon, where a non-juror Bishop lay hid for years in a priest's hole above the church's porch, hard by an outside piscina used during the plague and a muralled tomb where rests the heart of a Crusader. . . .

And on a January morning, to the reflective observer who stands on Bredon's top, the frost delineates in sparkling tinsel the veritable setting of all these bygone dramas, and the cold, pale limelight of the winter sun discloses their spacious scenery and faintly gilds the little time-worn spires which guard the unheeded graves of their forgotten actors.

The Valley of the Teme

In the wild land west of Severn the Teme, that Brett Young called 'Severn's wild daughter — a wayward child', winds through the old borderland of Wales and England. All around, memories of old wars and sudden raids still hang on the deep woods and fat meadows, where old farmsteads and ancient churches stand atop of hills like fortresses, ready to give warning of raids.

Today, unspoilt peace lies over the dark woods awaiting the burst of spring, for then the woods are all ablaze with wild daffodils, and when those flowers are over, the apple and the cherry orchards, and the great perry pear trees, a unique feature of the district, make a fairyland of rich blossom. Hopyards and cornfields are spread everywhere between orchards and woodlands, and the ever rich soil gleams through the verdure.

There are few vales in Britain possessing so many and diversified charms as that of the River Teme, and possibly none less known. From its source to its confluence with the Severn below Worcester, it passes through a land of ancient strife, but one which is beautiful in the extreme, and at certain points more than rivalling the Dart or the Wye.

The Forest of Wyre

Between the Severn and Clee Hills stretches the ancient Forest of Wyre. In former times there was much border warfare in the district and in the village of Arley there was a law which allowed the men to deal with any marauding Welshmen as they wished without fear of punishment.

The Wyre Forest was intersected by highways and byways and later by two railways. Its great oaks have given employment to many: local tanners looked to the forest for supplies of bark and wagon-loads of bark used to be a common sight in late spring when the bark was peeled. Charcoal burners — wood colliers, as they were known (hence the Wood Colliers' Arms in Bewdley) — provided the fuel for the iron furnaces, living in the forest like gypsies. For centuries the forest provided the material for some of the old crafts such as the making of besoms and skips and clogs.

Wyre was one of King John's favourite hunting grounds. Castle Hill at Wolverley was once his shooting box and from there he would cross the stream at Kingsford, leaving behind Kinfare (King's Road) and continue to Shatterford (Shooter's Road). Deer are still to be found in the forest and fruit trees are fenced against them; there are beautiful and rare moths in the deep parts of the forest; and in the centre is a tree called the Sawb Tree, said to be the parent tree of the pear family known locally as the Whitty Pear.

The old inhabitants of the forest were not always law-abiding. A hundred years ago the Far Foresters were lawless folk, much of their time occupied in poaching, sheep-stealing and marauding. Uneducated and often unmarried, they lived in long huts, with a pigeon or two, sometimes a donkey and some pigs, which occupied the end of the hut. In 1833 three determined overseers of Bewdley set off to carry out the very difficult task of collecting the rates. They trudged the long distance to Far Forest and went from hut to hut; but not a penny could they get and not a man was to be seen. Abuse, contempt and jeers from the women greeted them as they served demand notes on the men and no-one offered refreshments. Hungry and footsore, they arrived back at Bewdley late that night with the bitter taunts of the women still in their ears, advising them to bring their coffins on their next visit as they would never leave the forest in their shoes.

Upper Arley – the church, castle and chain ferry

Upper Arley, the most northerly of Worcestershire parishes on the Severn, was noted for its ancient church, its picturesque castle and its chain ferry. Arley Church was a 'peculiar', that is to say, it was exempt from the jurisdiction of the bishop of the diocese (the parish itself always part of Staffordshire until 1896). In the church (twelfth-century in origin) are memorials to three soldiers from three wars, centuries apart. In the chancel is the effigy of a crusader knight, Walter de Balun, lying on a table-tomb, killed on his wedding day, taking part in a tournament at Southampton whilst awaiting embarkation for the Holy Land; opposite him is a sculpted portrait of a soldier killed in the Great War of 1914–18; and in the nave is a memorial to Henry Lyttleton, a Cavalier who fought at Worcester in 1651.

Arley Castle, now sadly gone, was built in the early years of the nineteenth century by Viscount Valentia, who spent vast sums converting the ancient manor house of the Lyttletons into a 'medieval castle', complete with four massive towers and a great hall in the best feudal tradition. Viscount Valentia, later Earl of Mountnorris, was a colourful character with many and varied interests. A great traveller, he was a pioneer explorer in Abyssinia. He was a keen naturalist and his collection of shells was reputed to have been the finest in the country. His ruling passion, however, was fireworks and he spent hundreds of pounds a year on them. He kept a personal 'powder monkey' whose sole function was to prepare set-pieces, rockets and squibs for his noble patron, who would stage firework displays at night without warning, startling the neighbourhood, causing people to leap out of their beds. He was a law unto himself, appropriating consecrated ground to enlarge his lawns and removing gravestones to use as shelves in his wine cellars.

The tower in Frenchman's Street Mountnorris built out of spite. The landlord of the village inn, Sam Willcox, owned a house in the street which Mountnorris wanted to purchase and Sam refused to sell; so the lord of the manor built a tower aimed

Upper Arley Ferry at the beginning of this century

entirely at spoiling the landlord's view up the village street — a fine tall castellated tower, complete with turret. Recently it was refurbished, but keeping its interior white stone walls; and in 1987 it was up for sale for £90,000.

Arley Ferry was the last county ferry to operate by chain or rope. The ferry is recorded as early as 1323 and originally was pulled across by means of a rope; but later it was secured by a long cable to another suspended from two uprights some two hundred yards up stream, and crossed the river without any motive power other than the current, its course being controlled by manipulation of the rudder. The ferryman was on call from 6 am to 10.30 pm except when floods made the crossing dangerous. The doctor and policeman had a traditional right to call for the ferry at any hour; and children going to school and people going to church travelled free. Three ferrymen were drowned while operating the boat in years gone by but there is no record of a passenger being lost. It was once a very busy crossing and on one Easter Monday four thousand five hundred passengers crossed the river in sixteen-and-a-half hours. But increasingly it operated at a loss and in 1964 it was closed and a footbridge built.

Blakeshall and 'the five wounds of Christ'

At Sebright Farm in Blakeshall, near Kidderminster, is a barn which had special significance for Roman Catholics in the past. The barn has many ventilation holes the size of a half-brick, but about six feet from the ground are five larger holes,

The barn at Sebright Farm, Blakeshall

evenly spaced and well seen from the road. A former owner, a local historian, explained that for generations they were known in his family as 'the five wounds of Christ' and had been specifically placed in the days of Catholic persecution to be seen and recognised by any Catholic who needed help and safe lodgings.

Two nineteenth-century land settlement schemes: O'Connor and Ruskin

THE NATIONAL LAND COMPANY IN WORCESTERSHIRE

In 1845 Feargus O'Connor, the leader of the Chartist Movement, founded the National Land Company, a scheme aimed at bringing industrial workers back to the land where they could support themselves and qualify to vote. The company had a capital of £130,000 in 100,000 shares of £1.6s each, and land was allotted to subscribers by ballot. The holder of *one* share balloted for one acre and an advance of £7.10s as working capital; and the holder of *two* shares balloted for two acres, a house and a £15 loan; the holder of *three* shares balloted for three acres, a house and £22.10s loan; and the holder of *four* shares balloted for four acres, a house and £30 loan.

Five estates were bought, two of them in Worcestershire – Lowbands and Snigs End at Redmarley D'Abitot (then in Worcestershire); and Great Dodford, near Bromsgrove. The Lowbands and Snigs End settlement was established in 1847 and consisted of two small farms, eighty-two houses and a school-cum-community hall. The scheme was a failure: the area was isolated and far from markets. Only a few succeeded and those mostly subsisted on the charity of local farmers.

At Dodford the land belonging to the old priory was acquired in 1849, some two hundred acres apportioned in one-to-four acre lots. But here, too, the scheme proved a failure. There were several reasons for this: the holders were chiefly factory hands, completely inexperienced in country life; they had insufficient capital; and the heavy clay soil at Dodford was almost unworkable. In 1850 O'Connor's company was dissolved and most of the settlers were dispersed. In the early 1860s John Wallace, a settler and formerly head gardener to the Earl of Plymouth, introduced strawberry growing to the remaining Dodford occupants which ultimately saved them from disaster. Wallace realised the Dodford soil was too heavy for potatoes and cereals but could be converted to market garden soil. Flowers and summer vegetables were grown as well as strawberries and garlic for Lea & Perrins's Worcestershire sauce factory.

To celebrate the opening of a new church room in 1900 a special song was composed which summarised the village's previous half-century:

> And yet again the scene is changed,
> 'Location Day' arrives,
> O'Connor's boys come settling here
> Like bees from busy hives.
> The gay procession wends its way,
> The wagons and the gigs,
> 'Feargus and Freedom' flaunts aloft,
> 'Less parsons and more pigs.'
>
> Sing of the land they bought and let,
> Sing of the poor men's share,
> Sing of allotments fair for each,
> Sing of the acres square.
> Sing of the ring of axe and spade,
> Sing of the fields they dug,
> Sing of the muddy roads they made,
> Sing of the homes so snug.
>
> Sing of the days when luck was gone,
> Sing of the winter cold,
> Sing of the hungry children's cries,
> Sing of the sticks all sold.
> Sing of the men who went away,
> Sing of the men who stayed,
> Sing of the days when luck returned,
> Sing of the garden trade.

RUSKINLAND

In the 1870s John Ruskin, art critic and social reformer, promoted a land settlement scheme under the banner of St George's Guild. He was assisted by Alderman George

Baker, the Mayor of Birmingham, who made a gift of twenty acres of land on the fringe of the Wyre Forest, just north of Bewdley (and still shown on the OS map). Several families were established on small parcels of land, each to be self-supporting, aiming to live by exchanging produce – 'to live by barter'. Ruskin had founded his St George's Guild to show how barren land could be utilised; to demonstrate what self-respect and education could achieve; and to convince the upper classes that 'people maintaining themselves by their own efforts were more noble than those engaged in the profession of war'.

In 1899 Baker built a house near to the settlement, Beaucastle, much in the style approved by Ruskin. Perched on a hilltop at the edge of the Wyre Forest, it was designed by William Doubleday and constructed from sandstone quarried on the estate, together with wood from the forest. Beaucastle has a somewhat fairytale appearance and contains many fine examples of the work of master craftsmen of the time. The observation tower offers 360° views over the forest.

Ruskin visited the settlement only once – to inspect the land – in July 1877. In the Guild's search for Utopia in England several settlements were established but most including this one failed lamentably. The land or the settlers – sometimes both – proved intractable, much to Ruskin's disappointment.

The Black Country – the first industrialised area

When the world's first steam engine was erected near Dudley Castle in 1712 to pump out water at one of Lord Dudley's mines, it marked the beginning of the shift in industrial life which eventually led to the growth of the great industrial towns. Industry, which until then had been located in rural valleys so as to take advantage of water power to drive the machines, now went to the coalfields. Iron to make the machines was the material of the Industrial Revolution and now coal became the fuel and steam the power. The abundance and accessibility of the iron, coal, limestone and fire clay around Dudley resulted in mines, forges and factories being built close together, and the houses of the workers crowded against the pit banks and factory walls without thought of health or sanitation.

That part of Worcestershire and Staffordshire was the first in the world to suffer the impact of change which we call the Industrial Revolution. The small hamlets around Dudley, Oldbury, Old Hills, Lye, Stourbridge and Halesowen merged with those on the Staffordshire side of the border to become a great industrial *wen* which came to be known as the Black Country; and with good reason, for it was scarred, burned, blackened and torn apart. The mines disgorged their waste and coal dust over everything for miles. The furnaces and forges added to the fumes and smoke; and through it all wound the black arteries of the canals which were the lifelines transporting raw materials and heavy goods.

Travellers to the Black Country from home and abroad have recorded their amazement at the scene: 'From a hill near Bilston, towards Sedgley at night, 200 blast furnaces for the smelting of iron may be seen. The rushing and roaring of the blasts of the furnaces, the thunderous blows of the ponderous forge hammers, the clanking and crashing of the steam engines, and the pulley chains and the ropes of the pits, all give a stranger the most fearful and awful notions of the place.'

Earl of Dudley's Round Oak Ironworks. An engraving from the official guide to the Great Western Railway, 1860.

A description of Oldbury in Worcestershire around the mid-nineteenth century gives some idea of what the Black Country must have looked like:

> The area around Oldbury was a region of furnaces, ovens and kilns, of forges, of factories and iron mills. The landscape varied from heaps of cinder, slag or pit refuse, fed by canals the colour of pea-soup, which, near the great furnaces, steamed. Night and day the pulsations of the mighty engines, the monotonous thud, thud, of heavy machines. At night the sky was illuminated by the lurid glare of countless furnaces (blood-red flames of the puddling furnace; streaked white and red of the blast furnace, and yellow and blue of the copper works). In Oldbury itself were the 'Four Moons Furnaces', so called because the glare set up by them illuminated the whole town sufficiently for the governing body to dispense with street lamps. The flaming gases were the result of wasteful processes, and were later captured and re-used. By day, dense clouds of smoke and corroding gases from the chemical works in the town blighted all plant life. Metal tarnished in a single night, and gradually corroded away.

This vivid picture of the Black Country comes from the American Elihu Burritt whose book *Walks in the Black Country and its Green Border-land* was published in 1868.

> The Black Country, black by day and red by night, cannot be matched for vast and varied production by any other space or equal radius on the surface

of the globe ... One would be inclined to believe, on seeing the black forest of chimneys over large towns and villages, as well as the flayed spaces between, that all the coal and iron in the district must be used up. The furnaces, foundries and manufactures seem almost countless, and the vastness and variety of their production infinite ... By night and day, year in and year out, runs that stream (of manufactured goods and minerals) with unabated flow. Narrow canals filled with water as black as the long sharp boats it floats, crossing each other here and there in the thick of furnaces, twist out into the green lands in different directions, laden with coal for distant cities and villages. The railways, crossing the canals and their creeping locomotion, dash off with vast loads to London and other great centres of consumption. And all the while the furnaces roar and glow by night and day, and the great steam-hammers thunder, and hammers from an ounce in weight to a ton, and every kind of machinery invented by man are ringing, clicking and whizzing, as if tasked to intercept all this raw material of the mines and impress on it all the labour and skill which human hands could give to it.

The mystery of the old county boundaries

County boundaries are often curious things, and before the changes which took place in 1930 there was no part of England more mysterious than the southernmost boundaries of Worcestershire which embraced the Cotswold Hills. If the old map of Worcestershire is imagined as a continent and the surrounding counties as seas, there is a distinct similarity to the northern part of the Mediterranean with its peninsulas and archipelago of islands.

Worcestershire had no less than five 'islands' in the adjoining counties to the south. The largest containing Shipston-on-Stour and Tredington, with Alderminster in the northern extension, lay entirely in Warwickshire, though it touched Gloucestershire at two points. The next largest, containing Blockley, lay in Gloucestershire, as did Cutsdean and the islets of Evenlode and Daylesford. Then there were seven 'peninsulas' stretching southwards into Gloucestershire, formed by the parishes of Chaceley, Bushley, Bredon, Teddington, Sedgeberrow, Broadway and Honeybourne, not to mention Oldberrow which projected northwards into Warwickshire. Gloucestershire and Warwickshire likewise had a number of islands in Worcestershire. In the north of the county there were similar islands, among them the large Worcestershire island of Dudley inside Staffordshire, and the Shropshire island containing Halesowen situated entirely in Worcestershire. Most curious was Tardebigge: for a hundred years part of Staffordshire, for a further six hundred part of Warwickshire and only from 1844 part of Worcestershire.

The inconvenience of such boundaries is obvious, but it is an ill wind that blows nobody good and they must have been welcomed by fugitives from justice who could take shelter in these out-of-the-way corners and laugh at their pursuers till such times as the news of their arrival trickled through to the headquarters of a more or less distant shire and a second hue and cry was raised. Such curious boundaries pose a number of questions: why were there so many detached 'islands'? Why do parts of Worcestershire and Gloucestershire stretch beyond their natural boundaries, *i.e.* Worcestershire beyond the line of the Malvern Hills and Gloucestershire across the Severn to the Forest of Dean? Even more intriguing are early references to the county of *Winchcombeshire*. What happened to it?

THE OLD SEE OF WORCESTER

A clue to the puzzle may be found in the boundaries of the old See of Worcester. Worcestershire under the Saxons formed part of the kingdom of Hwicca, a kingdom which broke away from Wessex in about 591 and thereafter, under its own petty kings, was included in the great central kingdom of Mercia. When Christianity at last came to the Hwiccas, Archbishop Theodore of Tarsus in 680 placed the newly converted tribe in charge of a bishop, Bosel by name, whose jurisdiction naturally extended over the whole of their territory. Consequently the boundaries of their kingdom can be constructed from those of the old diocese of Worcester before the sees of Gloucester and Birmingham had been carved out of it.

The Danish invasion, though it just stopped short of the Hwiccas, wiped out the old organisation of the Mercian kingdom. When therefore the successors of Alfred finally regained it in the tenth century, it had to be entirely rearranged for administrative purposes. The districts were cut into shires, each usually containing a burgh, or fortified place, which later became the county town and gave its name to the shire.

WHY THE FOREST OF DEAN IS IN GLOUCESTERSHIRE

As the Hwiccan kingdom was too large to be treated as a single unit, it was sheared into four parts – Worcestershire, Gloucestershire, Warwickshire and Winchcombeshire (a lost shire of which more anon). It would seem that they were intended to be roughly equal for the purposes of taxation and military service, and that they contained on average twelve hundred hides, which became units of taxation. But Winchcombe, lying in the hilly and unproductive Cotswold country, though it may have been assessed at about the same number of hides, was probably larger in area than the more fertile lowlands of Worcestershire or Warwickshire. Now these four shires, taken together, are considerably larger than the old kingdom of Hwicca, because in order to bring them up to the standard size they were given territory taken from their neighbours. So Gloucestershire stretched out across the Severn and took in the Forest of Dean, while Worcestershire extended its territory beyond the line of the Malvern and Abberley hills, which had been the boundary of the Hwiccas, as far as the Teme.

THE LOST COUNTY OF WINCHCOMBESHIRE

Before the Norman Conquest a great alteration had taken place. In the Domesday Survey we find only three counties, Worcestershire with 1,189 hides, Warwickshire with 1,338 and Gloucestershire with 2,388. Winchcombeshire does not appear at all. It looks as though something drastic had occurred; for Gloucester, enacting the part of a boa constrictor, had swallowed its neighbour whole (except for a few scraps which may have been snapped up by Worcester) and is unduly extended in consequence.

So far the existence of Winchcombeshire has been assumed but the evidence, though slight, seems sufficient. It rests on the Worcester Cartulary of Heming, compiled somewhat later than the Conquest, in which one document, purporting to go back to the ninth century, is headed 'Into Wincelcumb scire'. In the same collection a passage in another document refers to the powers assumed by Edric Streona, the treacherous minister of Ethelred the Unready, which may be translated as follows: 'He lorded it like a petty king, to such an extent that he joined village to village and county to county as it pleased him; for he annexed the County of Wincelcumb, which was then independent to Gloucester.' Such high-handed proceedings may have played some part in the dislocation of the boundaries which remained to the twentieth century.

The key to the problem lies in the observation that with few exceptions the peninsulas and islands belonged to the great abbeys of Worcestershire and Gloucestershire, which were the largest landowners in the district; and it would certainly have been to their convenience to have the outlying pieces of their property annexed to the shire in which they were situated. St Mary of Worcester (the cathedral priory) owned practically all the islands, along with three peninsulas. The Abbey of St Mary of Pershore held Alderminster and the peninsula of Broadway. A notable incidence of the principle may be seen in the case of Honeybourne. Of the two manors into which the township was divided, Church Honeybourne belonged to the Abbey of Evesham and therefore was attached to Worcestershire; Cow Honeybourne belonged to the Abbey of Winchcombe and would have been in Winchcombeshire but fell to Gloucestershire.

This arrangement or, rather, disarrangement, had been made before the Domesday Survey and Heming's Cartulary gives the clue to the date. If, as it asserts, Edric Streona wiped Winchcombeshire off the map in the days of Ethelred the Unready, it might well have been his policy to conciliate the great landowners of the district by reshaping the boundaries of Worcestershire and Gloucestershire without much regard for the convenience of the sheriffs or the Crown. This would put the date somewhere about AD1000 and, whatever his motives may have been, it must be admitted that it stood the test of time for a long, long period.

CHANGES IN THE COUNTY BOUNDARIES

Worcestershire had more 'islands' than any other county, but 1930 saw a drastic change in the county borders of Warwickshire, Worcestershire and Gloucestershire.

Losses to Warwick: Alderminster, Shipston-on-Stour, Tidmington, Tredington
Losses to Gloucester: Blockley, Chaceley, Cutsdean, Daylesford, Evenlode, Redmarley D'Abitot, Staunton and Teddington

Gains from Warwick: Ipsley, Bickmarsh (part)

Gains from Gloucester: Ashton-under-Hill, Aston Somerville, Childs-wickham, Cow Honeybourne, Hinton-on-the-Green, Kemerton, Pebworth, Beckford (part) and Forthampton (part)

Worcestershire did not do well by the exchange, losing 5,832 acres. Gloucestershire, already by far the largest of the three counties, seems to have gained most. One change in particular infuriated Worcester people, the loss of Daylesford, the home of the great Worcestershire hero, Warren Hastings. Other changes were keenly resented, for there were strong, centuries-old loyalties, especially at Blockley and Shipston — and, of course, the unique Four Shires Stone is no longer in four counties.

BOUNDARIES IN THE NORTH OF THE COUNTY

It was not the first change in the boundaries of Worcestershire, for in the north it was not until the reign of Henry VIII that Bewdley became part of the county. Until then it had been part of the Welsh Marches and for that reason enjoyed the privilege, through the Lord High Steward, of approaching the sovereign direct to lay any grievance. And there used to be two Warleys, Warley Salop and Warley Wigorn. The former, part of the great manor of Halesowen, was included with that town in Shropshire; the latter formed part of Worcestershire.

Boundaries were oddly mixed up and in the past there were places whose borders no-one could be sure of, for what maps existed were primitive and unreliable. This led in places to a 'no-man's-land', as in parts of Kinver Forest, a safe haven for robbers and highwaymen, where magistrates were uncertain of their authority. There were attempts to mark boundaries by trees and large stones. At Bromsgrove there is a line of ancient boulders at Wildmoor that divides the parishes of Bromsgrove and Belbroughton; and three boulders once stood in the High Street, dividing the manor of the rectory and that of Bromsgrove manor.

The Worcestershire hundreds

At the time of the Domesday Survey the counties were divided into Hundreds and their distribution gives an indication of their relative settlements and populations. The Hundreds were certainly in existence before the Norman Conquest. Each possessed a court and officers, and the court was usually held in the open at some ancient site where a stone or great tree was prominent — such as at Doddingtree.

Worcestershire was divided into twelve Hundreds. The bishop and monks of Worcester had three in their triple Hundred of Oswaldslow, the district around Worcester; the church of Westminster had two in the neighbourhood of Pershore; and the churches of Evesham and Pershore one each. The remaining five were the Hundreds of Came, Clent, Cresselaw, Doddingtree and Esch. Came included Bromsgrove and Kings Norton; Cresselaw included Kidderminster; Doddingtree the western part of the county; and Esch the area around Feckenham. By the thirteenth century these twelve Hundreds had been reduced to five. Oswaldslow and

Doddingtree alone retained their ancient names and boundaries; the Westminster and Pershore lands had become the Hundred of Pershore; Evesham was known as Blackenhurst; while Came, Clent and Esch were amalgamated into Halfshire.

The term *Hundred of Halfshire* is particularly applied to an ancient Anglo-Saxon territorial division and was the basis for military service and the administration of government taxes. The Hundred of Halfshire was made up of about forty towns and villages, the court of the lower division sometimes held at Church Hill and Feckenham under a great tree.

Skating on the frozen Severn at Worcester in the severe winter of 1890/91

Worcestershire place names

Worcestershire has more than its fair share of strange place names. It is surprising how easily many villages named in the Domesday Book can be identified today.

Bentley Pauncefoot	Dead Man's Ait	Happy Land
Atherstone-super-Stour	Drinkers End	Loggerheads
Bristitune	Shavers End	Mathon Melly
Cakebould	Edvin Loach	Solcum
Catchems End	Fastocheselde	Upton Snodsbury
Cank and Cobley	Flyford Flavell	Vigo
Clerkenleap	Golafers	Morton Folliot
Cutlers Rough	Gilgal	Leopard's Grange

The spelling of course is different, but all spelling until the eighteenth century was fairly arbitrary and a writer would use different forms in the same piece of writing. The publication of dictionaries gradually produced standardisation of ordinary words, and in the early nineteenth century the Ordnance Survey provided standardisation of place names. The early surveyors were extremely careful in their choice of spelling and though documentary evidence then used has been lost or destroyed (mostly by bombing in the 1939–45 War) the Ordnance Survey spelling has been generally adopted.

Officialdom needs to have accurate names, and there are at least thirty place names in Worcestershire which caused controversy. Wyre Piddle asked the county council in 1905 to reduce its name to Wyre, but as the powers did not exist at that time no action was taken. Stourport asked to have 'on-Severn' officially added and in 1914 Tenbury asked for the addition of 'Wells'. Though the county council had no objection nothing was done, and officially the place is still Tenbury. In 1933 the law recognised the need for local residents to have a considerable say in deciding the name by which their village or town should be known and in 1934 Stourport became Stourport-on-Severn.

One of the strangest place names in Worcestershire is that of the hamlet of *Paris* on Bredon Hill, near Ashton-under-Hill. Baldwyn, Count of Flanders, a retainer of William the Conqueror, originally owned the estate and is reputed to have built and named the hamlet shortly after the Norman Conquest.

There are a number of hamlets with the name *Lench* or *Link*. Near Evesham there is a group: Rous Lench, Church Lench, Atch Lench, Sheriff's Lench and Ab Lench (this last now called Abbot's Lench). At Malvern there is Malvern Link. Lench is a variation of lych, linck and linchet, words signifying a ledge or ridge, a hillside terrace which was once cultivated. In the days of open-field cultivation, where there were steep slopes, it was the practice to plough horizontally, the grass banks between preventing the soil from slipping from one strip to another.

Strange field names

In the early nineteenth century a survey of field names in the Kinver and Cookley area was recorded. Some obviously described the nature of the land, such as Weedy Piece, Linseed Field, Oaktree Piece, Wet Furlong; but some are very strange indeed and one wonders how they were so named:

Neckhandkerchief	*Spiteful Piece*	*Neckcloth*
Hitter High Field	*Bolt Stone*	*Worlds End Field*
The Stocking	*Kamskatcha*	*Little and Big Wigley*
Botany Bay	*Jacob's Well*	*Smoky-Billy Piece*
Mount Ephraim	*Slash*	*Big Moscow*
Clapper Piece	*Bible Meadow*	*The Bath*
Crumpit Piece	*Piccadilly*	*Siberia*
France Plantation	*Messmates*	*Bomb Castle*
Giants Well Piece	*Lampern*	*Big Higgins Flat*

CHAPTER TWO

History and Legend
Great Events and Great People

I N THE NINETEENTH century a school of historians, by a severe exercise of the critical faculty, reduced history to a science of dry facts and the results were wholly destructive. Their histories, anyway, were mostly of kings and their ministers, of nobles and their politics: legends, passed down the centuries by oral tradition, had no place.

Modern historians hold a different view. Most are convinced that a great many legends have a sounder historical basis than was at first believed. The countryman never doubted it. Stanley Baldwin said in 1930: 'I can remember that we were taught that the story of Troy was only a myth, yet modern research has proved the story of Troy to be exactly true. I put my money every time on country tradition — that is where true history is to be found.'

Massacre at Bredon

Landscape and folklore are closely linked. It is around famous landscapes that legends cluster thickest. In Worcestershire nowhere is this more so than on Bredon Hill whose topmost elevation, crowned by an Iron-Age camp, has been the source of many legends from the distant past — of attacks, disasters, massacres, sacrifices and of witchcraft. The camp is some twenty-two acres in area, one of a line of twenty-seven forts which can be distinctly traced from Clifton Downs to Bredon Hill, a distance of forty miles — each within signal distance. They were built by the Dobruni to guard against their warlike neighbours, the Silures of South Wales.

In the centre of the camp are the Bambury Stones. The stones were originally one, standing on the edge of a large cavity. But in the nineteenth century the earth moved and the stone split into three or four pieces, one of these known locally as the Elephant Stone because of its resemblance to a kneeling elephant. Until recent times sickly children were passed between the stones as a cure; but stranger and more weird ceremonies have been enacted. For here out ancestors sought to account for the strange happenings they did not understand and, by the magic of fire and dance, sought to entice the spirits out of the ground or frighten the evil spirits away.

Tales long told often embody a communal memory which archaeological digs confirm. Stories of fierce and bloody encounters surround this ancient site and excavations made at the lower *vallum*, to ascertain the exact position of the gateway into the camp on the southern side, revealed that the gate had been forced and the defenders massacred, their legs, arms and bodies found lying about in all directions near the burnt-down gateway. Excavated pottery tells of occupation between 100 BC and 100 AD, but none was Roman. It is thought that the inhabitants were massacred by the Belgae, a warlike tribe from the Continent who invaded Britain early in the first century BC.

Augustine's Oak

One of the most historic of meetings was that between St Augustine and the bishops of the Britons in the summer of 603 AD. When the Romans left, Britain was by no means abandoned to paganism. The Christian faith established in the days of Roman dominion survived in unbroken continuity. But St Augustine, having established the authority of the Roman hierarchy in Saxon and Anglian parts, was keen to bring the British Christians into line.

In his *History of the English Church* Bede says: 'Augustine, with the help of King Ethelbert, drew together to confer with him the Bishops and Doctors of the next provinces of the Britons at a place which is called to this day Augustine's Ac (Oak), on the borders of the Hwiccas and the west Saxons.' Tradition has it that British bishops, hearing that Augustine was a haughty and proud man and not of the humility of Christ, watched with care the way he received them. If he remained seated on his throne as they approached, they would know that his was not the true way of Christ; and, since Augustine made no attempt to rise and meet them, they returned across the river and he went back empty-handed.

Where did the meeting take place? Five places have been stoutly contested as the scene of the meeting: Aust Cleeve in Gloucestershire; Martin Hussingtree (anciently Aussuntree); Alfric (Acfric); Rock; and the Mitre Oak, Hartlebury. In the opinion of past antiquaries Rock had a superior claim, for in Saxon days the village was called Ther Ac (The Oak), whilst in the Domesday Survey it is given as Halac (Holy Oak). And indeed, a famous oak of great antiquity stood there until it came to an untimely end in 1757. The trunk had become quite hollow and, during the rebuilding of the tollkeeper's house which stood near, the gatekeeper took up his abode in the hollowed-out tree trunk. One bitterly cold night he made up a roaring fire inside it, the tree took light and in a few hours was entirely consumed.

Other traditions have just as strongly held that the meeting was at the Mitre Oak, and for this reason was specially chosen in 1575 for the bishop and clergy of Worcester to meet Queen Elizabeth on her visit to the county. It would certainly fit in with the claim that the British bishops crossed the Severn. At one stage the great oak was used by the gatekeeper, Thomas Morris, as a stable for his three donkeys. The tree that stands today, at the side of the busy Worcester-Kidderminster road, is said to be a sapling from the original, but still very old. It is surrounded by an iron fence, for the land on which it stands is held on condition that the tree is not interfered with.

The lost town of Kenelmstowe

In the north of the county, at the foot of the Clent Hills, is the site of the lost township of Kenelmstowe. It was a populous town held in great regard in medieval times and visited by great numbers of pilgrims, for it was the scene of an atrocious royal murder and of the miracle that led to its discovery.

Kenulf, King of Mercia, died in 819, leaving three children, Kenelm, seven years of age, and two daughters, Quendryda and Burgenhilda. The young prince was entrusted to the guardianship of his elder sister, Quendryda, during his minority and in the summer months much of their time was spent on the Clent Hills where Kenulf had built a royal hunting lodge. The sister conspired with her lover, Ascobert, to kill the boy and so gain the kingdom; and while riding one day in the wild Cowbach Valley, between the Clent and Romsley hills, the lad was treacherously murdered and his head struck off. The corpse was buried in a hastily scratched grave under a thorn bush, with the blood-stained weapon by his side. The murderers returned to Winchcombe with the story that the prince had mysteriously disappeared and Quendryda succeeded to the kingdom. But she was under a shadow and, maddened by the suspicions of courtiers and citizens, she eventually decreed that anyone who looked for the prince, or even named him, would be beheaded.

It was then that strange things began to happen. The Pope was officiating in St Peter's at Rome one morning when a snow-white dove entered, bearing in its beak a scroll which it placed on the high altar before flying away. The words on the scroll were written in English:

> *In Clent, in Cowbach, lyeth under a thorn,*
> *His head off-shorn, Kenelm, King born.*

The Pope sent messengers to England, ordering Wilfred, Archbishop of Canterbury, to investigate the mystery and bring justice to the criminals. The investigators came to the Clent Hills and explored the little valley (still known by the name of Cowbach) and were guided to the place by the lowing of a white cow. The corpse and the blood-stained knife were disinterred; and on the removal of the body a fountain gushed out which for centuries afterwards was celebrated as a holy well, attracting pilgrims from all parts of the kingdom, and many notable miracles were said to have been performed there.

The body of the prince was conveyed to Winchcombe, though not without difficulty for the cortege was met at Pyriford, near Pershore, by armed men from Worcester who tried to prevent its progress. It is recorded that on sight of the coffin Quendryda's eyes fell from their sockets onto the page of the psalter from which she had been reading; and she died shortly afterwards, shunned by all. No-one could be persuaded to bury her and her corpse was flung into an open ditch to be devoured by wolves and birds of prey. The little prince was buried by the side of his father in the east end of the abbey, and through the centuries pilgrims from all parts flocked to their shrines.

Many medieval manuscripts have told the story of St Kenelm, the earliest of which seems to be the Douce Manuscript, said to be written by a monk at Worcester at the time of St Oswald, about a century after the event, who also claimed that Quendryda's psalter was still in existence at that time, stained with blood from her eyes. Like most medieval accounts, it appears to be a blending of fact and legend. Excavations made at the site of Winchcombe Abbey in 1815 disclosed the stone coffins of Kenulf and Kenelm, the bodies crumbling into dust soon after exposure to the air. In the child's coffin was a long-bladed knife, a mass of rust which fell to pieces. These, together with the coffins, were removed to the parish church.

It is at the church of St Kenelm, in the parish of Romsley on the Clent Hills, that the legend lives on, for the church stands *over* a stream. It is supported on arches on the slopes of a deep ravine, a most unlikely site — unless it had special significance. The populous town of Kenelmstowe grew up around it and in 1215 was granted a four-day fair on the feast of St Kenelm (17 July) which continued until the mid-nineteenth century. After the Reformation, however, the pilgrims ceased and later the main road between Bromsgrove and Dudley, which for centuries passed through Kenelmstowe, was diverted and the town declined. Today no trace of the township remains and the stream has been diverted from the church.

The skin of the Dane

'From the fury of the Norsemen, good Lord, deliver us.' During the period of the Danish raids Worcester had cause to call for deliverance in those dark days of terror. More than once in the tenth century their black-dragon boats anchored in the shallows of Diglis within sight of the city walls. The city was poorly defended and at the sight of the ferocious warriors the monks, and those citizens who could, fled for safety to the woods.

The Danes swarmed over the walls, looting whatever valuables they found in the city and church, murdering the old people left behind, setting fire to the place and returning to their boats, drunk and laden with booty. But one Dane, more avaricious than the rest, stayed behind and found the Sanctus bell of the cathedral. The monks and citizens returned with help and caught him before he could reach his ship. Furious at the murders and sacrilege, they fell upon him and, it is said, flayed him alive. When the raiders had gone the Dane's skin was tanned and nailed upon the inner side of the great doors of the cathedral as a warning to the sacrilegious and to marauding Danes in particular.

Tradition has it that the skin remained on the door down the centuries for all to see. 'I recollect when a boy at school, between 1780 and 90,' wrote Dr Prattinton of Bewdley, 'being shown what they said was human skin on the inside of the north door.' During restorations in the early nineteenth century the old door was removed and its whereabouts lost track of. In the 1850s Jabez Allies, a Worcester antiquarian, obtained permission to search the cathedral and found part of an old door and, beneath a strengthening bar of wood, a parchment-like substance. He sent it to the

Royal College of Surgeons who confirmed it was human skin and the hairs on it those of a light-haired person. A piece of the skin can be seen in the cathedral library to this day.

The Cathedral Ferry (established for the monks' convenience) c1910

Simon de Montfort

In the Barons' War of the thirteenth century Worcestershire was in the thick of things — just as it would be in the Civil War four centuries later. Fighting began in 1263 with an attack on Worcester by a baronial force which took the city after repeated assaults. The cathedral was spared but the destruction of the Jewry is particularly recorded. After the Battle of Lewes in 1264 Simon de Montfort was made head of state and King Henry III and his son, Prince Edward, were taken prisoner. On 13 December 1264 from his imprisonment the king summoned his council and, as was usual, included only nobles and bishops. De Montfort, probably after consultation with his friend, Walter de Cantelupe, Bishop of Worcester, sent a further summons and in London on 28 January 1265 there assembled in one great chamber — besides the twenty-three peers, eleven bishops and a hundred of the clergy — two knights for each county and two representatives from each city, cinque port and large town. It was a momentous gathering.

De Montfort did not enjoy his triumph for long as some of his most powerful supporters went over to the king's side. At dawn on 4 August 1265 Simon found himself trapped in a loop of the Avon at Evesham and vastly outnumbered. His position was hopeless. But Cantelupe did not desert his friend, encouraging his troops and giving plenary absolution. It was a day of violent thunderstorms but the battle raged fiercely and the barons fought desperately for hours. With de Montfort was the king, a prisoner still and wearing an ordinary suit of armour. In the fray he was wounded and would have been killed had he not cried out, 'I am Henry of Winchester, your king, kill me not!' To the last Simon, alone with his son, stood in defiance, wielding his great two-handed sword, refusing to yield until he was struck down from behind. It was the last round of the Barons' War, though described by the chronicler, Robert of Gloucester, as 'the murther of Evesham, for battle none it was'.

That night the head and hands of de Montfort were sent to Roger Mortimer's wife who was at Worcester Castle, and what remained of his dreadfully mutilated body was brought through the bloodstained and muddy tracks into Evesham Abbey where he and his son were reverently buried by the monks.

Medieval funerals

The final scene in man's life has been marked by many strange customs and conventions and, on special occasions, with great pomp and ceremony. In medieval times to have a great or saintly personage buried in one's church was not only a mark of prestige but of considerable financial advantage; for usually the dead man left land to the church and his family made gifts of money; and pilgrims and visitors came to these 'holy' places, leaving money and tokens.

Today some stories are difficult to believe, yet at Worcester an old tradition involving a king has been proved to be well founded. In the cathedral library is King John's written command that he should be buried between Worcester's two great saints, Oswald and Wulstan. But local tradition has it that he also ordered his royal robes to be covered by a monk's habit and the cowl to be pulled over his face, so that at the Resurrection the glory of his two companions and his own disguise might enable him to evade the vigilance of the gatekeepers of Heaven — for the wickedness of his life gave him little chance of being admitted on merit. When the tomb was opened in 1797 to ascertain the truth, the skull was indeed found to be covered with the remains of a monk's cowl, and over the royal robes were the remains of a monk's habit.

There was great rivalry between religious foundations in the middle ages. Tombs were watched night and day to see that no part of the saintly skeleton was stolen. In Worcester Cathedral the watchman's window, where the sacrist could watch the high altar and tombs, still remains. On the death of William de Beauchamp, Earl of Warwick and Castellan of Worcester, it was announced that his body was to be buried in the Greyfriars burial ground. This caused bitter ecclesiastical argument and bad feeling for the cathedral authorities wanted the body buried in their ground —

and not just for the prestige. There was a practical reason for it. When Edward II was buried at Gloucester the monks there soon began to make it known that 'miracles' were taking place at the murdered king's tomb. This so diverted the pilgrims visiting the tombs of Oswald and Wulstan at Worcester that the loss of revenue held up the remodelling of the nave of the cathedral.

The most magnificent funeral ever seen at Worcester was that of Prince Arthur, the eldest son of King Henry VII, who died at Ludlow Castle in 1502. The embalmed body was brought in a great procession to Worcester Cathedral for burial. At the town's liberties (Castle Street) the Order of Friars censed the corpse and when the procession reached the gate it was met by the bailiffs, all the prominent citizens and all the clergy, both regular and secular, of the town. The streets were lined with weeping maidens and mothers.

At the lychgate no fewer than four bishops, in rich copes, censed the corpse. It was conveyed under a canopy with banners into the churchyard where it was received by the abbots and priors of Worcester, Gloucester, Evesham, Chester, Shrewsbury, Hailes, Tewkesbury and Bordesley. The dead prince's favourite horse, adorned in rich trappings, was ridden up the cathedral into the choir where the Abbot of Tewkesbury received it as an offering. That night 'there was a goodly watch of lords, knights, esquires, gentlemen ushers, officers at arms, yeomen, and many others'.

The next day three masses were sung and the corpse was censed again and laid in the grave. It was one of the greatest scenes of pomp and ceremony ever witnessed in the cathedral and one of the most moving. The chronicler wrote: '. . . but to have seene the weepinge when the offringe was done, he had a hard heart that wept not . . .' Then the prince was laid in the tomb

> with weepinge and sore lamentation . . . the orisons were said by the Bishop of Lincoln also sore weeping. He sette the cross over the chest, and cast holy water and earth thereon. His officer of armes, sore weepinge, took off his coat of arms and cast it along over the chest right lamentably. Then Sir William Ovedall, Comptroller of His household, sore weeping and crying, tooke the staffe of his office by both endes and over his own head break it and cast it into the grave . . .

Interestingly, no members of the royal family were present at the funeral because they feared the plague was rampant in these parts. Nor was the Bishop of Worcester – he was a non-resident Italian.

'Remember, remember, the fifth of November'

No national political celebration is so generally observed as the *Gunpowder Plot*, 'a holiday forever in thankfulness to God for our deliverance and detestation of all Papists'. The following song was still in use in Worcestershire into the twentieth century:

Guy Fawkes and his companions did contrive
To blow the Houses of Parliament up alive,
With three-score barrels of powder below,
To prove Old England's wicked overthrow;
But by God's mercy all of them got catched
With their dark lanterns and their lighted match.
Ladies and gentlemen sitting by the fire,
Please put hands in pocket and give us our desire;
While you can drink one glass, we can drink two,
The better for we and none the worse for you.
        Rumour, rumour, pump-a-derry
     Prick his heart and burn his body,
      And send his soul to Purgatory.

Huddington Court, probably the most historic and romantic house in Worcestershire, stands in a maze of narrow lanes and grass-bordered tracks, a half-timbered moated house with velvet lawns, set in an old-world garden glowing with flowers. Yet, this delightful place was the scene of one of the saddest tragedies, for it was at the very centre of the Gunpowder Plot of 1605. The arch conspirator, Robert Catesby, was the cousin of Robert and Thomas Wyntour of Huddington, and it was here that thirteen conspirators, all gentlemen of wealth and breeding, laid plans to blow up Parliament. Thomas, one of the three Wyntour brothers, was sent to Flanders to secure help and there enlisted the support of Guy Fawkes who had experience with explosives. By May 1605 the tunnelling was complete and the gunpowder was collected in the vaults under the House of Lords.

Huddington Court, 1991

Catesby and Robert Wyntour met at Huddington Court to arrange the final plans: Guy Fawkes, having fired the mine, was to escape to Flanders by boat; on 5 November Sir Everard Digby was to arrange a hunting party on Dunsmoor Heath, near Rugby, where the invited Midland Catholic gentry would hear of the success or failure of the plot; arms and armour, ammunition and horses were to be collected at Norwood, near Warwick, and similar preparations were entrusted to Robert Wyntour at Huddington; relays of speedy horses were to be placed along the road from London to Dunchurch; and finally the Princess Elizabeth, who was staying at Coombe Abbey, near Coventry, was in the event of success to be proclaimed queen with a Catholic regent.

There have been many theories as to how the plot leaked out. One was that Mrs Habington of Hindlip Hall at the last minute warned her brother, Lord Mounteagle. But it seems more likely that the government was well aware of what was going on and waited long enough to catch the conspirators in the act. The news of failure reached Huddington where most were assembled. There was great consternation and thirty desperate men prepared themselves for the death they knew full well would speedily overtake them. All thirty attended Mass before leaving Huddington and retreating as an armed band towards Wales. They rode via Hewell Grange, Clent, Hagley and Wolverhampton. From Lord Windsor's house at Hewell they obtained, or stole, arms and gunpowder, but the roads were very foul and due to the continuous downpour the gunpowder became damp.

They reached Holbeach House, just over the Staffordshire border, at ten at night. Some had already deserted to attempt a solitary escape and to add to their misery the gunpowder, which had been spread out in trays before a fire, blew up, severely injuring Catesby and others. The mishap completely unnerved them and when, about eleven o'clock, the Sheriff of Worcester with an armed force of two hundred men surrounded the house, there was but brief resistance. Several were killed and the rest brought back to Worcester. Robert Wyntour and Stephen Lyttleton hid in barns and farmhouses for two months but were eventually given away and captured. Humphrey Lyttleton, also involved, sought unsuccessfully to evade death by giving information about hiding places at Hindlip Hall and, as a result, Father Garnett and Father Oldcorne were also taken.

'Prick his heart and burn his body', the line in the old song, shows the intense popular fury against the papists — and that was indeed the fate of the conspirators, for they were all hung, drawn and quartered: Robert and Thomas Wyntour and Father Garnett in London; the others, including John Wyntour, Humphrey Lyttleton and Father Oldcorne, at Red Hill, Worcester.

Such events leave their legends. When Oldcorne was butchered at Worcester his head and quarters were set upon poles in different parts of the city and his heart and intestines were cast into a fire, whence legend has it they sent forth a lively flame for sixteen days, notwithstanding continuous rain, when the public had to smother them with earth. Scratched on the glass of the diamond-paned windows of Huddington Court, in Jacobean writing, are 'Robert' and 'Thom'; and, on another pane, the words 'Past care, past care'. They are said to have been written by Lady

Wyntour, the wife of Robert, who it has been claimed 'still haunts the walk by the moat, waiting for the return of her husband'.

Worcestershire's pilgrim fathers

One of Worcestershire's most outstanding sons was among that stalwart band of religious discontents who sailed from England in 1620 and founded New England. He was *Edward Winslow*, described as a gentleman from Droitwich and accompanied by his younger brother, Gilbert. The Winslow family emerged from obscurity in Tudor times at Earls Croombe. A branch of it settled at Kerswell in Kempsey, and one of its members moved on marriage in 1594 to St Peter's parish in Droitwich. He was a man of some substance, a landowner and a farmer, and he sent his son Edward to be educated at the King's School, Worcester. In 1613 Edward was apprenticed to a London printer, but seems to have broken his indentures for he went to the University of Leyden in Holland and helped to set up a press for the little colony of Englishmen who had exiled themselves for conscience sake. The books he helped to print gave such offence to King James that they led to the seizure of the press.

Winslow then joined a group who planned to start a colony in the New World, free from religious interference. The *Mayflower* left Plymouth after many delays, the one hundred and two Pilgrims under the leadership of John Carver. Edward Winslow was twenty-five and accompanied by his wife and his brother Gilbert, then twenty years old. The ship was overcrowded, whole families sleeping on the bare deck; and the voyage must have seemed unending: forty-seven days before they left Plymouth, sixty-six days on the Atlantic crossing and another hundred and thirty-one days before the last settlers went to live ashore. Yet only one passenger died on the voyage and a male child was born and fittingly christened Oceanus.

THE FIRST WINTER

In the explorations of the first winter Edward Winslow took a leading part, establishing friendly relations with the natives and later thwarting a plot against another settlement. When the land was laid out he ranked third, only Governor Carver and the Ruling Elder Brewster taking precedence. During that first dreadful winter his wife died, but he drowned his sorrows in work and kept a journal in which he recorded: 'Of a hundred persons scarce fifty remain, the living scarce able to bury the dead.' Winslow's journal was sent over to England in the spring, and as the official account of the colony was lost it was hurriedly edited in 1622 so as to attract more settlers.

In April John Carver died and William Bradford was elected governor; and in May the first wedding took place: Edward Winslow, though only six weeks a widower, married Susanna White who had lost her husband and had been left with two small children. It was probably a means of survival for both of them. In the autumn of 1623 Winslow came home and sought to attract more colonists by publishing *Good News from New England*, in which he continued his journal till September 1623.

Returning next year he was chosen as assistant to the governor and re-elected every year except in 1633, 1636 and 1644 when he was elected as the colony's governor. Ten miles north of New Plymouth two of Edward's brothers christened a new town Kerswell after the family's farm near Kempsey.

THE TRUSTED AMBASSADOR

By 1635 Edward Winslow was a trusted ambassador of the infant colony and returned to London to unwind financial tangles with the London merchants and to confute before Archbishop Laud's new Council for the Regulation of Plantations the many calumnies spread at home about Plymouth Colony. Cromwell, who clearly thought highly of him, used him as a negotiator and in 1655 he sailed as chief commissioner for the West Indies to supervise the wresting of Jamaica and other islands from Spain. But Winslow's small expedition burnt its fingers badly in attacking Santo Domingo in Haiti. It drew off to repair damage and to prepare to assail Jamaica, and in those few days Winslow died on board the flagship. Some put his death down to a 'strong fever', but one sailor who kept a diary adds: 'Some say it was with grief.' Indeed, the whole undertaking was no triumph and Winslow's colleagues, General Venables and Admiral Penn, the father of William Penn of Pennsylvania, were imprisoned in the Tower of London for mismanagement when they reached home. 'The buriall of Commissioner Winslow', the sailor wrote, 'was performed as solemnly as might bee at sea, his grave being the oshen sea . . . our ship gave him 20 gunnes.'

The Civil War

No county was more involved in the violence of the Civil War than Worcestershire, and no city suffered more for its loyalty to the Crown than Worcester. The city was the first to declare for the king and the last to surrender. And further, the welcome given to Charles II five years later in 1651 brought the fury of the Parliament upon it. Only in Ireland did Cromwell's troopers wreak such vengeance and destruction.

THE FIRST BATTLE OF THE CIVIL WAR

The Battle of Powick Bridge on 22 September 1642 was the first skirmish of the Civil War, and though on a small scale was of great importance. Colonel Fiennes with a force of Parliamentary troops had been shadowing a convoy of gold and silver plate from the Oxford colleges which, at the suggestion of Bishop Prideaux, Bishop of Worcester and Vice-Chancellor of Oxford, was sent to the king to raise an army. The convoy reached Worcester en route for Shrewsbury and sheltered behind the defences of the city. Fiennes meantime had established a largish force on Powick Ham, all of which was very interesting to the citizens, crowds of them walking out 'to see the soldiers'.

Prince Rupert had been detached to escort the convoy but had bypassed Worcester and turned down Swinton Lane into Wick Fields. There he and his men rested on that hot afternoon without even setting a sentry. Neither side knew of the other's whereabouts. Receiving information that the convoy had started from Worcester, Fiennes marshalled his men on Powick Bridge, sang a psalm and set off for Worcester. Almost immediately they stumbled on Rupert's force. Both sides were astonished, but Fiennes was on the move and should have had the advantage. He was a poor leader, however, and it was the Cavaliers who mounted their horses and charged. With the narrow bridge behind him, Fiennes could not form up to meet the attack. It was a short fight, probably no more than a quarter-of-an-hour, but it was fierce while it lasted. More than fifty Parliamentary troopers were killed or drowned in the Teme and the rest retired in disorder towards Upton. All the Royalist officers were wounded except Rupert; they did not bother to record the casualties in the lower ranks.

GENERAL WALLER AND THE TRUMPETER

One of the most exciting episodes, featuring an unnamed trumpeter, is rarely mentioned in history books. In 1643 General Sir William Waller came with three thousand men and eight guns to take the city of Worcester for the Parliament, halting his forces at the rise of Greenhill. But the city's defences had been greatly strengthened and the garrison stood at fifteen hundred men with three hundred citizens all trained and ready.

As was the custom, Waller sent his trumpeter to Sidbury Gate to demand the surrender of the city. Colonel Sandys of Ombersley, the acting governor, told him in no uncertain terms to be off. The trumpeter correctly refused to take this uncivil answer to his general. There was another harsh exchange and Sandys again told him to be off and left the gate. The trumpeter again refused to go: by the rules of war he was entitled to a civil answer. Sandys returned with a Captain Beaumont and the final heated exchange was decisive. Beaumont ordered the guard to fire at the trumpeter and he fell mortally wounded. Waller, considering the flag of truce had been violated, angrily went into immediate action, furiously attacking the Friary Gate. From Greenhill his guns began a bombardment of the city which lasted sixteen hours; but the Royalist guns were superior and the city maintained the ascendancy. Waller then switched his attack to Diglis where, after a hard fight, he captured William Berkeley's house which provided him with cover for firing. Sandys, realising the danger it presented, made a determined effort to regain it, driving the Roundheads out and burning the house down to stop it being used again. To follow this success a sortie of Royalist horse from St Martin's Gate drove into Waller's flank, pushing the Parliamentarians back to Greenhill.

When Waller learned that Prince Maurice was on his way to cut off his retreat to Gloucester he called off his attack, commandeered barges, sent his baggage and wounded down river and withdrew. The fighting had been particularly fierce. The Parliament's losses were six captains and a hundred and sixty men and the wounded filled several barges. Royalist losses on the other hand were given as two men and three women. But they were probably higher.

'TINKER' FOX CAPTURES THE ROYALIST GOVERNOR OF BEWDLEY

Colonel Fox was an ironmaster, though according to Royalists a tinker by trade. He certainly was one of the most remarkable Parliamentary leaders. In 1643 he captured Edgbaston Hall from a Royalist force and made it his headquarters, and with his own troop of cavalry raided the Royalist garrisons around. His greatest exploit was his attack on Bewdley which reads like an episode from an adventure novel.

One spring day in 1644 he set off through enemy occupied territory with sixty selected troopers for Bewdley twenty-four miles away. The town was doubly important, for there was a strong force of Cavaliers stationed there and it commanded the Severn navigation. The governor, Sir Thomas Lyttleton, was a personal friend of the king and lived in Tickenhill Palace. Fox had timed his raid with great cunning, for Prince Rupert's army had just passed on to Shrewsbury and so the little troop of soldiers attracted no attention.

At the gatehouse on Bewdley Bridge Fox was challenged by the guard. He peremptorily ordered them to open the gates and 'admit the Prince's men'. The night was dark, the nearest enemy was supposed to be twenty miles away and the soldiers were accustomed to obey without question orders given in that authoritative tone. The gates were opened and the troop rode through. Soon all the sentries were disarmed and the bewildered Cavaliers rounded up. Bewdley was in Fox's hands and without the loss of a single man. Not a note of warning had been sent to the governor and the palace was attacked and taken with complete surprise. The governor was added to the prisoners and Fox speeded away with his booty. Eventually, a force of Royalists was sent to catch him — but they went to Edgbaston, while Fox rode to Coventry and safety.

BY THE SWORD DIVIDED

The Civil War divided families. So intense was the political division that brother fought against brother, son against father. Three Worcestershire families were all divided by the sword.

From *Thomas Wylde*, a Worcester clothier at the time of Henry VIII, descended three branches, one seated at the Commandery, another at Kempsey and a third at Droitwich. The Droitwich branch ended in the celebrated Chief Baron Wylde at the time of the Civil War who, according to Dr Nash, was 'very stiff for the Parliament', whereas his cousin at the Commandery, who was head of the family, was a strong Royalist and had to compound for his estate.

Alderman John Nash, whose fine half-timbered house still stands on the east side of New Street in Worcester, was a captain of horse for the Parliament. His brother, Richard, was also a Parliamentarian, whereas younger brother Thomas, a barrister of the Inner Temple and a man of great learning, was an equally zealous Royalist. Dr Treadway Nash, a descendant, writing of the triumvirate of brothers, observes: 'The family quarrel, on political accounts, which was carried on with the greatest animosity and most earnest desire to ruin each other, together with the decline of the King's affairs and particularly the execution of his person, so affected the spirits of Mr Thomas Nash that he determined not long to survive it.'

Nash's House, Worcester, showing trade signs and hardware, c1880.

During the occupation of Worcester by the Royalists John Nash fled the city and Colonel Dud Dudley occupied his house; but when the war ended Nash returned and turned Dud's wife out-of-doors. Colonel Dud Dudley was general of cannon during the great sieges of Worcester and produced shot for the garrison there. During a restoration of the house in 1963 the remains of a shot tower was found and destroyed.

The *Sandys* family had the doubtful distinction of suffering one of the first casualties of the Civil War. Colonel Edwin Sandys, of the Kentish branch of the family, fought for Parliament at the Battle of Powick Bridge in 1642 and was severely wounded. His wife came to Worcester to nurse him, but his wounds proved fatal and she died of grief, though one report suggested she contracted smallpox. They were buried together in the cathedral (though there is no authoritative record of this improbable burial). The Ombersley branch of the family were fierce Royalists. At the seige of Worcester in 1643 Colonel Samuel Sandys, Edwin's cousin, was acting governor of the city. He it was who harshly ordered General Waller's trumpeter to be off.

THE CAMISADE

> *And on Satterday, the 30 of August, William Guyes a Taylor who lived in the Broad Streete, was hanged on the Golden Crosse Signe Post, for his Treachery against the King.*

Another of the rarely told stories of the Civil War concerns a Worcester tailor. At the Battle of Worcester in 1651 Cromwell occupied all the high ground on the east of the city, and on a high knoll, still known to this day as Oliver's Knoll, the general had his forward post from which he personally directed operations. It was here, three days before the battle, that a disastrous camisade was made on Cromwell's camp, when fifteen hundred picked Royalist men were detailed to surprise and, if possible, capture the general. They wore white shirts (or camisoles) over their armour or leather coats so that in the dark they could recognise each other. But it also made them good targets for the Parliamentary forces had been forewarned and the surprisers were themselves surprised.

A Worcester tailor, William Guise, a strong supporter of Parliament, had lowered himself over the city wall by means of a knotted rope and in nearby Perry Wood had disclosed to Cromwell that a night attack was being prepared. The attack was made with great courage but with disastrous Royalist casualties, for the defences had been strengthened. One leader leapt a hedge and was impaled upon a stand of pikes. The ground around Battenhall was strewn with the dead — most of them being buried on the spot.

The Royalists, in revenge, hanged Guise from the signpost of the Golden Cross in Broad Street the very next day. But he was no traitor, and only six days after the battle Parliament gratefully granted to his widow an immediate cash payment of £200 (a large sum in those days) and a life annuity of equal amount. The coincidence that Cromwell died seven years to the day of his great victory at Worcester led later generations of Royalists to change his meeting with Guise in Perry Wood to a meeting with the Devil, and to assert he had bargained his soul for victory and seven years of life.

Oak-apple Day

For many years Oak-apple Day, 29 May, was celebrated by decorating the Guildhall gates with oak boughs from the Coventry estate in honour of the return of Charles II from exile. Oak apples or oak leaves recalled the Boscobel oak in which Charles hid after the Battle of Worcester. At the Restoration in 1660 Worcester had a great celebration, for it was thought that some special mark of appreciation would be shown to the city which had suffered so much during the Civil War. But Charles never returned to Worcester and many Royalist sympathisers were disillusioned by the king's selfishness and broken promises. During the Stuart rebellions of 1715 and 1745 the city was strongly Whig and Hanoverian.

The celebration of Oak-apple Day was revived by the Tory faction in the city at the end of the eighteenth century when political sentiments changed, mainly due to the French Revolution. In 1821 the mayor organised a pageant and procession of the corporation, trades and clubs, quite in the fashion of the original celebrations. In country districts village clubs 'walked'; while at Worcester the Diglis fishermen carried nets decked out with ribbons and oak branches, and sweeps from the Trinity and Bull Entry processed with the instruments of their trade. Oak-apple Day processions continued until the 1860s and boughs of oak were affixed over many doorways in different streets. The custom of decorating the Guildhall gates with oak boughs continues to this day.

Oak-apple gates, the Guildhall, Worcester c1932.

Captain Kidd and the Droitwich MP

The story of Captain Kidd, the most famous of pirates, has a strong Worcestershire link, for it was a Droitwich MP, Lord Bellamont, who unwittingly provided Kidd with the means to effect his piracy and it was he who made amends for his error of judgment by having Kidd arrested.

Lord Bellamont married Catherine Nanfan, the heiress of Birtsmorton Court, and on acquiring the Nanfan property settled in this county. In 1695 he was appointed Governor of New England with a special mission to put down piracy, then rife in the waters around the West Indies. Captain Kidd was recommended to him and as the king was unwilling to provide Kidd with a ship of war Bellamont helped him to fit out a privateer and induced the great Lord Somers, the Earl of Shrewsbury and others to contribute funds. Captain Kidd's ship was a joint stock venture and carried mainly Worcestershire money. If things had gone straight the speculation, it was said, would have been 'better than diamonds'.

There is a good deal of mystery about Kidd's exploits, but he certainly acquired a very evil reputation, attacking not only pirate vessels and foreigners but also the English ships he was supposed to protect. The truth will never be known, but in his absence Kidd was proclaimed a pirate and on hearing of the proclamation boldly sailed to Boston, Massachusetts, to learn the truth. There he was arrested by Bellamont, sent to England, tried at the Old Bailey and hanged at Execution Dock.

His trial was very irregular and the evidence on which he was executed ought not to have hanged a dog. He protested that his alleged piracies were legal prizes, taken under his commission as a privateersman. Perhaps, after all, he was merely a pawn in the game of politics; but his alleged excesses served as a convenient stick with which to beat the government. Somers was especially attacked as he had sealed Kidd's commission and any acquittal of Kidd would have been attributed to official influence. Kidd was thus left to his fate.

That he had some buried treasure which the government failed to recover seems certain but its amount was exaggerated, as were probably his villanies. 'He left a name at which the world grew pale', his contemporaries said of him. But the Worcestershire speculators in Kidd's stock did not make a total loss: they obtained a grant of all goods taken by Kidd from other pirates.

John Baskerville, printer and atheist

John Baskerville, one of the greatest innovators in the art of printing, was born at Sion Hill, Wolverley, in 1706. He was a confirmed atheist, yet he printed the most beautiful Bibles. His Bible of 1763 was the finest ever produced in England and one of the most beautiful books in the world. Baskerville died at Cradley, near Stourbridge, in 1775 and directed that his burial be in *unconsecrated* ground free from 'the idle fears of superstition and the wicked arts of priesthood'. Yet for all his gestures of defiance his plans came to nought. He was buried in his garden in Easy Row but sixteen years after his death his house was set on fire and gutted in the great Priestley riots of 1791. Then came the canal which cut through the grounds: in 1820 workmen found his coffin and moved it to a warehouse where it lay for several years and was inspected from time to time. In 1829 it was moved to a neighbouring shop. Finally, it was reburied in a vault in Christ Church, Victoria Square, and when that was demolished buried in the *consecrated* ground of Warston Lane Cemetery. Baskerville began type founding about 1750, and in 1757 there appeared, as Macaulay says, 'the first of those magnificent editions which went forth to astonish all the librarians of Europe'. The Baskerville typeface, very popular in the eighteenth and nineteenth centuries, is still widely used.

Warren Hastings

One of the greatest men Worcestershire has ever produced was Warren Hastings. He was the son of the Rector of Daylesford, then in south Worcestershire. When Daylesford became part of Gloucestershire in 1930 there was a great deal of anger and this account from *Berrow's Worcester Journal* shows the feeling of loss for a part of Worcestershire associated with the great man.

> The County Council have handed away Daylesford and its imperishable heritage. Yet the life story of Warren Hastings lives for ever as an honour to Worcestershire. As President of the Council of Bengal and as Governor General of India, he saved British power from destruction. He was accused of all sorts of things by his rivals, not least by a man named Francis, whom he had wounded in a duel. His impeachment for treason, which is one of the most notorious and shameful in political history, ended in a glorious

the most notorious and shameful in political history, ended in a glorious acquittal, and a burst of national applause. In the words of Prince Regent in 1814, he was the most ill-used man in the Dominions of the Crown. Hastings, in spite of the jealousy of other Indian administrators and of the pettiness of poltering politicians, founded the Indian Empire. And then, the meanest men among his opponents promoted and prosecuted his impeachment – which was at once the most vindictive and the most iniquitous trial in English history. It ruined a man who was a giant among his pygmy contemporaries, a man of transcendent genius whom posterity has been delighted to honour. His impeachment was worthy only of the pip-squeaks who lost our Empire in the west while Hastings was founding this new Empire in the east. Sir Austen Chamberlain (another old Worcestershire man) said: 'Never was an Englishman so ill-requited.' The impeachment cost him seventy eight thousand pounds, but his victory brought him national honour. He spent nearly thirty years at the end of his life at Daylesford, and died in 1818.

The Napoleonic threat

The threat of a Napoleonic invasion of England at the beginning of the nineteenth century marked the beginning of what was known as the Volunteer Movement. There was unparalleled enthusiasm for the vigorous prosecution of the war, and throughout the country some four hundred thousand men enrolled – seven hundred and twenty-two in one week in Worcester itself. Corps were formed at various places, such as Bewdley, Stourport, Kidderminster, Evesham, Pershore and Bromsgrove. The public subscribed funds for the volunteers' uniform and equipment and needlewomen worked with patriotic ardour, not only to make them clothing but to provide colours to inspire them. These colours were formally presented to the units by some great lady. The North Worcestershire Volunteers, for instance, were presented with its colours by Lady Beauchamp in a field at Bromsgrove. It had the monogram LWV (Loyal Worcester Volunteers) in a floral design of roses, thistles and shamrocks, and the motto 'Honi soit qui mal y pense' surmounted by a crown. After Nelson had defeated the French navy at Trafalgar the spectre of 'invasion by Boney' subsided. But general unrest – arising from accusations of corruption in Parliament and denunciation of flogging in the army – spread throughout the country and was the cause of mutiny in a number of places. An evening paper (name unknown) reported:

> We have dreadful confusion in this neighbourhood between the local militia and their officers, about the 'marching guinea'. The Loyal Worcesters on Sunday last laid down their arms, knocked down their Colonel, and many of their officers, broke open the depot and helped themselves to ball cartridges. An express (messenger) was immediately sent to Kidderminster for the 36th Regiment who put an end to the battle.
>   The Pershore and Evesham Militia soon caught the flame . . . The Colonel, in the heat of his passion, drew his sword which was instantly broken into

pieces. The men, with fixed bayonets, would have run him through, if he had not made his escape. By way of revenge, they went to his home, the windows of which were instantly demolished. A troop of Light Horse (from Tewkesbury) was sent for.

It appears that the colonel had offended some of them at Evesham and they had taken it into their heads to mutiny. Fortunately, no lives were lost; but the writer of the report feared the worst since Worcester seemed to be in a similar state of mutiny, and the same thing was likely to take place at Upton that very day.

The 'marching guinea', which appears to have been the immediate cause of the trouble, was the weekly pay which, in degree, officers and men received to cover expenses incurred when marching from one place to another.

Carlyle takes the water cure

Doctors James Wilson and James Manby Gully arrived at Malvern in 1842 to exploit the purity of the Malvern water. They turned a hillside village into a thriving Victorian spa by founding hydropathic establishments which charged large fees for treatment in which the only part that mattered was diet and exercise. Thousands of overfed visitors poured in for a few weeks each season to endure the torture of ice-cold baths, sleeping in wet sheets and a spartan diet.

The Malvern water cure: before and after. Engravings from Taking the Water Cure, *1855.*

Dr Wilson ruled his patients with a rod of iron. Generals, politicians and peers of the realm were as deferential as boys at school. Alcohol and tobacco were banned. Wilson rode the hills on a thoroughbred bay mare rounding up his patients like sheep. Lord Lytton, feeling the pangs of hunger, was tempted into a pastry shop where he bought a dozen rich tarts. Unexpectedly confronted by Dr Wilson, he revealed his purchase. 'Poison!' shouted the doctor. 'Throw them away at once, sir!' And Lytton did.

Dr Gully, in contrast, had a charming and persuasive manner. He was the more successful, numbering among his patients such eminent Victorians as Tennyson, Gladstone, Darwin, Florence Nightingale, Disraeli and Dickens. Dr Gully was an admirer of Carlyle and knowing of his chronic digestive troubles wrote again and again, inviting him to Malvern. 'Only come and I will cure you.' Carlyle went, and Mrs Carlyle too 'as a bodyguard, not as a patient'; but she got tired of looking on and became a patient 'for fun'. The doctor did his best to repeat on Carlyle the miracle he had worked on Bulwer Lytton; and Carlyle responded all he could, even banishing his bad temper. Mrs Carlyle, writing to William Allington soon after the cure began, said: 'A lady told me the other day that it was quite delightful to hear from the bathman that his only regret was that he (Carlyle) was not kept longer in the pack. So you see the cold water must be acting favourably on his faculty of patience and resignation, if on nothing else.'

But it was too late. The Edinburgh doctors of long ago, with their too plentiful mercury and castor oil, had done organic mischief beyond repair, and Carlyle's sufferings which had lasted thirty years lasted for thirty more. He was grateful to Dr Gully all the same, and so was his wife who said: 'The more I think of these people (Dr Gully, his daughter and staff) the more I admire their politeness and kindness to us. I don't remember ever in my life before to have stayed a whole month in anybody's house without ever wishing to be away.' They enjoyed the pure air and quiet and continued to use the water compressors, sitting bath and packings for a little longer. But in a month or two the tired dyspeptic was to let go the little hope he had and say the water cure had 'done me no ill, and not traceably very much good'.

Leaders of society

Of Worcestershire's aristocratic families in the 1980s, only three still lived in their ancestral homes: Lady Beauchamp at Madresfield Court, Viscount Cobham at Hagley Hall, and Lord Sandys at Ombersley Court. The Foleys and the Dudleys and Wards have gone from Witley Court, once the grandest of all Worcestershire houses, but now in ruins; the Coventrys have left Croome Court, now a school; the Pakingtons have departed from Westwood, which is divided into flats; Lord Plymouth has sold Hewell Grange, a borstal institution until very recently; Lord Hindlip has gone from Hindlip Hall, now the West Mercia Police Headquarters; and the Vernons have given Hanbury Hall to the National Trust.

Among the ancient families of squires remaining, the Berkeleys of Spetchley and the Holland Martins of Overbury still occupy their historic houses, but the Winningtons have abandoned Stanford-on-Teme, the Russells have left Strensham, the Berkeleys of Cotheridge have gone, their house now in flats as is Severn End, the former home of the Lechmeres, and most recently the Bearcrofts have sold Mere Hall.

Well into this century these families have continued to draw the pattern of Worcestershire history and have been at the hub of activity, especially in the political field. During the last three or four hundred years the same names recur time and again in Parliamentary elections and, like all other human groups, there were good and bad among them. But rise or fall, their personalities, their eccentricities, escapades and elopements have provided a continual source of interest. The following stories show the quaintness of a lifestyle now gone, and provide a picture of the whims and fancies and of the tragedies of some of Worcestershire's leaders of county society.

THE ELOPEMENT OF THE VERNON HEIRESS AND THE 'COTTAGE COUNTESS'

In 1776 Henry Cecil (afterwards the tenth Earl and Marquis of Exeter) married Emma Vernon, the sole heiress of the Vernons of Hanbury Hall, and took up residence at Hanbury. One child was born of this marriage but lived for only one month. The curate at the time was the Rev William Sneyd and on 14 June 1789 Mrs Henry Cecil eloped with him. The Cecil's marriage had lasted just thirteen years. There is no evidence to show what effect the elopement had on Cecil but by the end of June he appears to have left Hanbury and was at Great Bolas, Shropshire, where he sought shelter for the night at the Old Rectory House, then occupied by Thomas Hoggins, a farmer. Strangely, he gave his name as John Jones, and remained there for some time. The following year an interesting marriage entry in the parish register of Great Bolas was recorded: 'April 13, 1790. John Jones of this parish and Sarah Hoggins of this parish, were married in the church by license.' John Jones was described as of 'Bolas Magna, Yeoman', over twenty-one years of age and a bachelor.

At the time of the 'marriage' Henry Cecil had not been divorced from his first wife. Divorce at that time was only possible by a special Act of Parliament, and it was said that only when his divorce received the Royal Assent in June 1791 did 'Mr Jones' inform Sarah of the real position. On 3 October 1791 Henry Cecil, described again as a bachelor, married Sarah Hoggins a second time at St Mildred's Church, Bread Street, London, and so it was announced in the *Gentleman's Magazine* of the same month. Cecil bought land at Bolas and they lived there as Mr and Mrs Jones. A collection of love letters in Burghley House, Stamford, shows Cecil's frustration at being away in town and his longing to be with Sarah in their cottage. In 1794 Henry Cecil succeeded as tenth earl and removed to Burghley House. The 'Cottage Countess', as Sarah became known, died a month after giving birth to her fourth child.

Within days of Henry's legal marriage to Sarah, Emma Vernon married her curate; and later a third husband, John Phillips, of Winterdyn, Bewdley. She died in 1818, aged sixty-five, and was buried 'by her own desire' at the north edge of Hanbury churchyard, and not in the Vernon vault with her ancestors. She chose this unworthy place for her sepulchre, it is said, because of her misdoings. She left no issue and the manor of Hanbury and her estates passed to her second cousin, Thomas Shrawley Vernon.

THE FALL OF THE HOUSE OF FOLEY

The great wealth of the politically powerful Foley family of Witley Court came from extensive ironworks in North Worcestershire. They were ironmasters to the navy throughout the seventeenth century, to their great profit, and received a peerage in 1733. The peerage died out in 1766 but was later revived for a kinsman. The decline of this great house began in the last years of the eighteenth century when the two sons of the first Lord Foley (of the second creation), according to the *Royal Register*, 'embittered the latter years of an excellent parent. In the annals of modern extravagance there has not been such extensive and useless dissipation as has been contrived by the two elder sons of the family'.

The second baron, who figured in Regency caricature as Lord Balloon, 'by a most rapid course of debauchery, extravagance and gambling involved himself in a state of distress from the misery and disgrace of which he could never be extricated'. He was such an inveterate gambler, says the *Complete Peerage*, 'that his father disinherited him, and left the estate to his grandson'. But the third baron followed the family pattern, and became the most extravagant member of the Carlton House set. Of the Foleys, Mr Creevey wrote in 1829 that, 'his wife is said to be the most extravagant woman in England'. She was always attended by five maids. She wrote novels, and in the midst of their ruin was never known to degrade herself by putting on a pair of gloves or a ribbon a second time, who always had four ponies saddled and bridled ready for any entertainment or excursion that may come into her head. 'To say nothing of Foley, who with a ha'porth of income keeps the best house, and has planted more oak trees than any man in England, and by the influence of his name and popularity returns two members for Droitwich and one for the county.'

Life at Witley Court in the early nineteenth century was vividly described by a Mrs Bryant, a member of the Foley household. She spoke of Lady Foley's pride, so overwhelming that 'sliding panels were constructed at Witley, so that a servant meeting her ladyship could run for cover till she passed by'. Among the frequent visitors to Witley was the Prince of Wales (afterwards George IV) and some of Mrs Bryant's anecdotes reflected credit on neither prince nor peer. The billiard room was situated next to the chapel, and often in the lulls of a Sunday afternoon service could be heard 'the rattling of the balls, bad language and the gentlemanly oaths so fashionable at that period'.

When the third Lord Foley died in 1833, overwhelmed by debt, the fourth lord, a young man, sold Witley Court for £899,000 — the largest sum then on record for any English property.

A VICTORIAN MELODRAMA

The purchaser of Witley Court Estate in 1838 was Lord Ward, Baron of Birmingham, only eighteen when he succeeded to that title but with an income of £100,000. The teenage baron owned over two hundred mines in the Black Country and scores of iron- and chemical works. In the boom years of the Franco-Prussian War he made a profit of £1,000,000 on his iron and coal concerns alone. He also gave vast sums away: £30,000 for the restoration of Worcester Cathedral; at his own expense he fitted out a hospital ship for the Crimean War in which Florence Nightingale travelled from Balaclava to Scutari. His wealth was fabulous, yet he was always in debt. When advised on one occasion by his solicitor to retrench, he replied that it was not possible for him to live on £80,000 a year.

Garden party at Croome Court (Lord and Lady Coventry front row), 1909.

He had a particular mania for jewels and spent £60,000 on jewellery at the Vienna Exhibition. At Christmas parties Witley Court was a 'vision of magnificence with strings of jewels hung from branch to branch of the Christmas tree', all gifts from Cartier of Bond Street. It is related that at the time of the French Exhibition of 1867, when the famous Dudley jewels were exhibited, he could not be induced away from the cases containing them — until he was taken into custody for 'loitering' by a zealous sergeant of police.

In 1851 Lord Ward had married Constance de Burgh, very beautiful and extraordinarily rich, but an unwilling bride. She had given her heart elsewhere but her parents insisted on the match which led within a few months to disaster and the death of the bride. The Countess of Cardigan, a friend of Constance, later related the details of the story which had all the features of a Victorian melodrama.

> Constance was of great beauty and Ward worshipped her beauty, and had strange ideas how to treat a wife; and Constance was not tactful or accommodating. He treated her like a lovely slave he had bought. He had a barbaric passion for precious stones and lavished them on her; she appeared literally ablaze with diamonds. He had a strange peculiarity which alarmed his wife. When alone, he expected her to sit for hours, unclothed except for ropes of pearls, on a black satin-covered couch, admiring her beauty. She was at first terrified and disgusted, and appealed to her father. Lord Ward

was a kind man and very rich, and the parents decided these peculiarities came within the marriage vows, and told her to submit.

Constance had a lover, Lord Dupplin, and was pregnant. Ward coming home from a ball one night saw Dupplin leaving his house. He immediately went up to his wife's bedroom and accused her of adultery. 'Get up, madam ... my house is no longer yours; arrangements shall be made for your future, but henceforth you are no wife of mine.' Tears and entreaties were useless. She was obliged to dress and led past the scandalised servants waiting downstairs and turned out of doors.

The frightened young woman managed to reach her parents' house and implored them to give her shelter, but they were as heartless as the husband, and would not do so. More dead than alive, she went to the house of her singing master where he allowed her to stay until the next day, when she went to Ostend. She died in childbirth on the Continent. Ward brought her body home and, bizarre to the end, forced a friend to observe the fact that his dead wife had rotten teeth by forcing her mouth open to see.

In 1865 Ward married again, and by this time he was the Earl of Dudley, the first by a new creation. His second wife was Georgina, one of eight beautiful sisters, painted as a child by Millais in a picture called 'Apple Blossom'. She was seventeen, he was forty-eight.

THE GYPSY COUNTESS

Enville Hall, near Stourbridge, was the seat of the Earls of Stamford. It lies just over the border in Staffordshire, but the family owned a great deal of property in Stourbridge and always regarded the Worcestershire town as their home town. In 1848 George Harry Grey, seventh Earl of Stamford and Baron of Groby, was twenty-one and at Cambridge. He had taken as his mistress the college bootman's daughter, Bessie Billage. Hearing that two other young students, Lords Strathmore and Munster, were competing for her favours, Harry Stamford, to the consternation of his friends, took her off to Brighton and married her.

She was a very simple person, unlettered, unteachable and terrified of the platoons of footmen, servants and gardeners at Enville Hall. Lord Stamford was patron of nine livings, and it was hoped that the clergymen's wives would befriend Bessie; but it was most embarrassing for everyone for she would call these ladies 'Madam', and bob and curtsey to them. Eventually he took her away to a mansion at Hove where they saw few people and where, after six years of marriage and to the relief of many, Bessie died.

It was assumed that Stamford had learnt a lesson; but with one year's grace he married again and his second choice was as strange as the first. He married Catherine Cox whose mother was a gypsy with a tribe of wild sons and daughters. One son, Israel, was in Dorchester gaol for horse-stealing; Tamar, the eldest girl, had produced three love children in five years, all born in the workhouse; and Mrs Cox had landed in Wimborne poorhouse, only to be removed to the bridewell for 'misbehaviour'. Catherine and her younger sisters became a popular equestrian act (the celebrated

'Fleming Sisters') in Astley's Royal Circus. They were very good-looking and the talk of the town, not only for their act but for their private lives, for they were all mistresses of the high-spending aristocratic military set. Catherine lived with the second son of the Earl of Denby, Captain Fielding, and in 1854, just after the captain had embarked for the Crimea, she gave birth to a daughter. It was shortly after this that Stamford saw her and married her.

It was a year before Harry Stamford took his new wife to Enville, and at her request great celebrations were held. There was a feast for the tenants, fireworks and a German band, and the grounds were thrown open to some sixty thousand workers from the Black Country. The parsons' and farmers' wives were expecting another Bessie, for they had heard all about her family. They were in for a shock. They found instead a fine, handsome, fashionably-dressed lady of about thirty, fearless and unperturbed. She was determined to be a countess and missed no opportunity for opening their country seats at Enville and at Bradgate Park, near Leicester, meeting the tenants and doing good works. On birthdays, at harvest and Christmas she would drive among her curtseying and forelock-pulling dependants, laden with boots and blankets for the needy. She opened ornate Gothic schools bearing her name, even held Bible classes for the grooms and stable lads. She brought all her family to Enville, including their many love children, but never her own child, though she did see her from time to time.

Lord Stamford was Master of the Quorn, and Catherine was queen of the hunt — for she could outride any other lady there. Yet after the meet she was completely ignored: the huntswomen would have nothing to do with Stamford's 'hippodrome dolly'. Worse, she was barred from Court by Queen Victoria; but her subsequent battle with the queen entertained both London and Stourbridge. She secured the box at the opera immediately adjoining the queen's, a move the latter did not relish, especially as Lady Stamford was wont to behave in a rather lively fashion there as if to show that she was in no way impressed by royalty. Eventually, the queen declined to attend the opera as long as Lady Stamford continued to figure so conspicuously in the adjoining loge, and as the countess refused all requests of the management to exchange her box for another the queen saw no opera for two seasons.

In 1883 Lord Stamford died. Catherine lived on, but always an outlaw beyond her estates. Even at the races she sat in lonely grandeur in her carriage. No lady ever approached her, no-one spoke to her. In 1904 Enville Hall was destroyed by fire. Two months later Catherine was dead.

THE MP WHO BOUGHT UP LEICESTER SQUARE

Few people know that London's famous Leicester Square was presented to the nation by the MP for Kidderminster, Baron Grant. He was a wizard of finance, the earliest of great company promoters, at whose touch millions came and went and ethereal shining projects and fabulous mines became as real to the hard-headed men of the City as the carriages and horses Cinderella's fairy godmother produced.

Baron Grant had so many gifts and talents that one is inclined to regret honesty was not one of them; but that old-fashioned quality would have been out of place in the grand company he kept. In the 1870s he was not merely beating his competitors, he was soaring unique and resplendent in spheres they could not approach. £24,000,000 (think of that in 1870) found its way into his coffers from the earnings of trustful people.

Albert Grant, born in Dublin in 1830, was the son of a certain Guttheimer, a German Jew, who kept a little shop of fancy wares in Newgate Street, London. Albert was educated on the Continent and spoke several languages fluently. He was a very presentable man, a man of taste and altogether a man of the world. His great genius was in floating companies which appealed to the very moderate savers, clergymen, civil servants, saving widows, better-off artisans.

His enterprises sounded wonderfully exotic: Cadiz Waterworks, Central Uruguay Railway, Labuan Coal Company, City of Milan Improvements, Odessa Waterworks, names which took captive the bourgeois souls of the palmy days of Queen Victoria; and he dressed his shop window with a glittering array of directors who seemed en masse to have stepped out of the pages of *Debrett's Peerage*. The high watermark of this wonderful man was reached in 1871 when the Emma Silver Mine Company was floated. Where the mine was no-one knew, and no-one thought to question the man who had been Kidderminster's MP since 1865 and who had recently been ennobled by the King of Italy for services rendered to Milan. The shares were a modest £20 and £1,000,000 was subscribed in a day. The baron made £100,000 by the transaction — but within a few months the shares were going for one shilling a piece.

The collapse of the company, however, did not destroy his reputation, and cleverly he bought Leicester Square for £30,000, erected the first open-air statue to Shakespeare there, and gave it to the nation. He also paid £8,000 for the portrait of Sir Walter Scott by Landseer and presented it to the National Portrait Gallery of Scotland. Though the dogs of fate were on his heels he built the largest house in London, Kensington House; but it was used only once before being seized by his creditors and pulled down. Misfortunes arrived with a rush. His pictures were sold at Christie's and for years he was never out of the law courts. Ninety actions were launched against him and there were many more still pending when at length in 1899, worn out, disgraced, penniless, he died.

Stanley Baldwin

THREE TIMES PRIME MINISTER

Though son of an MP Stanley Baldwin did not seek high office but reached the highest peak in British politics not just once but three times (1923, 1924 and 1935), and much to his friends' surprise. At the beginning of his political career in 1908 the editor of the *Daily Express* wrote: 'I met Rudyard Kipling with his cousin, Stanley Baldwin, the young ironmaster from the West Country (actually Bewdley) who hopes to get into Parliament like his father before him ... He is rather shy and not at all politician-like in his manner, and I do not suppose he will ever do more than follow his leader if he ever gets in. But I call him pleasant, cultured and conscientious, but a badly dressed man without much desire to sit in the limelight; also he has a sense of humour, and when he smiles it lights up the face that is rugged and interesting.'

Baldwin came in for much criticism during his career. Birkenhead said bitter things, but later came to pay tribute to his character and wisdom; and Churchill did the same. He held office in incredibly difficult times. They were the days of a national strike, of a national government, the rise of dictatorship abroad, the peace movement at home and the abdication crisis of Edward VIII. Atticus of the *Sunday Times* wrote in 1936: 'It is difficult to estimate how the future will judge us. But Mr Baldwin need have no worries. This man of climax and anti-climax, who has upset the conventions of party leadership, who has turned Parliament from a place of warring factions into a Council of State, who has been bitterly attacked, who has faltered and blundered and emerged more powerful after every crisis — his place in history is secure. His baffled enemies say he is cunning, but is it cunning for a countryman to know when the rain is coming, or a storm is at hand?'

Malvern Cycling Club at the Hundred House, Great Witley, welcomed by Stanley Baldwin (in the straw hat), c1890.

Stanley Baldwin liked telling stories against himself. The following example is remarkable considering that he had been Prime Minister for a number of years. He was once travelling from Worcester to London by train, the only occupant of the carriage. The train stopped and a gentleman entered and sat opposite. He began to look hard at Mr Baldwin who was examining some papers. After a while the man leant over and tapped Baldwin on the knee. 'Excuse me, is it Baldwin? Harrow 1884? Trinity College, Cambridge 1886?' 'Yes,' said Mr Baldwin. 'Well, well,' replied the stranger. 'I thought I recognised you. I'm Thompson, Harrow and Cambridge. *What are you doing now?*'

OLIVER BALDWIN AND THE GYPSY

Wilden lies just off Hartlebury Common where for at least a century a community of gypsies has camped. Oliver Baldwin (later the second earl who, holding different political views from those of his father, joined the Labour Party) once said:

> I am the godfather of a gypsy, and proud of it. While driving my car across Hartlebury Common, I overtook a gypsy running in the direction of Stourport. I stopped and enquired the reason for his unusual haste. He wanted a midwife. I fetched one, and the grateful gypsy started to dig under his tent for the price of a drink. 'No,' I told him, 'if your wife presents you with a son name him after me.' And there he is, a bare-footed, single-braced little rascal, running about the common, and rejoicing in the name of Oliver Baldwin Coleman.

Mrs Satan and 'the Sisters of Sin'

In 1927 Mrs Victoria Woodhull Martin, wealthy lady of the manor, died at Bredon Norton. Held in great regard by those who knew her, she achieved posthumous distinction when in 1943 the Bishop of Gloucester dedicated a memorial tablet to her in Tewkesbury Abbey which she had loved and supported so generously. She had come a very long way from Homer, Ohio, where she was born nearly ninety years earlier.

Victoria Claflin and her sister Tennessee had a crude and primitive upbringing. In their teens they moved from place to place, claiming to be clairvoyant physicians, able to cure cancer and other diseases, always one move ahead of the law and dissatisfied clients. At the age of sixteen Victoria was married by her parents to a middle-aged habitually intoxicated womaniser named Woodhull who, conveniently for Victoria, disappeared from time to time. In 1868 the two handsome sisters fell in with Cornelius Vanderbilt, the elderly millionaire broker whose wife had just died. As clairvoyants and obliging ladies they consoled him so effectively that at the age of seventy-six he proposed marriage to Tennessee. She considered marriage unnecessary while both received his support and he, recognising their keen intelligence, began to educate them socially. Gifts and tips for the stock market, which Vanderbilt almost controlled, flowed freely and soon they were very rich.

In the 1860s and 1870s the sisters achieved fame as bankers and brokers, something in those days unheard of. Both became active in politics, supported women's rights, produced their own newspaper and lectured all over the States on free love. Puritan America was horrified and the churches responded with a furious attack. Yet Victoria had supporters; she was the first woman to address the Congressional Committee, and in 1872 was nominated for the presidency of the United States by the Equal Rights Party (running against General Grant), the only woman ever nominated for this highest office.

A scandal disclosed in her newspaper, however, resulted in the sisters' arrest and imprisonment for obscene libel. Opposition newspapers called them 'the Sisters of Sin' and in an illustration in 1872 Victoria was called Mrs Satan. When released from gaol, they decided to leave America and in 1877 Victoria, her sister and her two children sailed for England.

In England they changed. They made no effort to join the women's suffrage movement and Victoria even denounced free love. They moved easily in English society. In 1885 Tennessee married Mr Francis Cook who was later knighted. Victoria, twice divorced, captured the heart of John Biddulph Martin, aged 36, a partner in Martin's Bank. It took six years to convince the Worcestershire Martin family that she was respectable, but friendship with the Prince and Princess of Wales, and especially Lord Coventry, overcame opposition. The Martins lived mostly in London, but on John's death Victoria came to live permanently at Bredon Norton; and as Mrs Woodhull Martin began her reign as lady of the manor. With reforming zeal she restored the old manor house and workers' houses on the estate. She built a village school and in 1906 turned a farm on the estate into a ladies' agricultural college. She took up the cause of world peace; she was instrumental in forming the Aerial League of Great Britain, offering $5,000 to anyone who flew the Atlantic. When war was declared in 1914 Tennessee (Lady Cook) and Victoria crossed the Atlantic to get American support for Britain, and when the USA entered the war in 1917 Victoria flew the Stars and Stripes alongside the Union Jack over Bredon Norton.

She died just after Lindberg had flown the Atlantic. Those in America who had known her as Mrs Satan must have been amazed at the position she had achieved.

Sir George Vernon: the man who gave away Hanbury Hall

Sir George Vernon, the last of the Vernons of Hanbury Hall, was an unconventional character. He left the hall and £66,000 to his estate foreman's daughter, Ruth Powick, whom he had taken as his mistress. Ruth was sixteen when one day Sir George came to her father's cottage and, in his blunt way, said, 'Ted, I want to borrow your daughter for six months. Things are in a mess at the hall.' At the time Lady Vernon was living in London. So Ruth learned shorthand and bookkeeping and travelled the world with her father's employer. 'Ten years later,' Ruth recalled, 'he again called on my father. This time, he was as blunt as ever. He said, "Ted, your daughter has been a treasure. I have decided to leave her everything. My one great wish is for Ruth to take the Vernon name. What do you say, Ted?" So my name was changed by deed poll and Sir George introduced me everywhere as his daughter.'

Sir George had a hatred of the Established Church and carried on a bitter campaign against church tithes. Every year he staged a performance in the forecourt at Hanbury

Hall as bits of furniture were auctioned, ostensibly in payment of tithe dues. In protest, he gave instructions that he was not to be buried in the local churchyard but in unconsecrated ground: 'No parson is going to read any service over me!'; and in 1940 he was found dead in his bedroom with a revolver beside him. For some time he had associated himself with Sir Oswald Mosley and the British fascist organisation; and moves were in hand to arrest him.

The Powick family, long-term servants of the Vernons, honoured Sir George's request to be buried in Shrawley Wood, part of the Vernon estate. Ruth became the mistress of the twenty-roomed Vernon mansion at Shrawley, while Lady Vernon lived on at the hall. Later Ruth married Frederick Horton and was known as Mrs Vernon Horton. In 1953 the hall was given to the National Trust.

CHAPTER THREE

Village Life

The Worcestershire dialect

STANLEY BALDWIN PUBLICLY COMPLAINED of 'the education which flattens out the countryside, which destroys dialect, and so destroys our old tongue. This schoolboard education has robbed us of our dialect, and told us we must not talk in broad Worcester.' But the county has more than one dialect, for north of Bromsgrove and Stourbridge it is distinctly 'Black Country'; and the student can easily detect the difference between east and west for Shakespeare's dialect of the Avon Valley is broader than that of the very western edges of the county.

In the Severn Vale a 'foreigner' once asked a local publican about five pear trees growing in a hedge near Tewkesbury. He got this reply:

> They pear trees wuz fust planted in a fine meadow near Pershore, where the land be very kind to pears, an' good bearings of capital fruit they had on 'em. But misfortune fur the farmer mon as owned 'em, theer wuz an owd rookery in some owd elms overanight 'em, an' soon as they pears wuz ripe, they domned owd crows 'ud come an' settle on the branches of they pear trees, an' peck-peck-peck they 'ud goo till they a' yut a' the fruit there wuz.

The farmer, so the tale proceeded, set a trap for the crows with bird-lime and one warm sunny day the crows settled on the trees and 'could move ne'er a foot'.

> 'Lummydays,' sez the farmer mon, 'I ha' got 'em this time. I'll git my owd gun an' shut the lot on 'em.' So off he guz to fetch 'un. They owd crows heerd what wuz said, an' set up a-cawin' an' a-flappin' theer wings fit to bust; an' as soon as they see the farmer mon come back wi' 'is muzzle-loader, they made sich a termenjous desperate flappin' that up come all five pear trees by the roots, an' whiffley-whiffley-whiffley off they flies, pear trees an' all, over along the river to Tewkesbury. Arter they bin agooin' fur a while, there come a smartish shower o' rain an' that washed most o' the bird-lime away, an' clunk-clunk-clunk, down drops they pear trees into a 'edge by the high road to'ards Newent. Took good root they did, too, an' theer they be to this day. But domme if I knows what happened to they owd crows arterwards.

A cottage flower garden

Country women take great pride in their gardens and many of them are very learned in the folklore of flowers. In a village near Evesham there used to be an old lady,

Mrs Oliver, living alone, whose garden was particularly interesting. She worked in the fields to earn a living and the garden was her hobby. Most of her time was spent in the open air. 'Laws,' she would say, 'I couldn't bide in the house. In the rain, in the shine, in the cowd an' the 'eat, I mun be out in the fields. The farmers coulden do wivout me labour. If I en't mangel trimmin' or swede pullin', I be tater pickin', and if I en't stone pickin' or 'op tyin', I be carrot weedin', and if I en't pea pickin', I be currant pickin'. Seed time an' harvest, summer an' winter, I be allus doin' summat.'

In the spring the old lady made money out of her flower garden. In January her garden was a show of snowdrops which she picked and bunched for market. The snowdrops were succeeded by 'daffydowndillies and primmiroses'. Violets, cissies, crocuses and gillyflowers followed on and as a rule these were the last of the marketable flowers.

Gleaning in South Worcestershire in the 1880s.

She collected the old-fashioned flowers that flourished throughout the summer and loved their quaint names which invested them with poetry and almost human personalities. There were columbines and marigolds, honesty and snow-on-the-mountain, hen-and-chicken daisies, sweet-scented lad's love and blue-eyed forget-me-nots. There were Canterbury bells, Solomon's seals, moss and tea rose trees. Seven sisters twined round the little parlour window and nearby were turn-again-gentlemen, love-lies-bleeding, love-in-a-mist, sweet williams, yellow bachelor's-buttons, white and red lady's-needlework, old-lady's-nightcap, white and yellow bedstraw, dame's rocket and thrift, touch-me-not, and evening 'primmiroses'. On the sunny side of the potato patch were tiger lilies, everlastings, poppies, monkey musk, snapdragons, rainbow flowers, monkshood, larkspur, red-hot pokers; and in September and October she had marguerites, michaelmas daisies and the flowers farewell-summer which, she said, were truly named for they were a fine sight until November.

The village water supply

The Rev Oswald G Knapp wrote an interesting account of village life in the mid-nineteenth century, recalling conditions at Honeybourne:

> The water supply in villages was often shockingly bad. I don't think any of the cottages near our vicarage had a well. Ours could only be used for washing; all water for drinking or cooking was fetched every day by a boy from the only public well which was in Cow Honeybourne, a mile away, in a two-gallon cider jar, loaded on a three-wheeled trolley made by my father. In a drought it would get so low that one had to wait a good while before enough collected to fill the bucket.
>
> Our neighbours got theirs from a brook which ran at the bottom of our garden. Before it reached us, at Mr Hiorn's farm, the stream was held up by a stone dam, and this portion was known as 'The Moat', though I doubt if it ever served any defensive purpose. The dam was pierced by a wooden spout which let the water into the pool below, where the annual sheep wash took place. On these occasions, the shepherd, Caleb Holford, took his stand in the wooden 'pulpit' which stood in the water alongside the spout, and drew each sheep beneath the water. At such times, of course, the water in the brook was undrinkable, and the cottagers had to take a yoke and pair of buckets to the moat above. Things were even worse when the brook was in flood and the water the colour of peasoup. All that could be done then was to let the bucket stand till the worst of the sediment had dropped down. It is small wonder that water, as a beverage, was unpopular.
>
> Owing perhaps to the wet clay soil, croup was prevalent among the infants in the Honeybourne district, and my father's prescription of a hot bath at first caused consternation among the mothers, who were fully persuaded that to plunge an infant into such an unusual environment would mean certain death, and he had to see the water was properly heated and the child immersed in order to get his treatment carried out. But when they saw the instant relief it afforded they gradually got over their horror.
>
> Indeed, water, hot or cold, was regarded as something which required to be cautiously and sparingly applied, whether internally or externally. For the latter feeling witness the story of a man who was set to clean out the village horse-pond. After taking off his shoes and stockings and turning up his trousers, he spent the morning raking out the mud. When he came out at dinner time and wiped the muck off his legs with grass, he was horrified to see that from the knee downwards they were *white*. He grasped at once what had happened. The horse-leeches, which inhabited the pond, had

fastened on his legs without his feeling them and sucked out all the blood.
Unless he could get a fresh supply pretty quick he was probably a dead man.
So he walked straight into Evesham for advice. Great was his indignation
when the unfeeling doctor not only laughed at his tale of woe, but sent him
home without even the comfort of a bottle of physic to make good his loss
of blood!

When water was used for washing it was used sparingly. John Morris, who collected
folk sayings in the Broadway district around 1900, was told by a farm labourer, 'I
never use water except for washing the top parts o'me — ; anyhow, a clean shirt
is as good as a wash'. A sad widow once told him: 'He washed his fit (feet) that
night, a thing he never done since we was married. I know'd as summat would
happen, and sure enough next mornin' he was djud.'

The village medical service

Honeybourne was very badly off in the matter of medical service. There were,
of course, reliable doctors at Evesham, but that was five miles away. One
of them, Dr J B Haynes, attended my mother when I was born. In those
days doctors did not go their rounds with a suitcase full of instruments and
remedies for all manner of emergencies. A watch and a couple of lancets
in the waist-coat pocket and a stethoscope screwed inside the top-hat
completed the usual outfit. The last was not always forthcoming. I fancy
the old doctor placed more reliance on his unaided ear, and I can recall
how I hated the tickling of his bushy whiskers when he pressed it to my
ribs. But I don't think he attended anyone else in the village, and the
cottagers would, of course, have been unable to pay his fee.

They were mainly dependent for treatment on the parish doctor who lived
up in the hills. He was rather rough and ready in his treatment, besides being
given to partake too freely of the refreshments which were offered to him
on his rounds. It was reported that when he felt it was unsafe to dismount
from his horse, in case he might not be able to regain the saddle, he would
pull up outside and shout to the patient to come to the window and put
out his tongue for inspection. Where a further inspection seemed necessary,
he flicked up his whiplash with directions to tie it round the patient's wrist,
in order to take his pulse.

Under these circumstances, it was fortunate that my father had a fair
knowledge of elementary surgery and medicine. (This because his brother
was studying at Worcester Infirmary, and the information had rubbed off on
him.) It stood him in good stead in a country parish at a time when new
agricultural machinery was coming into use. All accident cases were sent
to the vicarage for treatment, and the amateur doctor took risks which a
professional might have declined. The village blacksmith, who was much
in request as the pig ringer, one day let his forefinger slip between the jaws
of a sow on which he was operating, and came to the vicarage with the
upper part of the finger barely connected with the lower half. He refused

my father's advice to go to a surgeon. 'He'll take 'un off, an' I shall lose my best finger. You put 'un on, parson, an' I'll chance it.' So the finger was put on and strapped up and brought for dressing every day. He was a healthy man, and the new tissue formed and the finger was saved. Of course, it was stiff, but he could get a grip on it with his thumb, which was his main concern.

Village trades

Great changes have taken place in the social and economic life of the village during the last hundred or so years, and it is with surprise that one realises the number and variety of trades that once flourished in the village. In 1843 *Ombersley*, for instance, with a population of just over two thousand, had fourteen carpenters, two builders, two millers, four tailors, ten bootmakers, two milliners, two drapers, three butchers, two grocers, six blacksmiths, four wheelwrights, two saddlers, four doctors, seven academies of learning, and sixty-three farmers.

Some villages, it seems, managed with a jack-of-all-trades. At *Harvington*, near Evesham, in 1823 James Tarrant hung up his sign from a barber's pole which announced:

> *James Tarrant*, joiner, cabinet maker and builder, bricklayer and plasterer, repairs all kinds of machinery, keeps a journeyman carpenter to do all sorts of blacksmith's work; hangs church bells, pig killer, rings pigs and spays, bellows mender, tooth drawer and hair dresser, well sinker, and thatcher, jobbing gardener. NB Gamekeeper to the Manor of Norton and Linchwick.

Two trades once found in the larger villages were those of cerecloth and shroud maker. At *Broadway* in the first half of the nineteenth century Thomas Shuffery melted in his chandlery furnace bleached wax in which long strips of fine linen were dipped, and afterwards smoothed out with a polishing stone. The last cerements made there were for the body of Squire Phillips of Middle Hill. This explains the tradition that the old squire was buried in white wax.

The trade of shroud maker was carried on at Broadway until the latter part of the last century by the female members of the Keyte family who made the woollen garments with which, according to law, every corpse had to be habited. It is well that the law was repealed and a better custom adopted, for the antiquated shroud and hood, frilled and beribboned, emphasised the pallor of death and made its majesty grotesque.

Clogs were made in remote coppices in Worcestershire and Herefordshire until the end of the 1939–45 War. They were worn by those working on the land and in factories where the floors were covered with oil. One of the last clogmakers was William Ashworth of *Tenbury*. The clogs had a sole of alder wood with leather uppers. Alder trees were coppiced and 'stooled' to produce poles of six to seven inches thick which were cut into short logs with a two-man bow-saw, then cleft by axe and beetle. They were then shaped green on a stock or clogging-knife. The stock was made by the local blacksmith and, being exceptionally sharp, was anchored by a hook onto a bench. The clogs were then stacked like a beehive for seasoning so that the air could circulate and dry them out. The uppers were secured by brass nails.

It is impossible to avoid a feeling of regret that so many trades that formerly provided a certain amount of independence to those who exercised them have now gone. Villages were certainly more self-contained communities than today. There were, of course, parishes that had no amenities or social life, but they were the exceptions that provided grounds for comment. *Warndon*, for instance, had no parson, no school, no shops, and no post; and *Broome*, wrote John Noake in 1868, had 'no manufacturers or public works, no local squire, no mansion, no Dissenters' Chapel, no church-rate disturbances, no Fenianism or agitation of any sort'.

Village tradesmen in South Worcestershire c1900.

The village alehouse in the seventeenth century

The village alehouse provided the opportunity in every village for a kind of social intercourse not obtainable elsewhere. When homes were so uncomfortable it is small wonder that the labourer and his wife sought the snug alehouse parlour with its good cheer and companionship where they could pass away the long winter evenings. Here they sat and talked, and laughed and drank their small beer, swore big oaths in company with the parson and his clerk. Here they played at 'mack and mall', 'table and dice' and cards.

The alehouse was usually kept by women (called tipplers), retailing home-brewed beer at a halfpenny a gallon, better quality at double that figure and the best at fourpence a gallon. Every night the hostess was called upon to hang a lantern over the door till nine o'clock when the doors would be closed and business suspended. This rule, however, was continually evaded, and customers lingered over their ale pots till dawn, pledging their clothes and mortgaging their future wages.

Chaddesley Corbett had twenty dwellings in 1606, eight of which were alehouses, some of bad repute. One especially harboured thieves and the like, for robbery and prostitution, even murder, took place there and the innkeeper was accused of 'keeping of men in "huddimucke" while their wives are looking for them'.

In 1612 a memorial signed by nineteen inhabitants of Bayton was sent to the Worcestershire Sessions setting forth 'that John Kempster and Thomas Byrd do not sell their ale according to the law, but doe sell a pynte for a penny, and doe make ytt soe extraordynarye strong that it draweth dyvers ydle p(er)sons into the said alehouses, by reason whereof sondry assaults, affrayes, bloodsheds, and other misdemeanors are there dalie comytted by ydle and drunken companie which doe thither resort and there contynue in their dronkeness three dayes and three nights together, and also dyvers men's sonnes and servants doe often resort and contynue drinking in the said houses daye and night, whereupon dyvers disorders and abuses are offered to the inhabitants of Bayton aforesaid, as in pulling down styles, in carrying away yertes, in throwing men's waynes, plowes, and such things into pools, wells, and other bye places, and putting their yolks for their oxen into lakes and mystery places'.

Rural 'progress'

Before the enclosures of the eighteenth century, when land was scattered in strips in the great common fields and no farmer could call any particular strip his own, the house of the yeoman farmer stood in the village, the exception being the medieval manor house. Broadway is a very good example with the farmhouses lining the main street. But after the enclosures it became possible for the farmer to live on his own land, a development which accounts for most farmhouses being Georgian in style. Before the enclosures the farmer and his family ate with the servants; in the eighteenth century a dining parlour became the room for the family. 'Progress' continued, and the eighteenth-century farmer lived as the gentry had a century before. The *Worcester Herald* quoted from an old farmer's diary, under the heading of 'Rural Progress':

1743	*1843*
Man to the Plough,	Man Tally Ho!
Wife to the Cow,	Miss Piano
Girl to the Yarn,	Wife Silk and Satin
Boy to the Barn,	Boy Greek and Latin
And your rent will be Netted!	And you'll all be Gazetted!

Of course, not all farmers forgot the soil. Most had their feet firmly on the ground, steeped in old-fashioned pride and full of common sense. As one of them wrote:

I hate long stories and short ears of corn,
A costly farmhouse and a shabby barn;
More curs than pigs, no books but many guns,
Tight boots, sore toes, old debts and paper duns.
I hate tight lacing and loose conversation;
Abundant gab and little conversation;
A man who sings in bed and snores in meetings,
Who laughs while talking and talks while eating.

The enclosures in Worcestershire

Much of Worcestershire was unenclosed until the last decades of the eighteenth century and until then, according to the local tradition, a man could ride from the Gate Inn, Honeybourne Bridge, to the Fish at Broadway, or from the Fish and Anchor at Harvington to Long Marston across open fields without encountering a single fence. South of the Malverns from early days it was a wilderness 'where a man on horseback could ride from Malvern to the Bredons without impediment, except for the Severn'. Not until the drainage of Longdon Marsh in 1861 was common land there enclosed.

Shooting party at Blakedown, with the squire, Philip Addison Williams, in the carriage, c1895

The enclosures that took place between 1760 and 1870 were among the grossest injustices to the English peasantry, the large landowners – and their hired lawyers – the benefitters of a development that set the pattern of the countryside as we know it now. Enclosure made agriculture more efficient and the land beautiful, but it often amounted to sheer robbery. The ordinary commoner lost land and became a rent-paying tenant, for the cost of opposing enclosures was beyond him. Appeals for justice were useless; the JPs themselves were among the enclosers and the parson was usually a relative of, or dependent on, the squire — or even the squire himself. By 1870 the enclosures had virtually ceased and Worcestershire assumed its present aspect.

Those who enclosed, supported by law, were quick to react to any encroachment by the poor. In the Wyre Forest, William Smith, a landowner and magistrate, wrote in his diary for 1783: 'Henry Harris, Rochford, came with me to the Forest of Wyre, there we detected one Edwards, with 9 or 10 others, erecting a house up at Buckridge. I took it down.'

But not everyone accepted enclosures without a fight. After the Leigh award of January 1778 a group of people at Malvern Link 'did feloniously appear on the High Road; and upon the uninclosed part of the Link ... with their faces blackened, and being otherwise disguised, and armed with guns and other offensive weapons; and in the most daring manner did cut down, burn, and entirely destroy all posts, gates and rails'.

Agricultural wages in the mid-nineteenth century

Jessie Shervington of Salford Priors recalled the not-so 'good old days' of mid-Victorian times:

> In 1852, my first out to service, I went as a carter's lad to Mr Pearce, Grove Farm, Peopleton. I was hired for the year and was paid 30s. In the winter I had to be up to help the master chaffcutting at 4 a.m., and often I was on shoe, and knife and fork cleaning until 10 p.m. After that, I went to another farm called Ham Dene for nine months at 2½d per day; then I was hired the next year (1854) for 50s. My wage kept rising slowly after that until 1861. Then I married, and followed the occupation of a shepherd, and during a period of two years I received 8s per week of seven days. Of course, I had breakfast allowed me on Sunday mornings, and a Cotswold "hovel" rent free, and two quarts of beer daily. Harvest wages were 50s for a month, and dinner each day, and one got home at night with about enough time to spare to prepare food, and start off again for the next day's work.
>
> Between 1861 and 1872 my wages rose to 11s a week, and I was obliged by the Education Act to send seven of my nine children to school. I believe that in 1865 or 1866 we paid 9d for a 4lb. loaf. I do not think there are many people who would like to go back to the "good old days" after all, although I am always thankful and happy to think it is not hard work that kills people. At any rate, it has not killed me, for I have not lost one day's work through sickness since I started wage earning, nor have I had 10 whole days of holiday in that time.

Ploughing by oxen

Oxen were used to draw the plough until 1907 at Ripple, and were still in use elsewhere. They were certainly slow but they had their advantages: they were very strong, they were never shod and they could work on the land while the horses went to market. When the men had their lunch at midday, the oxen lay down in their gear and chewed the cud. The farmers worked them until they were four or five years old, then fattened them for the London market where the beef was reckoned to be the best. At Childswickham, in the days of the old village constable, a prisoner who had to be taken to Gloucester absolutely refused to walk, and as no other conveyance was available he was taken there astride the back of an ox.

Sir John Throckmorton's coat

Landowners took great pride in their livestock in the early nineteenth century. William Cobbett stayed with John Price at Ryall, near Upton-on-Severn, in 1826 and wrote: 'I am here among the finest cattle (Hereford), and the finest of sheep of the Leicester kind, I ever saw.' In 1840 Price, in a letter to the *Farmer's Magazine*, issued a challenge for a £100 to all breeders and feeders in Britain to pit the merits of a bull and twenty cows, all bred by himself, against any other breeder of cattle in the country. His challenge, however, was not taken up.

A challenge of another sort came from Sir John Throckmorton in 1811, which caused much sensation at the time and has often been referred to since. Though it took place at Newbury, it possessed special local interest because Sir John came from one of the most notable Worcestershire families and was the owner of Harvington Hall, near Kidderminster. He made a wager, upon which no less than a thousand guineas were staked, that he would wear a coat at dinner in the evening made from the fleeces growing on the sheep's back in the morning. It was won easily, the time actually occupied in shearing, spinning, dyeing, weaving and tailoring, including all subsidiary processes, being only thirteen and a quarter hours. Concurrently with this manufacturing feat, a large-scale cooking exercise went on. The two fleeced sheep were roasted whole and all who helped to win the wager sat down to eat them, with Sir John as the guest of the evening wearing his new damson-coloured coat.

Love haul at Chastleton

Another type of combined operation was seen in the Broadway district. Mr Whitmore Jones who owned Chastleton House had ceased to farm in 1845, but in the spring of 1850 Chastleton Hill Farm was suddenly thrown on his hands owing to the death of the tenant. Mr Jones was quite at a loss as to how to cultivate the land for a season, and at Evesham market casually mentioned his difficulties to one or two neighbouring farmers; whereupon, they offered, if he provided seedcorn and bread, cheese and beer, to give him a 'love haul'.

A day was fixed, 6 April, and in the morning Mr Whitmore Jones went up the hill to see the men at work. He had expected to find three or four ploughs there – but there were sixty-eight, ten of them double ones! The horses were decked out in ribbons, and the men wore clean white smock-frocks; altogether the scene looked like a gigantic ploughing match. A hundred acres were ploughed, harrowed and very nearly sown that day; the drillers could not quite complete their work and three came over the next morning to finish it. Mr Whitmore Jones was afterwards told that great regret had been expressed that the 'love haul' had not been made more generally known or double the number of teams would have been there.

Farmhouse fare in the 1860s

In 1924 John Morris looked back to the farmhouse fare in the Broadway district in the 1860s which, though plain and with little variety, was ample:

> On the ceilings of the farmhouses in those days were hung bacon racks on which were flitches, ribs, chines, collars and heads, dried and yellow . . . . Over a large part of the area the old dining custom was observed of eating pudding first to save the meat. The pudding course was sometimes 'skimmer lads', round-shaped flattened pieces of dough, boiled loose in the pot, and afterwards anointed with butter or treacle, and often rough dough puddings boiled in a cloth and similarly dressed; both formed substantial foundations and the latter pudding required strenuous efforts to get it down. The second course was . . . usually 'pigsty beef', varied with an occasional fowl. There were ample rations of vegetables, but the butcher's cart seldom called, and after bacon the great stand-by was cheese. The master of the house often dwelt with pride on the fact that all on the table was the produce of his own land. But in a wet season, even in the farmhouse, the home-baked bread made from sprouted corn was dark in colour with a crust outside that, when broken, revealed a darker sticky mess within, that was said to have looked like cow-dung. An old labourer, who was then 'livin' in sarvice' said, 'If we hadn't had plenty of grease an' bacon an' tack we wouldn't have got it down, an' if we'd throw'd it across the kitchen it would have stuck agen the wall'.

A farm feast at Leigh

There was a toast used at farm feasts and harvest home which went: 'May we all have friends as numerous as the leaves of the oak, with hearts as firm as its butt.' In Worcestershire, even in the 1930s, a farm feast was by no means a thing of the past:

> At Leigh, six miles from Worcester, where the Teme floods over Bransford Bridge and the Leigh Brook makes one half of the parish difficult of access to the other, annually there is a gathering of farmhands — men and women and children. The long hop-room, gaily decorated with brilliant streamers, its walls and windows draped with softer hues, is the scene of the annual feast. The fare is all prepared in the Great House kitchen, or in the cookhouse whose furnace boils the Christmas pudding and whose 'stick-oven' roasts the great joint of beef. The master, his light-grey suit protected by

a blue-striped apron, carves, and the wide plates circle to receive from busy helpers potatoes, creamed swedes, brussels sprouts and gravy (such gravy, founded on boiled goose and stewed fowls).

Each guest, and there are at least seventy, is supposed to bring his own eating tools, but a pile is available for novices and the forgetful. Plum pudding and rum sauce are the second course, and mammoth jugs of beer and cider pass freely round the long trestle tables. When no-one can eat any more, the tables vanish and the fun waxes warm.

The guests are of both sexes and all ages and sizes; there are grandfathers and babies in arms, great strapping lads and bonny well-built lasses, and a host of small fry who scramble for the nuts, sweets and biscuits thrown to them. A professional entertainer with song and speech and dance performs on the dais, but the company furnish their own contributions too. The same songs, the same pieces are clamoured for each year . . . . Prizes are forthcoming — a pipe for the last man in Musical Chairs, and a cup, won for three years and therefore now the property of the master, makes the circuit of the workers who have helped to produce the champion hops in England. It is given to few ordinary folk nowadays to sup beer from a golden cup!

Just before midnight, everybody sings and prances to Auld Lang Syne, and after 'For he's a jolly good fellow', two threes of raising cheers, and God Save the King, the guests toddle home, all merry and bright, and in the moonlight.

Old farm worker with wooden rake, passing a 'split' — or oak-cleft — gate in Cradley, c1890.

Worcestershire hop growing

Hops were introduced into England in the reign of Henry VIII but extensive cultivation did not occur until about 1640 when there are references to hops in

South Lyttleton (near Badsey), Blackwell Farm, near Bromsgrove, and Homme or Ham Castle. In 1647 Joyce Jeffreys of Ham Castle bought 135 lbs of hops at £3 per hundred at Bromyard. At first regarded as a speculative crop, from about 1700 hops became popular and during the nineteenth century the growing of hops became more specialised.

Hop kilns (the Worcestershire term for oast houses) were at first no more than an outhouse of lath and plaster attached to the farmhouse, with a charcoal burner in the basement, or a brick furnace burning wood, allowing the heat to rise up through the slatted drying floor above. About 1840, more substantial kilns were built of brick and in the round, since it was thought a circular kiln would distribute the heat evenly. Later, this was proved false and square kilns, easier to construct, became the norm, with a brick furnace burning coal. The Worcestershire coal was found to be especially good, having a high sulphur content which yellowed and preserved the hops.

It is not easy to recognise an early kiln for they have only ventilators on the ridge. Cone roofs with timber cowls, pivoted to turn into the wind to produce an upward draft, came later. In 1871 T M Hopkins, a Worcester hop merchant, patented a steam-driven fan which cut the drying time from three to four days to seven-and-a-half hours; and in 1880 came the first machine for filling pockets (canvas bags). Coal, burnt on open fires, remained the predominant method of heating until the early 1930s when oil heating was introduced.

In the hopyards

Hop-picking was a great treat for the Black Country folk. From the dingy slums of Netherton, Dudley, Smethwick and Lye . . . families turned out with bundles and tin boxes for their annual excursion to the beautiful hop country of the Teme Valley. It began at Worcester, and the various stations on the railway in the Teme Valley, with the detraining of the tatterdemalion hordes with their buckets and pans and kettles and the rest of their quaint impedimenta. From the station they were picked up by farm wagons and taken to the hopyards.

It was something looked forward to for months by the Black Country folk, and yet the conditions of field life were not easy. They were not feather-bedded, they did not seek or demand the niceties of life. They slept in the open around a fire, or huddled together in tents, in cowsheds or pigsties called 'barracks'. . . . some farms seemed positively luxurious, the pickers slept in little shelters provided with bedding, and were each given a pint of soup for supper each night, and tea and sugar once a week. But they needed to be carefully overlooked, and they were locked in every night, for anything eatable or usable was regarded by some as public property and for their special use.

They brought with them the manners and the language of the roughest Black Country 'pit class'. Every year in the local papers there were squeals about the risks to modesty and morality through the casual mingling of the sexes. Many had grave doubts whether they ever had any modesty or sanitary ideas. 'Their ideas of decencies are barbaric,' wrote a clergyman to *Berrow's Worcester Journal*. 'During the working hours they sing hymns and swear and say obscene things, all in the same breath. During their leisure hours they attend the mission meetings, and try to steal the benches and chairs for firewood. What was at the same time painful and amusing, I saw one woman fetching the family tea in a corned beef tin, and another bathing her baby in a frying pan.'

On some farms, the last day of picking had its age-old ceremony of hoisting the last and best pole of hops, saved specially for the occasion. The pullers' caps and hats were decorated with rosettes, dahlias and asters and sprays of hops. Then a procession was formed, making its way to the farmhouse, headed by the busheller beating his metal measure as a drum, and followed by the pole-pullers, sack-holders and the pickers. At the farmhouse a feast was prepared and the farmer and his wife were toasted.

At the end of the weeks in the hopyards the transformation was complete. The colour was back into pale cheeks. The joy of the countryside, the effect of the open air, beamed in all the faces, from the buxom wrinkled old granny to the youngest grimy baby.

C E Daniels of Storridge recorded in 1914 that at a hopyard at Halesend, Cradley, then farmed by Mr Charles Purser, 'a gypsy, George Stanley, and his wife and very large family picked no fewer than 215 bushels in one day. The hops were bushelled by William Mansell and recorded by myself all in one book. Mr Stanley had two cribs which were bushelled and moved together. The rate on that day was at 5 to 1s. Mr Stanley never topped the two hundred other than that one day.'

Pea-picking in the Vale of Evesham

In 1912 a correspondent to the *Evesham Journal* sent a long description of the pea-picking season in the Vale. He wrote how in June in the Vale of Evesham all roads led to the peafields. The growers immediately around Evesham preferred to employ local labour, and on a good day it was a pleasant sight: the peas with their soft green shade; the pickers, women in blue and white blouses and big straw hats, men with their white shirts and sleeves rolled up over brown, brawny arms. But elsewhere in the Vale the peafields were bought by buyers from the large towns whose sole object was to get the peas picked as cheaply as possible. A horde of rough uncouth pullers from Birmingham and the Black Country descended on the area for the 'pulling'. They started in the early morning and often all the peas in that area were pulled by 3 pm. In that time the pickers would have picked two or three pots, according to the quality and quantity of peas, normally earning 1s to 1s 6d per pot. The next field could be twelve or sixteen miles away and the pickers had to pack up and tramp off.

The women were pale and coarse-faced, with dirty shawls over their shoulders, bedraggled skirts and leaky boots, carrying sacks containing their belongings. A few pushed old soap boxes on wheels which carried little children. Young girls in their teens cursed and sang ribald songs with gaunt-faced lads. Men, trousers rolled up to the knees, pulled savagely at the pods, cursing women who failed to pick the pots quickly enough.

> They sleep in barns or under the hedgerows, waking next morning shivering with ague and without a morsel of food in their sacks; in the barns they are overrun by rats. At mealtimes, little fires are made on which to boil a can of tea to go with the bread. On Sunday there might be a piece of scraggy mutton with potatoes 'pinched' from gardens.
>
> Out of the few thousand who come pea-picking, most are tramps and casual labourers (of both sexes) who will fill the casual wards of the workhouses. Last week Evesham had 80, and Stratford-on-Avon had 120, and they come verminous and unclean.

Black Country hop-pickers arriving at Holt Fleet, 1909.

Village Superstitions

At Charlton, a hamlet of Cropthorne, where the Dineley family lived, there was a curious custom that the house should never be without a mistletoe bough in the kitchen. When the new bough was put up at Christmas the old one was put in the oven and burnt and the servants supplied with something hot to keep out the cold.

At Mathon there was formerly a belief that if land was left unsown in a field there would be a death in the family within the year; and when the accident was discovered they did not sow it again. Old women were entrusted with the cure of burns by charming, which they did by repeating a certain number of times the old doggerel rhyme, 'There were two angels came from the north . . .'. Two other strange beliefs concerned women: if a woman cut her hair at the new moon, then it would grow thick; and no woman should go near 'curing hams' if in menstruation or the ham would go 'off'.

There were many other village superstitions. The Rev Oswald Knapp wrote of the Honeybourne area: 'I have seen the cast skin of a grass snake worn inside the hat as a protection against rheumatism. Death's Head moths were reputed to be exceedingly dangerous to handle. Once when one of the moths alighted on the step of the church porch during the service the whole congregation was held up, and as the situation seemed to require an extra strong man to deal with it word was passed back to the blacksmith. He with a fine disregard of the possible consequences to himself took a short run and a jump, landing with both feet on the deadly insect, which left only a smear on the stone. Then the congregation breathed freely and departed to their homes in peace.'

Stanford-on-Teme is full of curious place names such as Devil's Den, Hell Hole and Death's Dingle; and hereabouts grows the plant called Devil's Bit (*Succisa pratensis*) which, tradition says, was given to heal man of any deadly wounds; but when Satan saw what numbers of the human race it deprived him of he bit the roots off in spite, whereupon it miraculously grew without these usual necessary appendages; and this is the reason we find it growing apparently without roots.

A considerable amount of folklore features the apple, that most important of Worcestershire fruits. Speaking to members of the Worcestershire Naturalists' Club in 1878 Mr Edwin Lees said:

> Even now in rural localities, it is thought a sign of forthcoming death in a family if an apple-tree has fruit and flowers upon it at the same time; and if one of the apple-trees in the garden flowers a second time in the same year, it is considered a 'token' for death . . . .
>
> The sun shining on particular days was always time out of mind a favourite rural notion as regards good luck, and it is still a prevalent idea that if the sun shines through the apple-trees of the orchard on Christmas Day, there will be an abundant crop of apples the following year. But when the trees loaded with red-streaks are ready to be gathered, and rough winds might do much damage to the crop of fruit, the rustics cry with bated breath —

> September blow soft
> Till the apples are in th' loft.

Christmas and Twelfth-Night customs

An old Christmas rhyme was sung at Bewdley where it was the custom to allow servants and apprentices to lie late in bed on Christmas morn while the mistress got up and did all the work. The bellman used to go round the town ringing the bell and, after wishing everyone 'Good Morning', sang:

> Arise, mistresses, arise
> And make your tarts and pies,
> And let your maids lie still,
> For if they should rise
> And spoil your pies,
> You'd take it very ill.
> Whilst you are sleeping in your bed,
> I, the cold wintery nights must tread.

Twelfth-Night customs were kept in country districts until the end of the nineteenth century. The most important custom was the pilgrimage to see the 'holy thorn' bloom at midnight. There were 'holy thorns' at Ripple, Tardebigge and Newland in Worcestershire. The following account is of a visit to Ripple:

> The old men and women have gone silently from the village, with no light but the waning moon to see the mystery. The tree is in an open glade. It is twelve minutes to twelve. The moon past the full has not long risen, the sky is cloudless and the stars shine brilliantly, the air is still and sharp with frost. The thorn tree stands alone casting a long black shadow. Not far off, the old men and women stand still and quiet as a group of dark spectres.
>
> Suddenly the silence is broken by the far-off chimes of the village church. Twelve solemn strokes. The group rustles expectantly and with one accord draws nearer to the tree. Is it mesmerism or is it reality? By the uncertain light of the moon the little white buds of the thorn tree are seen. Slowly, weirdly, the buds unfold and in half-an-hour the holy tree is white and glistening as a hawthorn tree in main moonlight. The people kneel on the cold ground. The place and the hour are sacred. But one woman, too bold, breaks off a spray of the silver blossom, and lo, the petals drop and she is holding a bare winter twig. Until one o'clock the tree remains in bloom, then softly the petals drop like white snowflakes and the tree is black and gaunt and common once more. The old folk silently depart, overawed. Their faith in this demonstration is absolute and steadfast, for have they not seen?

Twelfth Night, or Old Christmas Eve, was when the ancient custom of *wassailing* was observed. On the banks of the Teme in the mid-nineteenth century a farmer and his neighbours 'proceeded to an elevated wheat field, where twelve small fires were lighted, and a large one in the centre, these fires being generally considered as representative of our Saviour and the twelve apostles, though in some places they bear the vulgar appellation of Old Meg and her daughters. Jugs of prime old cider having been brought, healths are joyously drunk with abundant hurrahing from a circle formed round the central fire. The party afterwards adjourn to an orchard, and there encircling one of the best bearing trees, and not forgetting cider, sprinkle the tree, while one of the party carols forth the following verse:

> Here's to thee, old apple tree,
> Whence thou may'st bud, and whence thou may'st blow ....'

Some old sayings

The wisdom of ages is concentrated in some of the sayings of country folk. John Morris in the early 1920s collected the following in the district south of Evesham:

> I be sorry for um, they be townsfolk an' don't know nuthin' (This about city dwellers who had settled in the village)
> If you've anything to say, keep your mouth shut
> Every crow thinks his feathers the blackest

On women some of the expressions were poetical:

> They was a makin' love like a pair o' pidgins
> Her was a picturesome girl
> It's no good a woman runnin' arter a mon, her need as well stop at home an' shut herself up, her'd be just as forrud
> I never knowed but one business woman, an' her husband hung hisself
> A pig and a woman and a donkey be contrary things, and a man can do nothing with um if he don't let um have their own way

Sayings by women about men:

> There was nothin' there, nothing but trousers
> He seemed like a thing as was put in a cage to be pecked at
> He en't the mon as is goin' to kill the pig (Not the man that matters)
> There was a lot in his face as was no good to anybody

When a grudge is remembered the remarks can carry a sting:

> She'd carry a stone for seven years and then throw it at you (about one who stored up ill-will)
> They carries their chins in the air, though the mice be a-runnin' their cupboards with tears in their eyes
> I wouldn't tell a lie to do anybody any harm, but if I can do anybody any good without doing anybody any harm, then I be prepared to swear

Weather lore

In the old days the countryman paid great attention to the weather. The upper and middle classes seldom troubled themselves unless a journey or an outing was involved; but with the poor it was different, for the farm labourer's wages usually depended on the clouds. The farmworker, in his untutored fashion, was often a meteorologist. From living almost constantly out-of-doors he had a habit of studying the sky and weather rhymes and proverbs, passed down from ancient times, were treasured up in every village. They are the result of long observation and that they contain some germs of truth is certain. Among those remembered in Worcestershire are:

> When Bredon's Hill puts on its hat,
> Men of the Vale beware of that.

> When Bredon Hill is fair and clear,
> Men of the Vale have nought to fear.

From Childswickham come the following:

> A mist round Broadway Tower,
> It'll rain within the hour

It looks too muddy in the Tewkesbury Hole to go far afield today

> We be going to have some drier times,
> For I've been hearing E'sam's chimes.

And three sayings with religious references:

> If it rains on Good Friday and Easter Day,
> There'll be plenty of grass, but little good hay.

It was a black wind which blew at the Crucifixion (A black wind was one from the north-east or east accompanied by dark lowering clouds)

> If Candlemas Day be cloudy and black,
> It carries the winter away on its back.

Two old villagers of Cradley, c1890.

Herbal medicines

Old country folk made much use of herbs as remedies. Here are some used in the Vale of Evesham:

Steeped *camomile* flowers used as a remedy for toothache

Marsh mallow root boiled and used as a plaster for boils, abscesses and so on

The stems of *arum* (called lords-and-ladies, or parson-in-the-pulpit, or cow-and-calves) steeped in water to give a liquid useful as an eyewash and very beneficial when put on gatherings

Steeped *cabbage* leaves used extensively as a remedy for toothache, earache and so on

Dandelion stems, the juice sucked out as a liver tonic

Coltsfoot, the dried flowers steeped to give a remedy for coughs

Onion, half-roasted and put in the ear to cure earache

Broom flowers boiled extensively as a remedy for dropsy

Rue tea widely used as a remedy for rheumatics, lumbago, and sciatica

Agrimony tea used as a purifier of the blood in cases of blotches

Wych elm bark used as a curative for eczema

In the Upton-on-Severn area teas made from *hyssop* and *horsehound* were regarded as excellent for coughs. *Rue, nettle* and *tansy*, taken while fasting, were regarded as beneficial for dealing with different forms of dyspepsia. The juice of *celandine* and *black bryony* removed corns and bruises; and *white lily* roots, *elderflowers* and *house leeks*, mixed with fresh liquor or cream, were believed to make excellent ointments and lotions.

All over Worcestershire a very common remedy for diarrhoea was a grated hot-cross bun baked on Good Friday and kept for a year.

Nuts and nutting

Nutting used to hold special delights. At Broadway there was an old countryman who was looked upon as an expert when it came to walnuts. 'There be two things about warnuts', he'd say, 'a warnut allus bears better if his boughs a' bin well threshed the year afore, an' if you want a warnut tree, don't plant it yuself, for nobody does any good arter plantin' a warnut tree fer themselves; they must get somebody else to plant it for 'un.'

> Time was (said an old lady) when there was a special day for nutting — the day of 'Holy Rood', the 14th of September, when, clad in the dress they had worn each year, the village lads and lasses used to troop to the woods and copses and hangers, to chase the squirrels through the trees, and pull down nuts together. But it was only a token, the nuts got then were got too soon; they should be left till the leaves of the hazel are golden-lined and the rooks are patching their nests for the winter, which is early in October. Then you will gather them when they are thoroughly ripe, and have true flavour. They will keep sound and good, and be fit for those mysteries, the rites of the 'Nutcracker Night', which was on All Hallows Eve, the last night in October. Sometimes it was called 'Heart-prophet Hallow Eve', for lovers pledged each other that night and sealed the secret in a nutshell. Ah! a nut can hold the story told on that night.

Benjamin Williams Leader: February Fill Dyke, 1881. (Believed to be Kempsey Common). Oil on canvas. Reproduced by permission of the Birmingham Museum and Art Gallery

Attributed to John Harris: Prospect of Worcester from the East, c1750. Oil on canvas. Reproduced by permission of the City Museum & Art Gallery, Worcester

W R Jennings: Bewdley Bridge, 1973. Oil on canvas. Reproduced by permission of Mrs S Beaman

E Dayes: Witley Court, 1810. Colour engraving. Reproduced by permission of the Wyre Forest Museum Service

'Urchins' and others

There are many references (with quaint spelling) in old churchwardens' accounts of the seventeenth and eighteenth centuries to *urchins* (hedgehogs), *fitchers* (polecats), *eadows* (probably jackdaws) and other wildlife. The original cause of such entries was the passing of an Act in 1532 by which, in order to keep down the great number of rooks, crows and choughs, every parish, township and hamlet had to supply itself with a net for the destruction of these birds. The nets were to be maintained for ten years, and a sum of tuppence was to be paid for every twelve old crows, or choughs, by the owner or occupier of the manor or lands. Later, another act supplemented this with 'three-a-penny for the heads of old crows, and for the heads of every six young crows, a penny; and for every six eggs unbroken, a penny; and likewise for every twelve starlings' heads, a penny'. The heads, after being seen by the churchwarden, had to be burned or cut up before him.

Other 'ravening birds and vermin' were scheduled with the price on their heads:

> For everie Head of Martyn Hawkes, Furskytte, Moldekytte, Busarde, Schagge, Carmerat, or Ryngtale (Hen Harrier) 2d; for everie Iron (Heron) or Osprayes Heade, fowerpence; for the Heade of everie Woodwall (Green Woodpecker), Pye, Jaye, Raven or Kyte, one penny; for the Heade of everie Byrde which is called the Kinges Fyssher, one penny; for the Heade of everie Bulfynche or other Byrde that devoureth the Blowth of Fruite, one penny; for the Heade of everie Foxe or Wilde Catte, twelve pence; for the Heade of everie Fitchere, Polecatte, Wesell, Stote, Fayre Bade, one penny; for the Heades of everie Otter or Hedgehogge, two pence; for the Heades of everie three Rattes or twelve Myse, one penny; for the Heade of everie Moldewarpe or Wante, half-penny.

From the churchwardens' accounts the mortality of such birds and vermin must have been very great in some districts. It would seem that the inoffensive 'urchins' were the most important capture among the vermin, although it is difficult to see why. But we know that hard things have been said about their egg-sucking proclivity, and therein may lie the reason.

Old Worcestershire bird names

In November 1987 Mr Joe Perry, aged 82, a gamekeeper, and his son Bill, aged 60, a man steeped in country lore, both from Cotheridge, sat over the kitchen table and wrote down this list of names of Worcestershire birds:

Blackbird	Blackie, Black Ousel, Black Thrush, Garden Ousel, Goldybill, Merle
Blackcap	Blackie Topper, Fauvette, Guernsey Nightingale, Haychat, Hayjack, Mock Nightingale, Nettlecreeper
Bullfinch	Bud Pricker, Bully, Nope
Buzzard	Puttock, Bloodhawk, Mousehawk

Chiffchaff	Chipchop, Maybird, Willow Wren, Thummie, Sallypicker
Chaffinch	Boldie, Chaffy, Piefinch, Pink-Pink-Pink, Tink, Twink, Wetbird
Robin	Bobbie, Tommy Liden, Ruddock
Goldfinch	Seven-Coloured-Linnet, Sweet William, Goldie, Thistlefinch, Coalhead, Goldspink, Proudtail, Draw-Water
Ringdove	Woodpigeon, Quice, Quist, Cushot, Culver, Rock Pigeon, Wrekin Dove, (Disagreement here: Bill named four — Ringdove, Rock Dove, Stock Dove and Turtledove. Joe named only Turtledove.)
Red-Backed Shrike	Butcherbird, Cheeter, Cuckoo's Maid, Flasher, Flusher, French Magpie, Jackbaker, Murdering Pie, Nine Killer, Whisky John
Great Tit	Oxeye
Bluetit	Tomtit
Long-Tailed Tit	Canabottle
Hedge Sparrow	(Bill gave thirty six names for a Hedge Sparrow) Black Wren, Billy, Blue Isaac, Blue Jamie, Blue Sparrow, Blue Tom, Bush Sparrow, Creepie, Cuddie, Dick Dunnock, Dicky, Doney, Dunnock, Dykesmauler, Dykie, Field Sparrow, Foolish Sparrow, Grosbeak, Hatcher, Hazock, Hedge Accenter, Hedge Bettie, Hedge Chanter, Hedge Chat, Hedge Chicken, Hedge Creeper, Hedge Mike, Hedge Warbler, Henpie, Muffitie, Phip, Pinnock, Shuffle Wing, Titline, Whin Sparrow, Winter Fauvette. (Joe gave only one name — Dunnock)
House Sparrow	Spug
Whitethroat	Jack Straw
Plover	Peewhit, Lapwing
Yellowhammer	Scribbling Schoolmaster (This because of the scribble on the eggs. Its song, says Joe, 'Little bit of bread and no cheese'.)

CHAPTER FOUR

Travel and Trade

Travelling the old roads

'THE CYCLE AND THE MOTOR CAR *have in some measure restored life to our highways, but our modern vehicles cannot invest the roads with the particoloured charm which they once possessed . . . . The country squire no longer goes to London in his family coach, with coachman in bright attire on the box. The High Sheriff and his javelin men do not meet Her Majesty's Judges on the City border. The coach and four does not break upon the quietude of the village with the guard's sonorous note. The village carrier's cart is still with us, but the heavy wain, protected by a powerful dog, carrying folk and heavy goods between large towns, has long disappeared. The packhorse does not bring salt from Droitwich, or take fish to Malvern. The pillioned pony, with mistress riding home from market, cannot be seen even in the Northern Dales. The small Welsh farmer does not drive his flock of turkeys through the Herefordshire lanes in the hope of getting a better market for them in Worcester . . . . Military companies may march from one centre to another, but uniforms are drab and changes have reduced the length and number of marches.'*

The Ridgeway

One of the oldest known roads in Britain lies at the eastern boundary of Worcestershire and was long ago called the Ridgeway. But as it pursues its way across the country it passes under a number of names – *Buckle Street* in the Cotswolds, *Ryckneild Street* when it runs across Worcestershire land and, as it nears Birmingham, *Ickneild Street* under which name it makes its way to Wall, near Lichfield, to join up with the Roman Watling Street. It was an important route used by the Iron-Age Celts and possibly by Cro-Magnon man some four thousand years ago; it served as a link between the Celtic settlements of Bredon, Woodbury Hill, Gadbury Hill, Hanbury Hill and the Malvern Camps; it undoubtedly saw use as a Roman road; and it facilitated travel in medieval times between the towns of the central Midlands and Evesham, most of the traffic destined for the abbeys of Bordesley and Evesham.

When Redditch's needle trade became big business in the early days of the nineteenth century the old Ridgeway road was still used as the main artery between Birmingham and the expanding country town. Indeed, traffic became so heavy that the old Coach and Horses Inn at the foot of Weatheroak Hill could no longer cater for such trade and a new inn, the Peacock, was built at the top of the Ridgeway incline. But the road at Weatheroak Hill was far too narrow to cope; lay-bys were cut into it at various points and wagons had to carry latten bells to give warning of their approach. Finally, a new road was created completely bypassing the former Ridgeway, and the old way became no more than a vague track marked on the Ordnance Survey map.

Roman roads in Worcestershire

Of the four greatest roads built by the Romans in Britain only one, the Fosse Way, touched the area of modern Worcestershire, and that at two outlying 'island' parts which have now been lost by the re-drawing of the county boundaries. The two most important crossings of the Severn took place south of the county at *Glevum* (Gloucester) and in the north near *Uriconium* (Shrewsbury), where Watling Street crosses the Severn.

The Romans left Britain a superb legacy of roads but the Saxons had little use for them, settling in forest hamlets near rivers, leaving the roads to disappear under encroaching weeds and grass and making use of them only as boundaries; for the parishes were formed then and, like brooks and rivers, the roads were ready-made demarcations of territory from point to point.

However, roads and boundaries can be obliterated, even moved, if there is someone powerful enough to override local opposition. There are two interesting examples of this in the Droitwich-Bromsgrove area, the first on the Roman road from Worcester to Bromsgrove which left Worcester up Rainbow Hill and headed in a direct line through the Saxon estate of Hindlip. In medieval times the road was blocked and redirected around the estate to Fernhill Heath, then back to join the old road at Sandy Way, Martin Hussingtree. The line of the Roman road continues through the estate, however, by way of the parish boundary and a footpath. The same thing happens at another ancient estate, Grafton Manor, just south of Bromsgrove. The Roman road runs straight from Droitwich but at Stoke Heath the road is blocked and a medieval road travels round the Grafton estate, rejoining the line of the old road at Rock Hill. Again, the line of the Roman road continues through the estate by way of the parish boundary and a footpath.

There is no documentary evidence as to when this happened. The earliest map of Worcestershire (Saxton's) dates from 1579, but no roads are indicated. Clues can be found, however, in the fact that at both estates, Hindlip and Grafton, the owner was the great Norman Sheriff of Worcester, Urse d'Abitot, cousin of William the Conqueror, and one of the most powerful men in the land.

Pilgrims on the road

As Christian settlements established themselves, so traffic in those areas increased. Monasteries attracted pilgrims who travelled to see the shrines and holy relics; and with the pilgrims went trade, money and goods.

In Worcestershire Christian settlements began to be established in the second half of the seventh century, clerical colonies which were off-shoots of the house at Worcester, mainly in the south of the county. One of the earliest was at Fladbury which resulted in a road from there to Worcester. Evesham was founded in 709 and by that time the road must have been well established. But these 'pilgrim' roads were in reality little more than tracks. For the solitary traveller they were also dangerous so that travellers journeyed in large companies, putting up for the night at inns spaced at easy distances of a day's walk. At pilgrim centres in the towns large hostels awaited them, either in religious inns such as the New Inn at Gloucester, or in religious establishments such as St Wulstan's Hospital (now the Commandery) at Worcester. With the pilgrims travelled many foreign merchants, bringing valuable currency to the Crown.

The roads in the south of the county and into Worcester were especially busy, for there were a number of shrines there of national importance. At Worcester the crush of pilgrims visiting the shrine of St Oswald in the crypt at Worcester Cathedral was so great that a one-way system had to be organised with an entrance at one end and an exit stairway at the other. Later, the shrine was removed to the chancel for convenience of access and when Wulstan was buried near Oswald Worcester became one of the most visited places in the West Midlands. A little further south, great numbers of pilgrims visited Evesham, Tewkesbury and Gloucester, and especially Hailes Abbey which was famed for its possession of a phial of the Holy Blood.

Pilgrim traffic and the trade that concentrated around the monasteries meant that roads in the south of the county were better maintained than those elsewhere. The monks built stone bridges over small streams such as Piddle Brook, near Pershore, and over the River Isbourne at Hampton, near Evesham; whereas in the north of the county the few bridges were of wood, but mostly there were only fords. But there was a further reason why roads in the east and west of the county were less developed: blocking the way were the royal forests of Feckenham in the east and Malvern Chase in the west, and any attempt to make a road through those would have brought severe punishment in the forest courts. A track of about eight-foot wide was cut through Feckenham Forest from Tibberton to Worcester some six hundred years ago and it remained a track until it was widened and improved under the turnpike acts.

Medieval market towns

It was the right to hold a fair or market that marked out the township from the ordinary village, a right only held by royal grant. Most of the market towns of Worcestershire grew up at ancient strategic sites, crossroads or at a ford over a river; and they appear to have been distributed at about ten miles' distance from each other, or what was a convenient riding distance for itinerant traders. Of the ancient market townships featured in the map below (all once in Worcestershire) thirteen are now no more than villages and one, Kenelmstowe, has disappeared completely (see page 25).

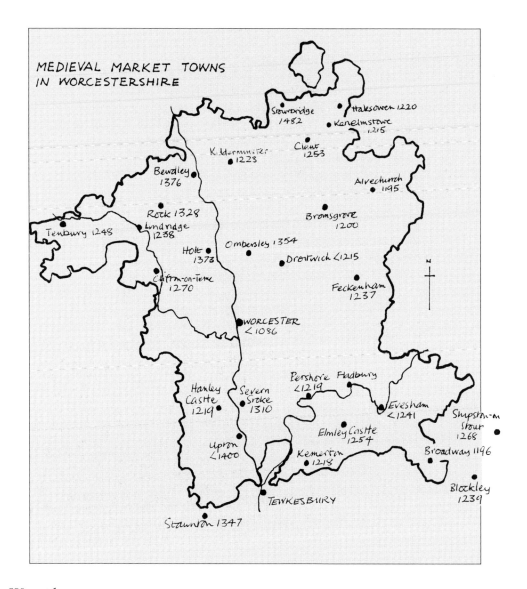

MEDIEVAL MARKET TOWNS
IN WORCESTERSHIRE

Wayside crosses

From the early days of Christianity it became the practice to place crosses along the highway where devout wayfarers might halt for a while and pray; where a coffin would be rested and a prayer said for the dead; and where in time of trouble, plague, famine or war people would gather to pray for relief. Even penances were performed at the cross, which is why stocks and a whipping post were sometimes placed alongside.

In 1229 William de Bleys, Bishop of Worcester, ordered that in every churchyard of the diocese should be erected a cross. These came to be known as *Palm Crosses*, as it was the custom on Palm Sunday to process to the cross from the church carrying palms. Many Palm Crosses remain today despite their destruction at times of religious upheaval.

Wayside crosses were erected where roads diverged, as at Wyre and Childswickham; at the fords across the Severn at Uckinghall and Hanley Castle; and on steep roads, such as the London road out of Worcester. Only a few remain for when coaches and larger wagons came into use the crosses were deemed to be dangerous obstacles and were removed. In the seventeenth and eighteenth centuries a cross was regarded as a papist symbol and most of those remaining were mutilated – which explains why so few, even in churchyards, are original. In the nineteenth century some were fitted with a new head and at Childswickham an elegant eighteenth-century urn was placed on top of the shaft.

Wayside cross at Ashton-under-Hill, capped with sundial, c1890.

Packhorse trails

No main roads were built in Britain from the time of the departure of the Romans to the making of the turnpike roads in the eighteenth century. Some paths were paved for special use (such as the 'Pilgrims' Path' through Ripple), but mostly the roads were the old untouched prehistoric trade routes and ridgeway paths.

Along these paths trains of heavily burdened pack animals carried essential goods, especially salt from Droitwich and wool from the Cotswolds. They can be traced by way of hollow roads worn by countless pack animals scrambling up rough steep tracks, or at crossing places where a flat rock ford enabled a river or stream to be crossed, except when in flood. At places like Bewdley caves afforded shelter for travellers.

Often these packhorse tracks have disappeared from long disuse; and memory and an intimate knowledge of the district are needed to trace them. At the crossings the hollow roads often give way to a firm built-up causeway to keep up the single-file formation leading to a bridge, as at Shell and Ripple. The bridges were narrow and often humpbacked which contributed to their strength, and the parapets were kept low so that loaded panniers would clear them. Some trains were very large and often whole villages would turn out to see them pass. Some villages acted as staging posts and their economy depended on the trains, supplying fodder for the animals and drinks and cheap beds in barns for the drivers. Along the routes can still be found packhorse alehouses and the old name for the line tracks called 'gals' or 'galloways', as at Gilgal at Stourport.

In the north of the county a network of trails led to Bewdley, the principal inland port during the period of the Industrial Revolution. They brought iron and charcoal from the Clees for the furnaces up Severn, and from the Black Country the finished ironware, pottery and other goods for shipping down Severn to Bristol. The railroads killed the packhorse trade, though in remote districts the trains continued until the 1914–18 War.

In 1766 Richard Whitworth in his book *The Advantages of Inland Navigation* listed some of the goods then brought by packhorse and barge to Bewdley: 'timber, coal, lead, iron, millstones, lime, alabaster, marble, Birmingham goods, fuller's earth, wool, pottery, glass, locally-grown products, manufactured goods and foreign imports. Potware – about 150 tons annually at 3s 10d per ton – from Burslem was carried in large crates on horseback to Bewdley. 150 horses came with woollen goods weekly from Manchester through Stafford to Bewdley'.

> Hundreds of packhorses were tethered nightly in the streets of Bewdley. Wyre Hill had hollow roads worn by the countless pack animals scrambling up the rough steep track. These pack roads can always be traced by the drinking places for animals along their verge. One is still on Lea Bank, another near Dowles Church, and again at the Black Man's Stitch (or Ditch) on Long Bank, where the old road runs in the fields south of the present road up the hill. Caves, too, were always found wherever suitable rock was, such as at Blakeshall, Cookley and around Bewdley. The price of carrying a ton of potware from Burslem to Bewdley was only 2s 10d. How many animals would it take to carry a ton, with boxes and packing?

In the north of the county great quantities of iron and coal were carried on packhorses from the Severn to the numerous forges in the Wyre Forest and in the Stour Valley. Along these 'iron roads' pig iron was brought up Severn from the Forest of Dean and finished goods were returned to the Severn for shipping down to Bristol and elsewhere. In the Wyre Forest 'iron roads' can be traced at Heightington, Cleobury and Coveley. Cleobury Lane is deep and was called 'Bloody Hollow'. From Halesowen forges 'iron roads' ran up Bundle Hill and down Huntingtree Lane to Stourport. Great loads of coal and iron were carried by packhorse along these deep lanes.

Drovers' roads

To this area of the West Midlands came drovers from Wales and the Welsh Border, using prehistoric ridgeways where possible and boasting that they could take cattle to Worcester and beyond to the London markets without paying a 'pike'. Their knowledge of the old green roads as an alternative to the turnpikes had been built up over centuries, a knowledge now sadly lost.

Drovers' roads can always be distinguished from packhorse trails by their width, for whereas packhorses travelled in single file, a drover would bring perhaps over two hundred animals in a mass and as many as two thousand geese in a single goose drive. The drovers' roads were from forty to ninety feet wide with grassy verges where cattle could graze when quietly making their journey, for even when conditions were good it was unusual for cattle to make more than twelve miles a day. Pigs were driven even shorter distances, the average no more than six miles a day.

Some drovers' roads can be identified near old inns where verges are double the normal width, or have a double hedgerow, the one farthest from the road having old trees and shrubs which indicate the original line of the road. 'Stances', or grassy hollows, remain near old inns, or fields of bright green grass (heavily manured) behind inns with names like 'Halfpenny Green' (½d per animal was charged for the night), or 'Cold Harbour', where the nightly charge per man fluctuated between 4d and 6d.

Long journeys on rough roads were hard on the hoofs of animals, and it was the practice to shoe bullocks and sheep. Along the main driving routes were smithies, usually near to a drovers' inn. Two of these still exist – on the road at Brinsley Common, just east of Bromyard, and next to the Red Lion Inn at Holt Heath. Geese were equipped for the journey by being driven through tar, then sawdust or sand to acquire 'boots'.

Drovers' inns

Along the routes were ancient inns, often very primitive. The Feathers Inn at Ledbury was a famous drovers' inn with its field behind where the cattle rested before being driven over the Malvern Hills, through the Holly Bush Pass, where there are wide verges all the way to Upton and the crossing of the Severn. (When the road was turnpiked other passes, such as the Gullet, were used.) From Upton the drive went by way of Fladbury and Broadway to Stow-on-the-Wold or Moreton-in-the-Marsh. Even the Lygon Arms (as the White Hart) was a drovers' halt before it became the great coaching inn; and before the days of hedges and enclosures it was the practice to plant one or two fir trees as a 'marker' at a drovers' inn, which is how the Fir Tree at Dunhampstead got its name.

There is a good description of the arrival of a drovers' group in 1855 at the New Inn at Cropthorne by G M Stratton:

> My father, C F Stratton, kept the New Inn at Cropthorne for many years. Some 70 years ago I well remember, as a boy, seeing as many as eight or ten Welsh drovers, several times driving as many as 300 and 400 of the Welsh

black cattle. Also at times, a similar quantity of the hardy Welsh ponies. These, so they told us, they were taking to London .... They always made our place a rest-place for themselves and animals for a night's stay, as we had a green field for the animals.

My mother and the principal drover would stand by the gate leading to the field, and count the animals to make sure that none were lost. She would have a quantity of peas in her pocket, and when the number 20 was reached she would then place one pea in another pocket and by that method of calculation she would know the number of animals for which she would charge.

Droving and packhorse trains reached their peak in the eighteenth century; but droving lasted longer for where there was no railway animals still had to be brought to market on the hoof. The Worcester Cattle Market was an important market for drovers from Herefordshire and the Teme Valley until well into the 1930s. A traffic survey over Worcester Bridge, taken on Wednesday, 24 November 1912, recorded fifty-nine herds of cattle driven on foot — yet *Monday* was market day.

Turnpikes and coaching

TRAVELLERS ON THE ROADS

Travelling on the roads before the turnpike age was often a dangerous business. A Worcester guide of 1816 stated: 'In early times the journey from Worcester to London was a matter of dread and was preceded by the making of Wills and the settling of wordly affairs.' The precautions taken for a journey are well emphasised in a note telling of the casual meeting at Stourbridge in 1717 with a gentleman about to set off for London:

Mr Foley, of Prestwood, came riding out of the Talbot archway. He was a fine-looking man on a black horse; his hat was gold-laced, and his white curled wig hung down to the shoulders of his blue coat. He wore great riding boots and a fine long sword; his cloak, his saddlecloth and pistol-holders were all stitched with gold. Behind him, three servants in livery rode, armed with swords and blunderbusses, for Mr Foley was a gentleman and was riding to London.

As the turnpike system developed and the roads improved, so the dangers and discomforts lessened. Coaches plied from all the main towns and though they travelled slowly in the eighteenth century the journey often left agreeable recollections of an entertaining companion, or of a welcome roadside hostelry. An account of the Shrewsbury Old Heavy which trundled through Worcestershire tells of those leisurely days:

Stoppages there were whenever necessity arose — a very slight one served the turn — such as the encountering of a friend either of the coachman or passengers, between whom conversation, varying in length from three to five minutes, took place without let or hindrance. A special tap of ale at any given hostelry was acknowledged sufficient excuse for delay; for instance, the Boar's Head at Severn Stoke was usually the scene of copious refreshment. But crowning mercy to the fasting and thirsty was vouchsafed at Alveley, half-way between Kidderminster and Bridgnorth. There, in front of the Squirrel Inn, on a solid stone horse-block, six feet square, the like of which I never saw elsewhere, flanked with steps for the accommodation of passengers both on the road and inside, the provident care of Mrs Hobbs, the landlady, spread daily a snow-white cloth. Thereon appeared a crusty loaf, a cheese, all the better for having seen service, and a dish of sandwiches, each one of which would have cut up into four in these degenerate days, flanked by a portentous jug replete with mighty ale; while Mrs Hobbs, glorious in parti-coloured garments, smilingly bade guests eat and dine, which they did and were thankful.

The Hibernia and the L'Hirondelle were considered the fastest coaches on the road. In the 1830s they raced each other all the way from Liverpool to Cheltenham, covering the distance of 136 miles in 9 hours 33 minutes, which included stoppages. On one occasion the Hibernia did the fourteen-mile journey from Kidderminster to Worcester in 40 minutes.

THE TOLLKEEPER WHO STOPPED THE KING

At the junction of Ombersley Road and Droitwich Road in Worcester stands the 'Round House', now an antiques shop but once the Barban Gate Tollhouse, famed throughout England in the late eighteenth century as the gate where Robert Sleath stopped King George III on his way to visit Bishop Hurd at Hartlebury.

The right of His Majesty to pass toll-free had cropped up in conversation in a large company at Worcester and Robert Sleath, an honest blunt man and keeper of Barban Gate, argued that the king in his private capacity was liable to pay and that, though he respected his Sovereign, if ever he came to Barban Gate he should not pass until the toll was paid. A short time after, His Majesty's equerry arrived at Barban Gate and, true to his word, Robert demanded the toll on the grounds that the king was travelling not at the head of an army but privately. Nor was Robert frightened by the ensuing threats. Finally, with the royal carriage now in sight, the attendant was reduced to polite entreaty and assured Robert that the person who followed His Majesty's carriage would pay the regular demand. So the gate was opened and the whole cavalcade passed. But Robert received not a penny.

Aware that His Majesty would return to Cheltenham the following day, he waited and as the royal equipage was approaching locked the gate and took his station as before. The same equerry again began to remonstrate, but Sleath swore roundly that no-one should pass until he had received the toll for both days. The royal attendant, perceiving he was not likely to prevail, paid Sleath, threatening to crush him with the weight of legal vengeance; but Robert pocketed the money and was never called to account. On his grave this epitaph was placed:

On Wednesday last old Robert Sleath
Passed through the Turnpike Gate of Death,
To him would Death no toll abate,
Who stopped the King at Wor'ster Gate.

SOME GREAT COACHING INNS

The first mention of a stagecoach in Worcester was in 1674. The roads were very bad and dangerous; and the journey from Worcester to London, a matter of dread, took four days, many coaches only undertaking it during the summer season. When Thomas Shakill of the *Bell* in Broad Street, Worcester, announced a stage landau to Birmingham in 1753, he advertised it as 'easy and genteel. Performed, if God permit.' On the route specific coaching inns were established. At Worcester, the *Crown*, the *Hop Pole*, the *Bell* and the *Star and Garter*; at Bewdley the *George* and the *Angel*; at Stourbridge the *Talbot*; at Kidderminster the *Lion*; at Bromsgrove the *Crown* – all became the established posting houses. Coaches improved vastly over the years. Innkeepers advertised their new road carriages as 'flying machines' or, if they had improved windowing, as 'glass machines'; and the first 'Worcester Flying Coach' set off for London from the *Crown* on 11 June 1733.

In the golden age of coaching, from 1820 to 1840, 700 Royal Mail coaches operated day and night; and well over 3,000 stagecoaches, with a remarkable ancillary organisation of inns and posting houses every ten to twelve miles to change horses and snatch refreshments. At Worcester in 1836 there were fifty-five four-horse mail coaches, and forty-nine two-horse vehicles.

The *Holly Bush* at Belbroughton was once a staging post for coaches plying the old Stourbridge to Bromsgrove road. It had stables and a smithy and must have been a welcome sight to many a traveller on that wild road. Legends that the inn was a refuge for highwaymen cannot be verified; but the lonely road would have been ideal terrain for such characters. Nearby, the old Hollies Hill gibbet, one of four around the Clent area, was in sight of the *Holly Bush* and drew considerable crowds of sensation-seekers to the tavern. In later years it was the favourite 'baiting house' for wagoners carting loads of nails from Bromsgrove to the Black Country, but its busiest days were those of the annual Bromsgrove Fair, an extremely popular event with tatters from Tipton and the Black Country and others interested in horses. The tavern was a traditional 'camp' for generations of Romany families and there was much horse-trading and fist-fights between the 'travellers and those from the dark region'.

The turnpike trusts in the eighteenth century led to new, more direct roads and the old devious roads were either abandoned or became mere lanes or bridle paths. The old road from Worcester north to Kidderminster ran *west* of Ombersley village and on through Uphampton and Lineholt, by way of a number of small hamlets where there was a host of wayside inns, now all private houses. At the point where the lane to Doverdale crosses the old road stood the *Half-Way House*. Presumably, the present *Half-Way House* on the A449 took the old inn's name, but it too was a very old house, half-timbered at the front and with a thatched rear roof. Near the front door used to be a little glazed hole where a lighted candle was placed.

A little further north on the A449, on the corner of the lane to Elmley Lovett, was another wayside inn of great age, the *Crown Inn* at Warsley in the parish of Hartlebury, but now gone. It was the *Crown* until the late nineteenth century when the Rev Benjamin Gibbons, Rector of Stourport, bought it and changed its name to the *Lion* which was on his crest; but it was demolished during a road-widening scheme in the 1930s.

On the A38 a regular stopping place for coaches was the *Copcut Elm*, Salwarpe. The name is derived from an ancient elm that once stood before its door, under which servants would gather for the hiring mop during the eighteenth and early nineteenth centuries. The *Swan* at Upton Warren was another important coaching inn. Before the railway came to Birmingham four coaches a day stopped at the inn en route from Worcester to Birmingham, but when the Birmingham to London railway opened in 1835 it was far quicker and cheaper to go to London by way of coach to Birmingham and traffic increased greatly; no less than twenty coaches a day called at the *Swan* and other inns on the road. Then the Gloucester–Birmingham line was completed in 1840, with a station at Spetchley for Worcester, and the coach trade disappeared almost overnight, these once busy coaching inns reverting to quiet wayside taverns.

Mrs Clay's stall against the Priory Gateway, Malvern. (From a stereoscopic slide, 1855–60).

AT THE 'SIGN OF THE DOG'

In *Berrow's Worcester Journal* of May 1754 there was an 'interesting' appeal for a lost person which mentions a tavern under the '*Sign of the Dog*' outside the turnpike gates which then stood at the bottom of Wheatsheaf Hill at the junction of the London and Tewkesbury roads. It reads:

> Whereas Jean Andre, a short, thick, French Woman, with a small pale Face, a Cast in one Eye, supposed to be disordered in her Mind, was miss'd by her Husband in the City last Sunday Morning about Ten o'Clock, and has not since been heard of. Whoever will bring her to her Husband, Maximillian Andre, at the Sign of the Dog, without Sidbury Turnpike, Worcester, shall have ½ Guinea Reward, and all reasonable Expenses.

Horse sense

William Shuard, recalling the days of horse transport in the 1870s, described his journey from Ombersley to Brettell Lane in the Black Country:

> At the age of 15 years, I went to live at a farmhouse called The Court Farm, Borley, near Holt Fleet and Ombersley. I had not been there long before the farmer greatly surprised me by telling me to come up the country to meet him on the Saturday morning with a load of fruit. When I had recovered a little from my astonishment, I told the farmer I did not know the way, and at the same time thinking I might perhaps get out of doing this. The farmer soon put matters right by telling me to bring a horse named Snip, turn its head under the Black Bridge at Hartlebury and that was all. That was as far as I happened to know, roughly three miles on the way. I knew that the farmer himself was going on the Friday to Brettell Lane in the Black Country.

(The following Saturday at one o'clock in the morning young William was woken up by the farmer's wife.)

> After breakfast, I had to fetch the horse from the stable to the barn where the cart was kept, and not being familiar, owing to my inexperience, in coupling the horse to the cart, the old lady showed me what had to be done. I bade the old lady goodbye before I commenced my journey, she taking once more to her bed. I then gave the necessary commands to my horse as I disappeared into the darkness of the winding lanes. I came to Bishop's Wood near Crossway Green, where I could plainly see a crimson glare in the sky from the blast furnaces of Staffordshire. I then came to the Black Bridge. This was as far as I knew of my journey, and at this point the horse showed its first sense of direction, for it wanted to go to Kidderminster, which was only a few miles, instead of the long journey into Staffordshire.
>
> Remembering my instructions, I turned the horse's head to the right, and after this, I placed myself entirely in the care of my dumb friend and guide as we plodded along up over the lonely Shenstone Lane and over the steep Barnett Hills. The load I had in the cart was a heavy one and the horse realised this, and to make things easier it would wind itself from one side of the road to the other, displaying another bit of horse sense.

I then passed through the village of Hagley, near the cattle market; afterwards I entered Stourbridge, where my dumb and faithful friend . . . amazed me by exactly passing the off-side wheel onto the near-side tramline and keeping it there for the remainder of the journey except, of course, to pull out to pass a tram, but the horse did not lose much time in getting back onto the line again. The trams themselves were driven by steam and ran from Stourbridge to Dudley.

At about the middle of Brettell Lane, my dumb friend had fulfilled its duty, for it suddenly turned off to the other side of the road and drew up at the kerb outside The Pheasant public house, and in a few minutes my master came out and bade me 'Good Morning', and so my journey came to an end.

On the return journey William went to sleep in the cart, but the old horse took him home even when, on waking up, he thought he was going out of his way and tried to turn the horse's head. It just refused to go, so William gave up and the horse went on and delivered him safely back at the farm and, as William realised later, by the shortest route.

The Severn watermen

In the days when the Severn was a great trading highway every riverside village had its quay for coals, bricks and other products; and always near the quays were inns, the favourite haunting places of the watermen who worked the river.

The earliest vessel on the Severn was the coracle, a small keelless boat with a basketwork frame, used mainly for getting from one side of the river to another. But later a special kind of barge was developed, the *trow*, unique to the River Severn. The trow was a flat-bottomed, steep-sided barge. In Bewdley bowhauliers — four at a time — used to pull the trows upstream, taken on at the *Mug House* on Severnside North and the transaction sealed with a mug of ale. Some teams of men would number as many as twenty, working for a wage of 2s 6d a day plus two meals and two mugs of ale.

At Upper Arley where the Severn enters Worcestershire there was an important ferry crossing and no less than six inns for the watermen to choose from: the *Valentia* (named after Viscount Valentia of Arley Castle), the *Crown*, famed for its cockfights, the *Cock* on the river bank near the vicarage garden, the *Nelson*, later the site of the village shop, the *Harbour Inn* on the west bank, and a cider house called *The Case is Altered*.

Further downstream, at Hampstall, the crossing was a dangerous one, borne out by a notice that used to hang outside the *Hampstall Ferry Inn* which read: 'Passengers cross here at their own risk.' On 4 August 1919 — a Bank Holiday Monday — the ferry with seventeen people aboard capsized and nine were drowned.

At Worcester, a busy inland port, it was no unusual sight to see well over a hundred sailing vessels tied up waiting for a 'fresh' to get them over the shallows or a 'fall' to get them under the bridge. The quays and the riverside area were full of watermen's taverns, dingy and some of doubtful repute, frequented by the bowhauliers and their women, and gangs of smugglers. The area was a maze of narrow alleys which stretched in a picturesque muddle right down to the quays. By day, it was a busy, evil-smelling warren, by night the taverns were alive with laughter and snatches of songs; but here, too, the press gang operated and the alleys were dark and dangerous to strangers. The worst one was Rush Alley which was cleared at the making of the new approach road to the bridge and called Bridge Street.

Worcester Bridge c1820. A rare print showing the method of bowhauling Severn trows upstream.

Among the mixture of good merchants' houses and squalid tenements were a number of better-class inns, such as the ancient half-timbered *Wherry* at the bottom of Copenhagen Street, which catered for the passenger traffic of the trows and wherries that plied a regular service from Bristol to Shrewsbury in the eighteenth century. The river journey was the easiest and cheapest way from the north to Bath, the mecca of fashion, and whole families moved to take the waters, carrying with them furniture and bedding and providing the inns with a very good quality trade. The *Wherry* was also a centre of smuggling activity, for with the 'Slip' at its door the unloading of goods by night was easy. Vessels came straight from the coast until the 1840s and there was a series of underground passages and caves by which goods landed by night could be in shops in the High Street by morning. In the cellars of the *Wherry* was a bricked-up passage which once led to the *Cock Inn*, a little higher up the street. It also had a huge cellar which, tradition has it, had a passage running underneath St Andrew's churchyard to Bull Entry and the *Red Cow*.

Towards the end of his journey along the Severn in Worcestershire the waterman would have to negotiate another thriving inland port, Upton-on-Severn. A cluster of inns on or near its quayside testifies to its busy past. The crossing of the river here is an ancient one on the route from Wales to the Avon Valley. The stone bridge (replacing an earlier wooden one) was severely damaged in the Civil War and never properly repaired. It created enormous problems, especially for sailing boats, for a shoal of some three-feet draft developed just below the bridge – regularly causing as many as two to three hundred vessels to go aground. Today's bridge has sides so high that no view of the river is possible when crossing.

Worcestershire railways

THE 'BATTLE OF THE GAUGES'

By 1845 over forty railway schemes were projected in Worcestershire, thirteen of them affecting the city. Only six received legislative sanction, most of the schemes subsequently dropped. The real struggle lay between the Oxford, Worcester and Wolverhampton Railway Company (OW&W for short), backed by the Great Western Railway, and a line from Worcester to Tring, supported by the London and North Western Railway. Worcestershire became the cockpit in which was fought out the battle of the rival systems of Stephenson and Brunel (the latter addressing a meeting in the Guildhall in 1844 in favour of the OW&W scheme). The contest became known in railway history as the 'Battle of the Gauges': the GWR with interests in Worcester had a gauge of seven feet; the other lines were four feet eight-and-a-half inches, a width deriving accidentally from the pit rails in the north.

Up to 1845 the broad gauge had not made way north of Gloucester, and the control of the valley of the Severn was expected to decide its future. The battle was long and costly, a battle of Titans. All the great engineers and the pick of the parliamentary bar were engaged; and Worcester was the scene of great public debate and packed meetings. The broad gauge champions won all along the line, largely through the help of Worcester witnesses, and there was tremendous rejoicing. But it was a hollow victory. The legal and engineering expenses amounted to £1,000 for every mile of the company's line, more than had been anticipated, and this led to disputes between the OW&W and the GWR who were providing the guarantee. The 'narrow gauge interest' intervened and offered to finance and work the railway, but the contract with the GWR proved a stumbling block. Peto and Betts, the great railway contractors, ultimately took the construction in hand and the line became known as 'a contractors' line', the cost being paid in shares at a discount; but the company fell into hopeless financial embarrassment, its shares plunged from £100 to £14 and by 1849 £2.5 million had been spent without opening one mile of track.

On the running side, too, things went very badly. The carriages were old and let in water, the ramshackle engines frequently broke down. On 18 October 1855 an express from Worcester was delayed at Hartlebury for over six hours – four engines detailed to take it on broke down. It is no wonder the OW&W line came to be known as the 'Old Worse and Worse' line.

WORCESTER: A RAILWAY CENTRE

It was not until 1850 that the railway came to Worcester. After years of frustration and mismanagement the OW&W appointed A C Sherriff, a former schoolmaster, but trained in railway management. As the Worcester station master he brought tremendous Yorkshire skill and energy to the job so that under his control chaos was reduced to order. Traffic developed, new lines were laid in the areas around, and Worcester became a really important railway centre. The OW&W became the West Midland Railway, absorbing the newly constructed Worcester and Hereford line, the Newport and Abergavenny and Hereford, and the Severn Valley Companies, ultimately controlling over two hundred miles of line. The West Midland was in turn absorbed by the GWR nineteen years after Brunel's first visit, a development which, ironically, proved the death knell of the broad gauge. Both gauges were tried on the OW&W in its independent career. For a time the mixed gauge operated of necessity but it was the narrow gauge that survived. If the broad gauge could have held out for another twenty years it might well have become permanent. 'Future generations', wrote Edward Corbett, 'will never know the delight and smoothness of the Broad Gauge.'

THE BIRMINGHAM AND GLOUCESTER RAILWAY

The Birmingham and Gloucester Railway (later the LMS) was the first to run through the county – several years earlier than the OW&W – but it did so with sublime indifference to any needs Worcestershire people might have had. Its promoters were bent only on getting the most direct line from the manufacturing West Midlands to the port of Bristol and so it ran inconveniently east of Bromsgrove, Droitwich and even the county town.

The Crown Inn in Broad Street, Worcester, one of the great coaching inns, has an interesting relic of the early railway days. For ten years while the OW&W struggled to get a line to Worcester would-be travellers had to take a horse omnibus to Spetchley Station, the nearest to the city. It was a lumbering conveyance with fifteen people huddled aboard for forty to sixty minutes of tedious jolting. The tickets for the journey were obtained from a semi-circular window in the yard of the Crown and despite all the changes to this fine old pub it is still there.

The LMS banking engine number 2290 (0-10-0), the only superheated decapod locomotive in Britain, assisted the trains up the famous three-mile Lickey Incline for more than thirty years. She was known as *Big Bertha*. The Lickey gradient of 1:37 between Bromsgrove and Blackwell Stations is one of the most difficult in the country. Loco No 2290 (first known as Big Emma) was built specifically for the task. She went into service in December 1919 and (ending as No 58100) was reckoned to have done 838,856 miles. During the 1939–45 War traffic increased greatly, with 650-ton trains of munitions, steel and coal. Bertha needed help and was given three assistants; and the four locos, all together in tandem, puffed and panted up the Lickey at the rate of two miles an hour. The noise, smoke, cinders and grass fires gave way in June 1956 to the diesel engine.

In 1840 the gradient had caused much criticism and the engineers were angry when American engines from Philadelphia were imported. The subsequent great rivalry led to a famous tragedy. The British engine *Surprise*, straining with its load, burst its boiler and the two engineers were killed. They are buried in Bromsgrove churchyard with tombstones depicting American locomotives. It appears that the mason going to Bromsgrove Station sketched the first locomotive he saw — which happened to be American.

'Hell-Fire Jack' Richards and his engine Gipsy Lass *at Great Malvern Station, 1861*

RAILWAY ACCIDENTS

In the 1880s the River Teme had its biggest flood for many years and at Bransford, on the Worcester-Hereford line, it sapped the foundations of the railway bridge. A passenger was so alarmed by the bridge's oscillations that, on arriving at Malvern Link Station, he warned the station master of the danger of continuing to run trains over it. The warning was disregarded and a goods train proved to be the final touch. When the bridge collapsed an old platelayer named Jack Richards, in his younger days a crack engine driver known to all on the line as *Hell-Fire Jack*, clambered across the only remaining beam that spanned the foaming torrent, ran along the line and prevented an oncoming train from plunging into the river.

The worst railway accident in Worcestershire took place on 23 August 1858, on the old OW&W line just north of Stourbridge, when commercial pressures and negligence led to a disregard for safety standards. An excursion train from Wolverhampton, consisting of two engines pulling thirty-nine carriages, left for

Worcester, carrying fifteen hundred people, half of them children. On the outward journey the couplings broke three times; on the return journey the excursion was split into two trains, the first with thirty carriages, the second with sixteen carriages. The first train had stopped on a slope at Pound Oak, just north of Stourbridge, when another coupling broke. The guard was not in his van and the brake was not on. Eighteen carriages set off down the incline and, gathering considerable speed, met the second train halfway up. Fourteen passengers were killed and over two hundred injured.

The Hon Evelyn Ellis's Daimler, the first motor vehicle to reach the top of the Worcestershire Beacon, 12 October 1897.

Early motorcars

Mr T C Santler of Donnybrook, Malvern, claimed to have made the first English petrol-driven car, the *Malvernia*, and drove it at Malvern Link in 1887. Only after tests were completed and the car had taken to the road was the Benz three-wheeler imported into this country. Mr Santler, educated at Lyttleton Grammar School in Malvern, made three of these early cars with the assistance of his brother, W R Santler. Despite the Red Flag Act, Mr Santler's cars used to attain the speed of 20 mph, and could be driven at an average speed of between 4 and 12 mph. Santler cars were made until 1922, though latterly the firm was a limited company; and the original model was in Leamington in 1946 and still roadworthy. Mrs Santler recalled that only once during more than fifty years of driving was her husband fined. That was in 1907 when his number plate fell off.

It is said that T C Santler also made the first freewheel fitted to a bicycle and that experiments in that direction started as early as 1879. Shortly afterwards, a bicycle made by him, with the assistance of another Midland inventor, Mr J Nicholls, was ridden successfully from Malvern to Presteigne and back, a distance of sixty miles.

The Worcestershire Exhibition of 1882

After the failure of the Worcester Engine Company, and the West Midlands Wagon Company that followed, the great engine works lay empty and desolate. But in July 1882 they came to life with a vengeance. Following the success of the Great Exhibition of 1851, provincial exhibitions had become popular and someone suggested the building would be ideal to house a Worcestershire exhibition, providing 54,000 square feet of space, much greater than similar provincial exhibitions had had. The engine-fitting shop – 239 feet long, 50 feet wide and 30 feet high – with its iron and glass roof was chosen as the main court of the exhibition and called the 'nave'.

Worcestershire Exhibition Catalogue, 1882.

The exhibition brought together Worcestershire people to an extent never previously known and was for months both entertaining and instructive. On show were old masters from many local collections, and modern works by Brook, Leader and others, together with historic relics and documents, many never before seen by the public. As to the industrial exhibits, only those from the county itself were accepted.

It is rare indeed that one finds so many branches of trade and manufacture within the confines of a single county, and the fact that many of them are art industries lends an additional charm to the Exhibition.

Thus proclaimed the *Worcestershire Chronicle* on 22 July 1882, shortly after the exhibition opened. Strangely, the most popular exhibit proved to be the patent staircase which could be pulled up to the ceiling. Thousands tramped up it just to be able to draw it up after them. But the device did not succeed commercially: one fitted in a Worcester factory jammed; and the fire risk was obvious.

On the opening day, 'an occasion of unusual jubilation throughout the City', bells were rung, flags were flown and the streets were decorated with streamers and bunting. Crowds lined the roads to watch the 'great' of the county arrive and to admire the parading soldiers, brass bands, mayors and other dignitaries. Inside, the invited audience listened to a number of speeches and, finally, a rendering of the Hallelujah Chorus. The exhibition remained open until October 1882 during which time it was visited by over two hundred thousand people. Its financial success rendered possible the subsidising of various educational schemes in Worcester, Kidderminster and elsewhere; and though its chief benefaction, the Victoria Institute in Worcester, was not the outcome of any single event, the exhibition helped to ripen public opinion in favour of the project.

Shops and their keepers

CANDLEMAKING AT EVESHAM

Until the mid-nineteenth century most people still lived where they worked; often the craftsman was the shopkeeper as well, working in the back with all the paraphernalia of his trade. Today, shops are cleaner and pleasanter but the shopkeeper is often no longer a judge and pricer of the goods he sells. In country towns the old-style shopkeeper-craftsman continued until the 1939–45 War, and goods now factory-made were still being made by hand in the backs of premises in the High Streets.

Mr G Gibbs of Bengeworth recalled watching in the 1860s candles and rushlights being made at the back of the premises of William Martin, a grocer in Bridge Street in Evesham: 'The hot tallow was poured into a long box on trestles. The wicks were fastened to a frame something like the straight back of a chair, all hanging free of each other. Then the frame was carefully lifted up and more carefully let down into the fat. When all had been dipped once, and hung up for the wicks to stiffen, the process was repeated until they were the right weight. There were 6, 8, 10, and up to 18 to a pound. The smell of course was dreadful ... in 1848, it was noticed that there were no cholera cases near the tallow works. Some attributed this to the smell from there, and some to the tanyard nearby.'

OLD SHOP SIGNS

At 25 Oat Street, Evesham, lived John Begley, the chimney sweep. This was clear for all to see, for on a large sign which almost obliterated his small cottage was depicted a house with its chimney on fire, and Mr Begley (presumably) arriving in great haste with a bundle of rods and brushes over his shoulder. Beneath the picture, removed about 1910, was the rhyme:

> John Begley does live here
> Sweeps chimneys clean and not too dear;
> He sweeps them well, up and down,
> Both in Country and in Town.
> And if your chimney is on fire
> He'll put it out if you desire.

John Rock of Cleeve Prior set an old shoemaker named Cull to work in a shop in Evesham. Cull had the following lines printed on a board to go over his door:

> Behold the shop where toils a cheerful snob,
> Tho' thankful to those who bring him a job,
> Full grateful he to those who bring the pence
> To pay each debt, e'er they depart from thence,
> Because the man who serves the shop with leather
> If he don't receive will sell up altogether.

> Moral
> The adage which good folks were wont to say
> A man that can't receive can never pay.

Mr Rock however did not approve of it being above the door, so it was placed just inside.

THREE WORCESTER TRADESMEN

In more leisurely days philosophy seemed to go hand in hand with craftsmanship. Two tradesmen of Sidbury, working in the shadow of Worcester Cathedral, were well known for contemplative remarks.

Samuel Burlingham was a bootmaker using part of the Commandery for his business, an old-fashioned, quaint Quaker tradesman, portrayed in Mrs Henry Wood's pages. She knew him well. He died about 1870, the last of the Burlinghams to belong to the Society of Friends. He is best remembered for his advice on the choice of a wife: 'Friends,' he would say to his bachelor acquaintances, 'never thee marry a woman past 30. My first wife was young, and when I asked her to do anything, she would say, "Sam, it shall be done". But my second wife was past 30, and when I ask anything of her, she answers, "Sam, thou art wrong".'

The old violin maker's shop was for a long time a feature of the cathedral precincts. In a quaint little workshop next to St Michael's Church in College Street, Henry Handley plied his craft of violin making, surrounded by the delightful litter of odds and ends of instruments and implements. He was the son of a brickmaker, reared in the country, and at the age of fourteen was apprenticed to the glove trade, but preferred the work of violin making. He had a fancy when a boy to make boats with a knife and was nearly forty years of age before he made a fiddle. In 1919 when he was in his eightieth year he completed his hundredth stringed instrument; the hundred included one cello and ten violas. Musical instrument makers from all over the country sent to him for repairs. He died in 1931, aged ninety-one. He dated his later violins by putting inside the following verse:

> 'Neath the shadow of Worcester Cathedral tower
> I worked on this fiddle for many an hour,
> In my eighty-third year I fashioned the whole,
> Now it needs but a player to bring out the soul.

In Sidbury Jonathan Jackson, the principal butcher of the county, had his shop. His was a good example of the life of a prominent tradesman in the first half of the nineteenth century, before the railways revolutionised travel in country areas. He used to ride to Ludlow Fair, one of the most important for meat sales, starting at two o'clock in the morning, and return to a midday dinner after a gallop of seventy miles and the transaction of big business. It was a dangerous business, too, for buyers were accustomed to carry large sums of money with them.

The old Violin Maker's Shop, College Street, Worcester. Demolished in 1956.

VICTORIA HOUSE: A FASHIONABLE ESTABLISHMENT

The most famous of Worcester's drapery and millinery establishments in the nineteenth century was Victoria House at the top of what is now Shore Street. Its premises were part of the old Hop Pole Hotel, one of the most famous posting establishments in the Midlands, which was taken over in 1842 by Mr J W Scott who, on a most ambitious scale, converted the building and launched into the business of drapery, dressmaking and millinery. Scott named his establishment Victoria House for Princess Victoria and her mother, the Duchess of Kent, had stayed at the Hop Pole.

The business prospered greatly, county folk flocking in to shop at the new establishment; even royalty gracing the firm with its patronage. In 1865 Mr Scott took Mr H Oram into the business, a partnership which lasted twenty years, until

Scott retired at an advanced age. In 1887 alterations and new premises were built, with a lantern roof and modern spring doors; and the occasion was celebrated with a champagne supper for the forty shop staff. Two years later Richard Westwood bought the business and in 1899 put Mr W K Hogben in charge. Hogben had held a post in New Bond Street, serving many famous people, including Gladstone and Bright, and under him the business continued to flourish. Many royals shopped at Victoria House, including Queen Adelaide when she was resident at Witley Court, Queen Alexandra when Princess of Wales, Princess Helena when she was Princess Christian, and even Queen Victoria, though it appears she shopped by proxy. Some idea of the extent of the business can be seen by the fact that at one time there were fifty dressmakers as well as milliners, mantle workers and makers of children's wear.

The glove trade

The glove trade of Worcester was very ancient. The first mention of a Glovers' Guild dates back to 1497 but the trade existed in Worcester before that. Down to the 1840s gloves were made in workshops where the master, an all-round man, laboured at the bench with three or four journeymen and apprentices, cutting out the gloves, the sewing done by outside workers as piecework in cottages all around Worcestershire. The gloves were then hawked around by the master who called on regular customers and attended fairs and markets. Even the Dents, prominent in civic affairs in the eighteenth century, carried on business like this, with John Dent concerned with the workshop and William Dent doing the travelling.

For some there was great wealth in glove making. Two Worcester glovers, Francis Fincher and Alexander Beardsley, were prominent Quakers who after much persecution sold all their possessions and emigrated in 1683 with several other local Quakers, their families and servants. They were the first purchasers of land in Pennsylvania. Fincher was elected the first Speaker under Penn, but declined the post; and there are still Finchers working in the glove trade there. John Dent and his three sons started a business which was to achieve world fame and for his family an historic county seat, Sudeley Castle; and John Allcroft, who at a later period became the controlling partner in the firm, also earned a handsome living from the trade and bought Stokesay Castle.

In 1796 it was estimated that not less than 5,000 people were employed in the glove trade in the city and adjacent villages. By 1825, the masters were estimated to number between 100 and 140 and the workers in villages and towns some 30,000. The export trade was very large. But in 1824, the turning point, foreign gloves were allowed in − undercutting the local trade which never recovered. Work in Worcester was almost brought to a standstill. The small master glovers were driven out of business and as the nineteenth century developed the trade was concentrated in a few large firms.

The Black Country in 1860

It was in the north of the county that the great explosion of heavy industry in the nineteenth century took place. Iron was the material of the Industrial Revolution and coal was the fuel that fired it, and the Black Country had these and other materials in abundance. What was equally of importance was that the people there had the ancient skills in ironworking, and a wonderful endurance in the mine or at the forge to produce coal and iron in vast quantities.

Much of the iron made was consumed locally in the neighbouring chain, cable and anchor works; in the nail shops of Cradley, Halesowen and Bromsgrove, and in the boiler yards of Birmingham and South Staffordshire. The manufacture of chains and cables was introduced into the district about 1824, and the anchors some fifteen to twenty years later, but by the 1850s they were well established. In the factories, larger chains and cables were made, with employment of about two thousand men and boys, and the annual output was about fifty thousand tons. There were also three hundred-odd small shops, usually attached to cottages, in which husband, wife and children carried on the manufacture of trace and small chains.

The Nine Locks Pit disaster

The difficulty of keeping water out of a pit was a constant worry. In places it was an everlasting battle to prevent vast quantities of water from flooding the workings.

One of the most sensational mining disasters in the area occurred at one of the Earl of Dudley's pits, the Nine Locks Pit in Brierley Hill, on 17 March 1869, when thirteen men were entombed for six days. The rescue of the men, cut off by a great subterranean lake of water, is one of the most thrilling in industrial history. The body of water was so great that the mighty engine which pumped five hundred and forty gallons a minute, together with others which were brought in, could make no impression on it for a time. The suffering of the miners and the heroism of the rescuers were great indeed. After four hours the only lights the trapped men had gave out and they were in total darkness. By the last light they wrote on a tobacco paper a message from each of them and put it in a tobacco tin. When they had consumed their food they chewed their bootlaces.

Of the thirteen miners trapped the eldest, a man over fifty, got separated and could not be reached. He went mad and was heard shouting most pitifully for his wife, Louisa; but he died. Another went temporarily mad but was restrained and recovered; the youngest was a boy of fourteen years of age. The miners measured the passage of time by noting when the thumps of the great Nine Locks forge hammer overhead stopped for a change of shift and the Sunday rest. At last after six days and incredible dangers and hardships the rescuers broke through and reached them. The twelve survivors were temporarily blind and could hardly move, but they were alive. There were great cheers from the crowd at the pithead as every man was brought out, and especially when the boy Sankey was carried out and asked: 'Have you sent to tell my mother?'

Child labour

Child labour was particularly horrifying in the factories during the first half of the nineteenth century. It is strange that people who were active in the campaign to abolish the slave trade could be so blind to the conditions of working children right under their noses. By 1841, however, a commission concerning itself with the employment of children in factories began collecting evidence from many English towns. The following comes from Kidderminster:

> James Porter, aged 12, stated in evidence, 'I am a drawer for Timothy Lloyd, at Mr Dobson's; I have been so employed for five years; I went to school very young and can read and write a little. My father is a master baker, I go to Sunday School every Sunday, morning and evening. Our usual hours of work are from 6 o'clock in the morning until 9 or 10 at night. We never go before 6 as we have to go through a private passage to go to work and the master's servant is never up before that. I have once worked all night − never more. I worked then because the work was in a hurry. I have never worked anywhere else all night. I have begun elsewhere as early as four in the morning and left off at 9 or 10 pm. I work six days a week.

> Another boy of the same age gave his hours as from 5.30 am to 11 at night, at which hour he was so tired he could hardly crawl through the streets to get home. He breakfasted when he was lucky on a piece of toast or dried bread, and dinner consisted of nothing but taters and salt. A quarter of bacon, shared by all the family, would complete the day's rations.

Around Bromsgrove, where the brick trade was second only to the nail trade in importance, women worked extensively in the brickyards, and the employment of small children in the yards was not abolished until 1872. An Inspector of Factories said of them: 'One may scarcely recognise either in the person, or in the mind and manner of the female clayworker, a feature of the sex to which she belongs.' Young girls were employed 'among rough and uneducated boys, carrying bricks up ladders, clay on their heads, with matted hair, carrying bricks in and out of the hot kiln, loading bricks in trucks, running bricks away from moulders − doing all this often in a semi-nude state, and without restriction as to the hours of labour'.

Butties, foggers and tommy-shops

Many Black Country trades a century ago were run on a subcontracting basis: the owner paid a lump sum to a 'butty' who was responsible for hiring and paying the workers directly under him. This was the case particularly in the mines.

The variant in other Black Country trades, such as nailmaking, was that of using out-workers, who were at the mercy of the 'foggers' or middlemen who took their nails. They supplied the nailers with iron rod on credit, and paid for the finished nails in 'truck' or goods. These butties, foggers and trucksters were in an extremely strong bargaining position which they were not slow to use. All sorts of devices and extortions were used by foggers: fraudulent scales, refusal to accept nails on pretence that they were not exact in size; and they often got twenty or thirty per cent of the nailer's wages. The nailer's unit of dealing was a thousand nails, but it had an elastic definition — by custom the nailer had to sell to the fogger at twelve hundred nails (paid, though, for only a thousand); while the master, also by custom, handed to the customer only eight hundred nails and thus acquired four hundred free.

Early in the nineteenth century it was common practice for foggers to operate 'tommy-shops' or 'truck-shops' and pay the nailers in cheques which could only be changed at their shops. If they did not care for this then they could look for another job. These shops only sold the necessities of life but were joined by inns and taverns, if not run by the fogger or butty then by a close relative. Moneylending was another activity, a common rate of interest being as high as 5s per £ per week — or thirteen hundred per cent per annum.

The lost trades of Bewdley

From the middle ages Bewdley was renowned for its tanning and working in leather. It was well situated, with the Wyre Forest at its back door with a practically inexhaustible supply of oak bark, a constant supply of skins from the droves of cattle from the Welsh Border country, a never-failing water supply and a great highway for transport in the River Severn. With the tanneries went the auxiliary leather trades — shoes, saddles, horn and buttons, candles and manure, all nearby, their products easily transported down river to Bristol. In 1770 a writer remembered twelve working tanners in the borough. The last tannery on Severnside was near the bottom of Lax Lane, but it closed in 1938.

When Bewdley was the centre of the tanning industry bark peeling was a seasonable occupation. It lasted for a month, usually from mid-May to mid-June, when the sap began to run in the young oak trees. After a tree had been felled the women would sit around it and do the barking, skilled work which resulted in the bark being stripped off in semi-cylindrical pieces. It was put on racks to dry, and then sent into Bewdley for use in the local tanning industry. Until the 1920s bark peeling was an event of some importance in Bewdley and employed forty-odd people, mainly women. In 1938 only four men and four women were still doing the work. Today tannic acid is used.

There was a curious custom among bark peelers — rather like 'heaving' in Worcester. Visitors who came to see the peeling had their shins 'barked'. One of the women would creep up and clap a piece of bark along the visitor's shin. There was much laughter and the visitor was expected to 'pay his footing' with a coin or two for refreshments. Usually the visitor had been warned beforehand and took it in good grace.

The trade of felt-hat and capmaking was a flourishing one from the reign of Elizabeth I. Before that time Monmouth was the centre of the trade, but a plague hit that town so badly that the workers migrated to Bewdley. The great age of

Bewdley hatters was the Regency period when 'beaver' hats were fashionable and were supplied in great quantity to London firms and to others in the country. The 'felt' was made from rabbit skins, and the gentry and their gamekeepers for miles around supplied the rabbits. The carcasses were packed in special crates for sale in the Black Country while the curing of the skins took place in the rear of the premises, one of which was in Park Lane. The hat trade was much wider, however, and is said to have occupied about a thousand people, all with special skills.

The glass trade at Stourbridge

Glass manufacturing was first introduced in Stourbridge in 1556 by refugees from Lorraine. There were earlier glassworks in Sussex but the forests there, which supplied the fuel, became exhausted and, like the iron trade, the glass trade migrated to Worcestershire where fuel was abundant (though here, too, by about 1630 the forests were fast disappearing and the use of wood was prohibited).

By the close of the sixteenth century the trade was well established, and among the Protestant refugees who came to Stourbridge there were two families, the Henzells and the Tyzackes, who have been credited with the development of the trade in North Worcestershire. Annanis Henzell and his son Joseph have been given the credit for inventing the 'covered' glasshouse pots which produced the purity and brilliance characteristic of good Stourbridge glass. John Tyzacke had glassworks at Lye and elsewhere in a district where for centuries glasshouse cones (kilns) were a feature of the area. But today gas furnaces are used, being very economical and easy to maintain.

In medieval times and later Venetian glass was supreme, but in the twentieth century the finest decorative glassware in the world was made in Stourbridge, an achievement underlined when, before the 1914–18 War, a fine cut-glass ewer and basin, to be presented to the Kaiser, had to be imported from England since no factory in Germany could reach the required standard of quality.

Droitwich salt and saltmakers

Droitwich owed its existence to the making of salt and it is believed that it was the Roman *Salinae*, one of the first settlements in Worcestershire. The brine was obtained from springs, and later from wells in a limited strip of land in the centre of the town. Between Dodderhill Church and Friar Street and High Street there are thirty-two recorded wells. Between the seventeenth and nineteenth centuries brine overflowed at the surface from sources eighty feet deep, but when salt was taken at Stoke Prior (in 1825) the overflow ceased, proving the connection between the two places. With the cessation of pumping in about 1970 the brine has risen to a common level over the saltfield.

Many Roman roads were kept open as saltways, for the Romans greatly prized the brine from Droitwich. Indeed, the word 'salary' comes from *salarium*, an allowance of salt made to legionaries. In Anglo-Saxon times a network of salt tracks radiating

Four pensioners from Droitwich Workhouse, 1909.

from Droitwich was established through the heavily wooded areas of Worcestershire, and along these salt was carried for great distances, leaving its mark in place names all over the country. Transportation was a great problem for the salt trade, for the roads were quite unfit for heavy traffic. Already in 1708 a plan for a pipeline from Droitwich to the Severn at Hawford had been suggested to overcome these difficulties; and in 1713 an Act (the first of the Turnpike Trust Acts in Worcestershire) for the repair and maintenance of the Droitwich to Worcester high road was passed following complaints that the road was useless for the carriage of salt for nine months of the year.

In 1767 James Brindley was asked to survey a route for a canal from Droitwich to the Severn. The idea was an old one for an attempt in 1662 by Andrew Yarranton to make the River Salwarpe navigable had almost succeeded, with five out of the six locks built. But in 1673 another £6,000 was spent to complete the work, without success. The canal opened on 12 March 1771 amidst great rejoicing when two vessels arrived loaded with coals. The distance was only six miles long; but the canal was a barge canal, not a narrow boat canal, taking Severn-going vessels of fourteen feet wide right to the saltwork wharves, and was regarded as a model of what a canal should be.

SUBSIDENCE

From *Rocks of Worcestershire* by G E Roberts, 1860:

> Two years ago the ground cracked along the axial line of the hill south-east of Droitwich so suddenly that sheep feeding in a field disappeared and had to be hauled up from a considerable depth.

From *Landslips in Salt Districts* by J Dickenson, 1873:

> At Droitwich, the town, railway and neighbourhood are going down rapidly .... The one (stream) from the south-east comes from St Peters where it is tearing up the ground ... crosses Queen Street and other parts of the town where the houses are sunk and shattered. The other main run comes from Brine Pits Farm, where active solution is going on near the farmhouse, and further south under the turnpike road, and in the fields of Ford Farm, at Rashwood Hill. (The rectory of Dodderhill) has been so recently damaged as to cause it to be abandoned.

DROITWICH NICKNAMES

A peculiarity of the saltmakers of Droitwich was their use of nicknames. Very few of the 'old Wyche people' were without one, and some were very curious. Names such as Padgy, Guggie, Cabbage, Teddybear, Cron, Cuckoo, Tom-cat, Sausage, Yotty and Tar-Tivy could be heard bandied about at the saltpans and in the pubs.

Until the First World War Droitwich was a tight little community of saltmakers, still regarding people from places such as Worcester and Birmingham as foreigners; and there was much inter-marrying. Consequently, some family surnames tended to proliferate, as parish registers and gravestones show. To have so many families with the same surname in such a small population was very confusing, and so a system of family and personal nicknames developed. They were certainly being used widely in the mid-nineteenth century and probably long before that.

The most prominent surname in Droitwich was Bourne and each Bourne family (and there were many) had a family nickname: there were Dandy Bournes, Luggan Bournes, Betsey Bournes, Pie Bournes, Gory Bournes, Bonaker Bournes and others. So you would find individuals with two nicknames such as Rabbit Dandy Bourne or Swank Betsey Bourne. Sometimes the individual nickname was used after the surname − George Bourne Molley, or Bonaker Bourne Tongy; and sometimes in the middle − Jack Spare-me Cottrill or Graft Rhubarb Smith.

Many of the individual nicknames could be explained by a physical peculiarity: Whiskers Bateman, or Ginger Gandy; and some family nicknames must have had occupational origins such as Grammar Harrison (schoolmaster), Water-tap Harrison (plumber) or Tom-cat Harrison. But how did Jimmy Brasso Price get his name, or Bab Ward Sausage Waters? How did Weighan Honeysuckle Young or Tommy Dadio Harrison come about?

Family nicknames were so widely used that some old Wyche folk hardly knew their real names − or so they said! In 1850 two saltworkers wer taken before the magistrate for refusing to give their names to the constable who had arrested them for fighting. When asked, they had given their nicknames, declaring they were so used to these that they had forgotten those their godfathers had given them. The magistrate found difficulty in believing this and fined them ten shillings each. A few years ago a native of Droitwich collected nearly a hundred and twenty family or personal nicknames and recalled that occupational names, used in the Welsh style — Evans *the* Blacksmith, Bourne *the* Barber — were common in the area but that the use of *the* was reserved only for practising tradesmen.

CHAPTER FIVE

Politics, Law and Disorder

I

THE COUNTY OF WORCESTERSHIRE can truly be said to have been in at the very beginnings of Parliament, for the writs from Simon de Montfort summoning the meeting of Parliament – which proved to contain the seeds of our present parliamentary system – were issued from Worcester.

In 1295 Worcestershire returned sixteen members to Parliament: two knights of the shire; two burgesses each for the city of Worcester and for the boroughs of Bromsgrove, Droitwich, Dudley, Evesham, Kidderminster and Pershore. The smaller communities were glad to be quit of the payment entailed by parliamentary privilege and let their membership lapse. Bromsgrove, Dudley and Kidderminster seem later to have lost their privilege until the reforms of 1832. Droitwich was represented until 1311, but not again until 1554. Evesham recovered its privilege of two members in 1604.

Bewdley was in a special position. It was a royal town in the Marches of Wales and not until the reign of Henry VIII did it become part of Worcestershire. Since it had the special privilege of approaching the Sovereign direct through the Lord High Steward it was deemed unnecessary to send a representative to Parliament and it was not until 1605, when the Crown sold its estates and presumably Bewdley lost its privilege, that the borough sent one representative to Parliament.

Whigs and Tories

A cartoon, accompanied by this slightly illiterate caption, was published after the Worcester parliamentary by-election of 1774 and poked fun at the Whigs after the election of Thomas Bates Rous was declared void. Rous, the 'Nabob' referred to, was chairman of the East India Company and had been elected as a Whig in November 1773 amid renewed accusations from the Tories that members of the East India Company had 'bought' seats at Worcester. In March 1774 Rous's election was declared void and Nicholas Lechmere, a Tory, won the ensuing election – which prompted the cartoon. In the Dyson Perrins Museum, Royal Porcelain Works, is a memento of the election in the shape of a spill jar with a picture of two hands holding each other inscribed underneath 'In spite of the Nabob's gold'.

But Rous was soon back in Parliament, re-elected in October 1774. His political allegiance was changeable, however. Six years later he won the Worcester seat again — but as a Tory.

Eighteenth-century elections: the person and the purse

In the eighteenth century, elections in Worcestershire — as elsewhere — were usually decided by the person and the purse, with politics rarely entering into it. The county was represented by the aristocratic families of Foley, Lygon, Winnington and Ward; elections at Droitwich and Bewdley, with their very small number of self-electing burgesses, rarely amounted to contests; but at Worcester and Evesham, where the electorate was much larger, fierce contests were fought and the issue decided by the amount of money available to rally support.

A high proportion of Worcester's citizens were freemen since from early days the trade guilds in the city had been very strong. As many of these freemen, however, lived in London and elsewhere their voting involved days of travel. But candidates defrayed the travelling and accommodation expenses not only of the voters but of wives and children, and families naturally looked on it as an opportunity to visit relatives and friends in Worcester. The non-resident freemen, with all expenses paid, were in no hurry to vote and the poll at the 1773 election was open for as long as six weeks.

The creation of bogus freemen and the distribution of bribes were normal features of the time and advertisements regularly appeared casting the most villainous aspersions upon the candidate's character. In 1747 an attempt was made to turn away the London voters by the erroneous information that the poll book was shut and the candidate had run away! At the 1784 election, when no less than 88% of the Worcester electorate, resident and non-resident, turned out to vote, the polling was reduced to fifteen days; but an observer reported on that occasion that the city completely surrendered itself to 'a saturnalia of infamy', and there were 'hideous scenes of debauchery and drunkenness'.

Old-time elections were noisy, violent and riotous occasions. At the hustings brick-ends, broken bottles, cabbages, bad eggs and other bits of rubbish were freely thrown about. Even if the electors lacked the fiery zeal expected of them, the party organisers were eager to join battle and raise their followers to fever pitch; and the gentlemen of the press were delighted when a 'rough house' provided them with copy. Here is part of a report from Bromsgrove:

> At eleven o'clock, John Bompers with many friends, began to throw cabbages and carrots about in front of the hustings. Many people were struck by these missiles and either left the place or retaliated by throwing them back at Bompers and his friends. Eventually, Bompers, being struck in the eye by the sharp end of one of his carrots, violently assaulted the thrower, a gentleman called Eustace, and a free fight ensued. Soon everybody in the neighbourhood joined in and pandemonium prevailed.

The Worcester election of 1835 was unusual in that the man elected, a rich Tory ironmaster, Mr Bailey, paid his first visit to the city *after* the election. His victory by fifteen votes had cost him £16,000 and afterwards dinners were provided for his supporters and eighty public houses were 'opened' for free beer in the evening. A petition on the grounds of corruption claimed that forty-one paupers had been brought in to vote, two persons had been impersonated — one was already dead — and twenty-three admitted being paid to vote. The investigating committee, comprising seven Tories and four Whigs, sat for seven days; but the Tories were determined to hold on to the seat and in the face of the strongest evidence gave the seat to Bailey by one vote.

Rival corporations and screaming women at Bewdley

At Bewdley in the early-eighteenth century a struggle developed between the Herberts and the Winningtons. It was made worse by the fact that fresh charters had been granted to the borough in 1685 by James II and in 1708 by Queen Anne, so complicating matters that for at least two years the situation would have done justice to any 'Gilbertian' scene. Two rival corporations elected themselves, taking their authority from the different charters, and then solemnly annulled and declared void one another's proceedings. It even led to a double election in 1708 when one corporation elected a Herbert, the other a Winnington. Eventually, a House of Commons committee declared for Herbert.

A century later Bewdley Corporation was bought up bag and baggage by Wilson A Roberts, a local solicitor who elected himself permanent bailiff and packed the corporation with his own personal dependants. For more than ten years Roberts sold the seat to the Lyttleton family and cemented his influence in the corporation by sharing the plunder, an action frankly acknowledged in the corporation's yearly accounts. In 1818 Roberts discontinued the sale and elected himself, retaining the seat until the Reform Bill swept him out of office.

After the Bewdley election of 1847 both parties petitioned for corruption, *both* were found guilty and the election, not surprisingly, declared void. One side had paid £15 (and as much rum and cider as could be drunk) for votes, while the other had opened twenty-seven inns, some supplying as much as a thousand gallons of free beer a day. In the course of the hearing it was revealed that the accounts included '12 guineas for Screaming Women, and £100 for 100 Watchers'. The 'Screaming Women' were specially retained to prevent the other side's speeches being heard from the hustings; and the 'Watchers' had the duty of watching men whose votes had been bought and preventing the other side from kidnapping them. (Pearce Baldwin, the local ironmaster, had paid a man £60 to spirit two voters away to London.) At Stourport (in the same division) the Whigs kept fifty navvies to keep things in check following the breaking open of houses by the Tories. The investigating committee reported 'that a most pernicious system of intimidation, kidnapping and treating prevailed in the borough'.

An election campaign using an old carriage, 1930.

County elections: 1831

With the exception of 1806, elections for the county's MPs before 1831 were without contest, the seats shared between the local families of Foley, Lygon and Ward. In 1806 the Lyttletons decided to assert their independence, upsetting all the quiet arrangements. It was the first contest in a county election since 1741 – but after five days of voting, with an unbeatable majority against him, Lyttleton withdrew.

One of the most important nineteenth-century elections occurred in 1831 when the great Reform Bill debate was at its height. Two candidates, neither aristocratic, were put forward by Reformers, principally to oppose Colonel Lygon (the dashing commander under Wellington at Waterloo) who was strongly against any reforms and had represented Worcestershire five times, always without opposition. Faced by this opposition, Lady Beauchamp, Lygon's mother, let it be known she was providing £50,000 to support her son in the election and the 'commoners' withdrew, unable to match such expense.

A few days before the election, however, another aristocratic candidate was found, Captain Spencer, brother of Lord Althorp, and the struggle commenced. The campaign was expensive and violent, the Lygon expenses, it was estimated, amounting to £2,000 a day. While canvassing in the Corn Market, Worcester, Lygon was attacked and compelled to take refuge in the Reindeer Inn. One of Lygon's friends, irritated by remarks shouted by the crowds in the street, threw a decanter at them from the window of the Bell Inn in Broad Street where the party had its city headquarters and rioting was particularly bad. In reply the infuriated mob stormed the inn and broke every window and fitting within reach.

All political roads led to the city of Worcester, bringing in the county's voters not only from the outlying places but from London and elsewhere; for there was only one poll and that at Worcester. The Tory agent boasted to have secured all the public conveyances from the north of the county; but eighty Dudley supporters of Captain Spencer chartered a canal boat and sailed to the poll 'provisioned against contrary winds' with three butts of ale, three hundredweights of roast beef, fifty-six loaves, tea, coffee, pipes and cigars. Colonel Lygon found the Reform enthusiasm so strong that all the significant hints that he had plenty of money to spend went unheeded; and on the seventh morning of the poll he withdrew. In accordance with time-honoured custom in the city men were sent out with brooms to search the gutters for the 'missing candidate' (a procedure carried out for the last time in 1859 when another candidate abandoned the field). Foley and Spencer formed a coalition and, following great rejoicing in the city, the Dudley men made a triumphal return voyage, welcomed by twenty thousand people.

Political propaganda

Political propaganda, ridiculing the opposition and raising the electoral 'temperature' to get supporters to the hustings, was very popular in the nineteenth century; and the nothern part of the county seems to have been particularly good at it. Memorable political pamphlets were issued by both sides in the 1830s and 40s.

At the 1874 parliamentary election Dudley Liberals succeeded in ousting the Conservatives and produced a 'death card' edged in black:

> *The mortal remains of Old Toryism were consigned to their last resting place on Wednesday, February 4th, 1874. The funeral cortege was formed at the Dudley Arms Hotel, and passed in solemn procession through the principal streets of the Town, and on arriving at the Public Hall, Brierley Hill (the Bell was very solemn), a Solemn Oration was delivered over the Defunct Quiet Trust Not. The Funeral Service was read over the Departed:*
>
> *'A man that is born of a Tory hath but a short time to live, and is full of Humbug; he springeth up like a fungus, and withereth like a cauliflower, and is seen no more; in the midst of life and hope he meets his death. Oh! Lord Dudley, have mercy on his foolishness and deliver him not again into the bitter pains and disappointments of Elections! For as much as it pleaseth the People of this our Borough to have mercy on the soul of our Brother here departed, we therefore commit his Body to the Flames in the sure and certain hope of*
>
> NO RESURRECTION'

The following 'squib' alludes to three Conservative candidates, all from the Worcestershire Allsop family, and thought to have been written by Gladstone's son:

> There were three jolly Allsops, who sallied forth to woo,
> One came to grief at Droitwich, and then there were two.
> Two jolly Allsops still for Parliament did run,
> But Stafford declined Charlie, then there was one.
> But one jolly Allsop would yet keep up the run,
> When East Worcester has settled, then there'll be none.

Some Worcestershire MPs

In the past Worcestershire has been represented in Parliament by some very eminent men, some of them parliamentary giants, some conspicuous for their oratory. Others, however, are now best remembered for the tragedy and drama surrounding their lives – like Sir Humphrey Stafford of Grafton, the soldier MP who was sent with insufficient forces to quell a rebellion in 1450 near Sevenoaks and in the subsequent fighting was killed; or the millionaire, Sir Manasseh Masseh Lopez who represented Evesham in 1807 when bribery and corruption were rampant and was found guilty of offering commissions in the local Yeomanry, and in some cases of paying £100 for votes given to him, a lavishness which, instead of returning him to the House of Commons, procured for him a considerably quieter environment in one of His Majesty's prisons.

In 1837 two of Evesham's MPs fought a duel and they were both on the same side! The Tories had put up a Mr P Borthwick for the Evesham division in 1835, but on the hustings he was charged with being a bankrupt bookseller and an excommunicated member of the Scottish United Seccessional Church. He denied this and after his election sued for libel; but it was proved that generally the charges were correct and that he had been in gaol and, worse, *he had been a performer on the stage, and unsuccessful!* At a dinner Borthwick attacked his late colleague, Mr Rushout, for abandoning him to the committee of enquiry, a challenge was issued and they met in a duel at Wormwood Scrubs. After a second discharge, without effect, Borthwick withdrew his offensive expression.

Strange election customs

Kidderminster has had more than the usual share of civic disturbances; but most curious was the custom of the 'Lawless Hour', recorded by Noake from a book published in 1790:

> At Kidderminster is a singular custom. On the election of a Bailiff the inhabitants assemble in the principal street to throw cabbage stalks at each other. The Town House bell gives the signal for the affray. This is called the Lawless Hour. This done (for it lasts an hour) the Bailiff-elect and the Corporation in their robes, preceded by drums and fifes, visit the old and

new bailiffs, constables etc, attended by the mob. In the meantime the most
respectable families in the neighbourhood are invited to meet and fling apples
at them at their entrance. I have known forty pots of apples expended at
one house.

Among a number of strange civic customs at Evesham was the 'Ditching of the Mayor
of Bewdley Street' in Whit week. The chosen 'mayor' was escorted in procession
to the George and Dragon Inn, where amidst celebrations he was liberally plied with
drinks. He was then placed on the back of a gardener's cart and drawn up and down
the street by the crowd who tried to shake him off. If he managed to hang on he
was taken back to the inn and further plied with drink; and eventually, after
consuming a vast quantity of ale and in no state to cling on, he was shot off into
a wide ditch at the bottom of the street. The custom continued until 1850.

Politics and pubs

In the first half of the nineteenth century all the parties had a special inn which
served as headquarters and these inns played an important part in the life of the area.

Over a century after William of Orange was dead, old political prejudices remained.
At Kidderminster, once a year, the Kidderminster Orangemen processed from the Rose
and Crown with great orange sashes and rosettes, flags of great size, a brass band, a coach
of children in white robes, and a lamb or two with them. In the procession was a man,
guarded by two men on horseback, carrying a Bible on a cushion. One of the horsemen
had a drawn sword, the other a horse pistol. They climbed the steep ascent to Horsefair
and, firing pistols, the demonstrators went into St Mary's Church.

Beer houses were plentiful in Kidderminster at the time of the 1841 election and
each party engaged men to go from pub to pub with drinking orders. The laurel
and the oak were party emblems and pubs were festooned to show party allegiance.
But a lot of fighting men were engaged on each side and some publicans would
change their greenery as soon as rows developed. The ironmaster, W O Foster, closed
his ironworks and his workers, coarse powerful men, went about the town calling
out 'Where are the weavers? We will kill all the − weavers!'. But the locals knew
the alleys and kept out of their way. Eventually a truce was agreed with the help
of strong ale from the Lion and off went the ironmen.

In Bromsgrove at the Whig public houses a Hanoverian song was still being sung
at the Court Leet dinners well into Victorian times:

> From all who dare to tyrannise,
> May heaven still defend us;
> And should another James arise,
> Another William send us.
> May Queens like ours forever reign,
> For highest worth distinguished,
> But Stuarts who our annals stain,
> May they be quite extinguished.

A vivid description of a riot at the Crown Inn, Bromsgrove, in 1859 is not without humour:

> A Mr Cotton told of the Peelers wearing shiny black tall hats, covered with a kind of black oil cloth, and in the riot the hats were flying about like footballs. The crowd was so dense in the Crown yard that people could not lift their legs to kick one another. He saw a magistrate attempt to read the Riot Act from one of the front windows, but a brickbat caused him to withdraw his head abruptly. A troop of Dragoons were brought in from Birmingham, and then the troubles cooled down, which caused the troopers to curse most volubly, having got their horses and accoutrements badly splashed for nothing. However, some ale appeased them, and they trotted back.

At Stourport the Swan Inn was the headquarters of the Whigs in the first half of the nineteenth century. There it was customary to employ a choir of fifty to sixty boys who sang:

> See Sir Thomas Winnington, riding in his chair.
> Let the Tories touch him, and touch him if they dare!

The song referred to the 'Chairing of the Member' which Hogarth depicted so dramatically. Each winning candidate was provocatively carried in a special chair through the streets from one pub to another. *At Worcester* in 1816 *Berrow's Worcester Journal* reported that 'the chair ws prematurely demolished by a mob in the High Street'; and, later, 'the elegant cars broken up at the bottom of Broad Street at imminent risk of the new Members' lives'. At the 1820 *Evesham* election thirty-two chairmen at 7s 6d, three net men at 9s (carrying nets to stop the brickbats), seventy-eight constables and ninety-eight flagmen were employed to protect the winning member.

THE DUKE OF YORK PUBLIC HOUSE AND THE 1906 ELECTION SCANDAL

The Duke of York in Angel Place, Worcester, was the focal point of a political scandal that hit the national headlines and led to the city of Worcester being disenfranchised for some years.

In 1905 George Allsop, MP for Worcester since 1885, announced that he would not stand for re-election. Election excitement was intense: it was a period of radical reforms and of great public meetings; party colours were in their heyday and provocatively displayed. Two years before this Henry Harben, the Liberal, had taken up residence locally and had nursed the constituency with care. The Conservatives were playing their cards close to their chest and not until the last moment did they nominate George Williamson, a local employer of great charm and handsome appearance, and with much public service to his credit. Williamson won with a majority of 129, but in the following month, February, Harben filed a petition alleging wholesale bribery, though not against Williamson personally.

The hearing took place at Shire Hall before two judges, and the Liberals showed they had long known of illegal practices. They had engaged a retired police officer from Peterborough as a 'spy', and with great skill he was able to bring evidence of blatant and widespread bribery. A procession of witnesses testified to receiving cash and being treated for voting Conservative, especially at the Duke of York where, after being taken to vote, they were invited to visit the toilet at the rear of the inn and collect the sum of money left on top of the wall.

The evidence was so overwhelming that on the third day Williamson threw in his hand. The judges declared the election void, but Harben was not awarded the seat. Instead, the Prime Minister announced a commission to investigate 'the extensive bribery at Worcester'. In August three judges sat as inquisitors and it was obvious that Worcester was on trial. Prominent personalities were called and softness was shown to none. The Conservative agent at the opening of the campaign could not explain his accounts and his successor admitted being convicted for being drunk and disorderly before polling day. The commission's censures were sharp and to the point, and as a result of their report the city was disenfranchised for the life of that Parliament.

THE DROITWICH RIOTS OF 1910

Probably the last Worcestershire public house to be involved in political violence was the Wagon & Horses at Droitwich in what came to be known as the Droitwich Riots of 1910.

Droitwich had always been a strong Liberal town, but at the 1910 general election unexpectedly a Tory was returned. A crowd of Liberal rowdies, about a thousand strong, marched through the town venting their annoyance, and broke the windows of the Tory headquarters, letting it be known that after dark worse was to follow. The places said to be marked for special attention were the Worcestershire Hotel, which was the residence of the Town Clerk, and the Wagon & Horses in the High Street where the landlord was an active Tory supporter. Extra police were called in and strategically placed in the back streets, and their presence seemed to have prevented attacks; but at 8 pm a stone was hurled through the window of the Wagon & Horses despite a heavy police guard on the building; and when the pubs closed the mob gathered and went on the attack. Stones started to fly until there was scarcely a window at the Wagon & Horses intact.

The police appealed for order and eventually, about midnight, the Riot Act was read by the light of a candle (held by the deputy chief constable) which was quickly put out by a flying stone. Whether in the clamour anyone could have heard the mayor is doubtful, but it enabled the police to act. They had withstood hours of assault and abuse and stood no nonsense once they had been given the order to clear the streets. Batons were drawn, and their action was swift and effective. The ringleaders disappeared into the dark alleys and the mob melted away.

That, more or less, was the end of the Droitwich Riots, except that a dozen men, mainly saltmakers, were later brought before the Worcester Assizes, charged with 'riotous and tumultuous assembly'. One of the twelve, John Sankey, was quoted as the ringleader but a politically unattached witness said Sankey had merely had too much to drink and indulged in cheap wit; and even a police inspector admitted Sankey's behaviour was at times very funny, keeping those around him in good humour. All were acquitted for lack of evidence though Sankey was censured. In any case, said the judge, he couldn't find *one* man guilty of a riot. The trial seems to have dispersed what bitterness there was; indeed, the affair was the source of much humour in the years that followed.

II

Today the State controls all aspects of the legal system; but in the past there were three distinct legal authorities which controlled rural life. Judges and local justices of the peace administered the laws of the land; local legal rules and customs were administered by manorial courts; and ecclesiastical law was enforced by the church courts. In small rural communities these three legal systems often appeared to overlap, often administered by the same people.

Dispensing the Sovereign's justice

In medieval times the king travelled about his domain dispensing justice, but in time it was necessary to appoint judges to represent him. Thus, the Assizes, the main court in each county, normally sitting four times a year, dispensed criminal and civil justice with an itinerant (or circuit) judge in attendance. It was for long the practice for the sheriff and the chief officers, accompanied by trumpeters and javelin men and supported by the county gentry, to meet the judge of assize at the city boundary at Red Hill and escort him into Worcester. A man was stationed on the cathedral tower to give notice of the approach of the party when the bells would be rung.

The same procession accompanied the judge to the cathedral on Assize Sunday, where he was met at the door by the dean. Should there be no case for the Assizes the judge was traditionally presented with a pair of white gloves.

By the 1830s the judge travelled in great style. In Worcester it was customary for him to be accompanied by a marshal, a clerk, a butler, a cook (to ensure his lordship's diet was not poisoned) and a marshal's man. Sometimes he brought his wife and her maid. The county furnished him with a house, butler, waiter, 'boots', two female domestics and the use of silver, glass and linen. The Judge's Lodgings are at the back of the Shire Hall and contain magnificent entertaining rooms.

A very grand jury

Mr Justice Byles once complained that the Sheriff of Worcester had summoned a grand jury who were deficient in rank. At the next Assizes for Worcestershire his lordship attended, the clerk read out the following high-sounding panel, pausing after the first name in each line:

Horatio	King of Alfrick	Joseph	Knight of Leigh
Henry	Prince of Bromsgrove	William	Abbot of Great Malvern
George	Duke of Chaddesley	Walter	Dean of Newland
William	Marquess of Dudley	John	Archdeacon of Oldbury
Edmund	Earl of Evesham	Peter	Squire of Pinvin
Richard	Baron of Feckenham	Edward	Friar of Quinton
Samuel	Pope of Grafton	Henry	Monk of Ribbesford
Stephen	Cardinal of Hadzor	Thomas	Gentleman of Suckley
Humphrey	Bishop of Illey	George	Priest of Tenbury
Robert	Lord of Knightwick		

There is no record of a comment from the judge — but presumably it was felt that Mr Justice Byles had a sense of humour.

Courts leet and courts baron

Courts leet and courts baron were important features of rural organisation in days past, and almost always the proceedings were enacted at the nearby inn. In towns business was sometimes conducted at the town hall, but there was always a social side at the principal inn. The court leet was a criminal court and a view of frankpledge, that is, a court where neighbours in groups of ten were answerable for each other's behaviour. It was held once or twice a year in every manor before the steward of the leet who was judge, the jury being composed of freemen within the jurisdiction. It was 'to afford suit and service to the Lord, for the preservation of the peace, and chastisement of divers minute offences'. The court baron was a court for trying civil actions.

In a number of manors in Worcestershire this antiquated system survived into the twentieth century. Mr Hyde of Worcester, a solicitor with a wide country practice, described the court dealings, somewhere around the turn of the century, held at the Crown and Sandys, Ombersley:

> The manorial court was usually held in a panelled room of a venerable village hostelry. A jury of older inhabitants, copyholders of the manor, were sworn. The bailiffs of the manor deposed the facts, having first been primed by the solicitor, the jury gave their assent to a 'presentation', which he had cut and dried in readiness, a long white stick was passed to and fro in a mysterious manner, much after the fashion of an enchantress's wand, certain cabalistic phrases were repeated which sounded like 'hey presto, cockolorum', and a good deal of money was paid for the entertainment, and then they all sat down to an old-fashioned country dinner of the solid English type, toasted the lord and steward, and wound up with long churchwarden pipes and songs of interminable length, like the ballad of Lord Bateman.

In 1904 the *Worcester Herald* of 28 May reported: 'At the Golden Cross Hotel, Bromsgrove, the Court Leet and Court Baron of Lord Windsor (lord of the manor) began its proceedings. There lunch was provided for the jurymen, then leaving the hotel the assembly, headed by the head burgess of the town, arrayed in scarlet uniform and carrying the Court Stave, marched in procession to the Town Hall where the business of the Court was transacted.'

In December 1928 the *Evesham Journal* reported: 'According to the old custom, the jury assembled under the oak tree on the Village Green, Feckenham, where the Steward read the notice convening the Court; the Manor Bailiff then read the proclamation, and the jurymen answered to their names. The adjournment was made to the Rose and Crown, where the jury was sworn in, and the business of the Court transacted.' And by November 1936 only the pub had changed for, after electing an ale-taster, bread-weigher, beadle and reeve, the steward formally discharged the jury and invited all those present to a dinner at the Red Lion, Bradley Green, to which Lord Coventry had sent a present of game.

Despite various Acts of Parliament – of 1922, 1925 and 1935 – which took away the court leet's ancient power, the courts continued, and some still continue, to meet for ceremonial and social purposes.

The last recorded 'trial by water'

Perhaps the most remarkable local survival of 'legal custom' was at Redmarley D'Abitot, a Worcestershire village before its transfer to Gloucestershire. William Lygon, the first Earl Beauchamp, was riding through his constituency in the 1820s when he came upon a throng of excited rustics and learnt that they were putting an alleged witch through the 'ordeal by water'. His horrified protest was resented and they were at great pains to assure him that everything was in proper order and according to traditional rules. Only by his prompt and unflinching assertion of authority as a county justice was he able to save the wretched victim who, a few minutes later, would have demonstrated her innocence by drowning.

The justices of the peace

The chief agents of local government were the justices of the peace, unpaid local gentlemen with considerable power and position. They dealt with all aspects of daily life from crime and its punishment, through the endless disputes over poor relief, bastardy, unlawful gaming and drunkenness, to the licensing of alehouses and the state of roads and bridges. From Tudor times they played the central role in local administration. They had the powers to try minor cases and to supervise the administration of the parish officers. The county justices met formally four times a year at the Quarter Sessions and the records that survive are among the most interesting of local records. They spent most of their time on minor offences and as recently as the 1880s the justices were sitting with all solemnity to investigate such awful sins as 'unlawfully wandering abroad without visible means of subsistence (which the law stated to be 4d), wandering abroad to beg and solicit alms'. There were many cases of drunkenness for the beer was intoxicating and very cheap, many cases of assault and many more cases of bad language.

Berrow's Worcester Journal of 1748 published a skit on the Quarter Sessions which went as follows:

> 3 or 4 Parsons, 3 or 4 Squires,
> 3 or 4 Lawyers, 3 or 4 Lyars,
> 3 or 4 Parishes bringing Appeals,
> 3 or 4 Hands and 3 or 4 Seals,
> 3 or 4 Bulls and 3 or 4 Cows,
> 3 or 4 Orders and 3 or 4 Bows,
> 3 or 4 Statutes not understood,
> 3 or 4 Paupers praying for food,
> 3 or 4 Roads that never were mended,
> 3 or 4 Scolds and the Session is ended.

A Halesowen diary

In the nineteenth century Joseph Smith was Registrar of Halesowen for forty years and kept a diary. His entries were brief but the following selection tells the not uneventful story of life in a small town in Worcestershire.

> 1840 Jan. 3 George Todd, son of the Rev. John Todd, was transported for housebreaking and for stealing a pig, for 10 years.
> Jan. 21 Frost, Williams and Jones were condemned to be hung, their heads taken off their bodies, quartered and disposed of as the Owen should think fit, for leading on the people to riot to Newport in Wales. (Since pardoned and sent to punishment for life)
> Jan. 27 New police introduced in Hales Owen.
> Sept. 21 Henry Taylor's wife at White Hall hanged herself on the bed's head.

Oct. 23 The situation of organist played for and awarded to young man from Ludlow. Lost the post myself through that wicked false man, Dr. Moore, because I inoculated the children for the smallpox. He is a wicked false man.

Nov. 23 William Golden walked into the Floodgate hole at Cradley Forge and was drowned.

1841 May 20 Old Wm. Caton drowned in his mill pool.

July 27 – – Buried. Quite worn out by high and debauched living.

Dec. Mr Attwood's coalpits at Hawne took fire when 1 man and 2 boys were burnt to death as well as 5 horses.

1845 July 26 Geo. Burges returned from 7 years transportation.

1849 Richard Hollies, commonly called Civil Dick, of the Warwicks Dick, hanged himself on a ladder at Waxland.

Mar. 3 Little Tom Siviter fell with his hand between 2 cog wheels and had his arm smashed up to the shoulder. The doctor cut it off.

July 14 John Walters died through eating large quantities of beans and bacon and drinking some buttermilk and also some cider.

1850 Mr. Henry Hodgkins died broken hearted through the drunken and lustful propensities of his wife. I was at his funeral and had hat band and gloves. He was 38 yrs. He hastened his death by intemperance.

Dec. 6 Thos. Knight, formerly hostler at the New Inn, lately of Talbot Inn, Stourbridge, was returning from Birmingham with a pair of horses. He rode into Hay Green Pool it is thought to wash the horses' legs and got too far and was drowned with one of the horses.

1857 Thos. Robertson died a poor miserable object after living a life of gross wickedness as constable, and being a policeman, swearing any way to please his party, which was a wicked one too. He was very bad when a boy at school, and tried to make others as bad as himself. His father was a poor drunken wicked parson at Harborne Church.

Oct. 16 Henry Smith of the Samson, killed by a fall from a blow while fighting in Spring Lane.

Church courts

The church courts exercised great power over rural life until 1860, dealing not only with church affairs but with matters affecting the whole life – marriage, adultery and all sexual sins; schools, witchcraft, slander, drunkenness, working on Sundays and failing to observe holy days. Offenders were brought to the notice of the church court by a *presentment* made by churchwardens and the court possessed the power of enforcement. There are vast quanities of presentments from the seventeenth and eighteenth centuries for the diocese of Worcester in the Worcester Record Office, and a few excerpts show what a valuable insight they give to the daily life of past generations.

At *Madresfield* in 1662 the presentment reads: 'One of our bells was taken by the soldiers of the – garrison and broken and rendered non-serviceable, and therefore sold to repair the church.'

Beating the bounds of St Helen's parish, Worcester. A young boy is bumped at the corner of the boundary, overseen by old parishioners, themselves bumped there as boys.

From *Berrow* comes a sad tale of 'deficiencies' attributed to lack of ministry: 'The fault is not in us but in our minister for he has not been in our church this seven weeks, neither do we know when he will and our parish is much dissatisfied at it . . . . Now he has gone again and did not take care for any other minister. And we had a dead corpse to be buried and nobody to bury her. We had a corpse lie in our church all night and have been forced to have a minister out of another county.'

Such complaints however were rare. Most presentments were like that at *Hanbury* in 1712: 'Our Minister is an ingenious and learned and sober man and such as will make himself and his parishioners happy . . . . We hope that he has a competent allowance and wish and pray that he may live long to enjoy the same.'

There were, too, complaints regarding parishioners. For misbehaviour in the church at *Claines* in 1697 John Randall and James Ford, Junior, were presented for breaking into the church and, 'for ringing and jangling the bells . . . The said Randall laying hands upon the clerk's wife, taking her fast by the throat and threatening that he would kill her if she should tell that she saw them in church'.

In the same year Richard Horniblow from *Church Hill* is presented for 'profaning the Lord's day in following the unjustifiable recreation of fishing . . . . I do likewise present him for his most abominable, most unseemly and unchristianlike behaviour towards me in that when, according to my duty, I privately reproved him for the above mentioned crime . . . instead of a Christianlike submission he broke forth into bitter, spiteful and malicious expressions, saying he cared not a fart for me and scornfully saying — do your worst'. Yet in 1705 Richard Horniblow signs the presentments as churchwarden!

There were many presentments for bastardy and adultery and from *Ipsley* in 1664 comes the form and procedure of penance:

> The said (penitent) shall come into the church aforesaid at the hearing of the first lesson at Morning Prayer arrayed in a white sheet over her wearing apparel, holding a candle . . . and . . . a white rod of an ell long in her hand and shall be placed in some eminent place near the minister's reading desk where she shall continue the time of Divine Service and Sermon and after the reading of the second lesson she shall make her humble confession unto Almighty God . . . .

By the eighteenth century the authority of the church courts began to wane and the penalties held less terror. At *Leigh* in 1701 Elizabeth Collins was presented for fornication, but 'it seems she has acted with as much confidence as though it had been as great a virtue as 'tis really a vice'. In 1728 Elizabeth Pudge of *Hanbury* had been 'publishing and solemnly and frequently declaring that she has been guilty of adultery with several persons . . .'. And from *Kidderminster* in 1705: 'Mary, wife of Samuel Robinson, (was presented) for taking away the good name and scandalising the late churchwarden for doing his office to her daughter Margaret who was in child and sent to Worcester, the place of her last legal settlement.'

The life of a country policeman

Crime in the first half of the nineteenth century was a grave problem. There was no police force in the modern sense of the word until the 1830s. To avoid looking military, policemen wore a blue serge uniform, almost civilian in style, with a top hat (this at a time when almost every respectable man wore a top hat); and were armed only with whistles and wooden truncheons.

George Checketts started as a constable in the county force in 1840 and retired as Deputy Chief Constable in 1889. Communications in those days could only be made on foot and the amount of walking the policeman had to do gave truth to the joke concerning his feet. It was sometimes necessary for Checketts to walk from Tenbury to Worcester and the next day to walk to Hereford and back. The police station at Tenbury was a kind of shed used as a lock-up. It was not very safe and a prisoner would be taken to the Ship Inn and handcuffed to an iron bar which had been fixed into one of the rooms for the purpose.

> On one occasion at Eldersfield, Checketts had nowhere to put a prisoner, so he took him to a private house and persuaded the proprietor to have the fellow handcuffed to him while he went in search of an accomplice. On another occasion, he knocked up a friend, a local tailor, and locked the friend and the prisoner together in the former's sitting room while he went to seek for help.
>
> Some idea of the walking done by the police in those days can be obtained

from Mr Checkett's experience on being promoted to the rank of sergeant in 1845. He walked to Shipston-on-Stour where he had been offered a sergeant's position, from there into Worcester, and from Worcester back to Martley. He had scarcely sat down to nurse his blistered feet when he saw some suspicious-looking men with dead fowls. He questioned the men and, not being satisfied, he marched them to White Ladies to the lock-up, and then walked home again. He spent the next two days scouring the countryside in search of the owners of the fowls, and found them at last at Knightwick.

In those days, and long after, a policeman dealt directly with delinquents. At Kingscote the village policeman had complaints of stealing from an orchard and put up a large notice: 'P C Brooks will attend daily, and God help them that he catches.'

Prisons and prisoners

THE OLD COUNTY JAIL

The old castle at Worcester was long used as the county prison but the building was old and extremely insecure. Plans to build a new jail were put forward time and again but always shelved because of the cost. In 1807, however, Chief Baron MacDonald arrived at Worcester for the Assizes and warned that the county would be heavily fined if matters were not put right. A new prison was built in 1813.

> The old prison had been one of the sights of Worcester, and on the Assize Sunday prisoners were shown to the crowds, the visitors giving sixpence to the jailer for pointing out those condemned to be executed. There was an open ironwork railing between the debtors and the felons and they could communicate as they pleased. There were no special rules for the condemned criminal; he was chained to a post by day near the door of the common-room chapel. There was a regular transference of prisoners to the 'transports' which went down river to Bristol, whence they were shipped out to the plantations.

So many felonies carried the death penalty that there was often a reluctance to carry out the sentence. Reprieves for the first twenty years of the nineteenth century in Worcestershire were as follows:

1800	23 sentenced, 6 hung
1801	22 sentenced, 1 hung
1817	20 sentenced for sheepstealing – all reprieved
1820	27 sentenced, 1 hung (for highway robbery)

John Howard, the prison reformer, had visited and condemned the old county gaol in 1788, especially the felons' dungeon: 'The felons' dungeon was 26 steps below ground, a circular building of 18ft diameter, lit only by a 3 ft skylight. Even in this strong and deep dungeon prisoners are all night chained together by heavy chains through the links of their fetters and iron rings fastened to the floor.'

The new County Gaol was built in the style of a medieval castle and held a variety of prisoners, from murderers and debtors to political agitators and men of religion who preached in the streets without a licence. It was an all male prison, and very secure. Only one prisoner is known to have escaped. He hid himself under sacks on the coal cart, and was driven out of gaol. He straightway went home for tea, and was promptly sent back by his wife. Even in those grim surroundings there were moments of humour. The prison governor, Major Blake, on his retirement told of the prison chaplain who reproduced an old sermon when addressing five hundred male convicts, including the paragraph which began 'Those of you who are mothers . . .'.

HANGMAN BERRY

Worcestershire played a prominent part in the national agitation for reform in the relations between the public and the hangman. In the nineteenth century the hangman was a public figure, and it was the fact that so often he behaved in an unseemly way that led to the demand that the Home Secretary should examine the position, culminating in a Worcestershire MP putting a question in parliament.

The hangman of the time was Berry, who had a considerable record of executions . . . in fact, Berry was in the terms used at the time 'a bit of a lad'. After previous executions he had enjoyed the limelight in pubs, telling how the men executed behaved, and giving tit-bits of information of the proceedings. It was Sir Edmund Lechmere, Member for West Worcestershire in 1888, who put a question on Berry's behaviour after an execution at Hereford, but it had little result, for though he had the backing of many high sheriffs throughout the country, there was little that could be done.

Berry had spent the night previous to the execution at Hereford as a guest at a smoking concert, and afterwards came to Worcester visiting public houses, giving accounts of the incidents concerned at the execution. When he came again to Worcester for an execution precautions were taken not to allow him the freedom of the City. From Shrub Hill he was whisked by cab to the prison, and given an opportunity to take an airing accompanied by a prison warder. After the execution, he was taken straight to the station to return immediately to his home in Bradford. Berry, however, bought a ticket only to Kidderminster, and there behaved in a way which aroused another scandal. He visited several public houses, told stories of executions and gave lectures on morality and phrenology.

At the next Assize the Grand Jury made a presentation to the Lord Chief Justice urging that the executioner should be under the direct control of the Home Office. The Home Office declined to take the authority away from the local authorities, recommending the High Sheriff should choose the right man for the job .... It appears, however, that Berry at last realised that his behaviour was resented, and he must have changed his ways, for he continued in office until 1892, carrying out a hundred and thirty four sentences.

Crimes Extraordinary

In the annals of old Worcestershire crimes two cases stand out as extraordinary. They have been the subject of learned papers, even radio plays. The first, known as the 'Campden Wonder Case', though seemingly in Gloucestershire in that strange shared borderland, involved triple executions (the only factual feature of the case) which took place on Broadway Hill. The second, that of the Oddingley murders, was perhaps even stranger.

THE CAMPDEN WONDER CASE

One August evening in 1660 William Harrison, steward to the Lady Campden of the day, started out from his home to collect some of her ladyship's rents. His house was on the edge of the little Cotswold market town of Campden (now Chipping Campden) and the tenants whom he proposed to visit lived at Charringworth, a village about two miles away. It was a mission which resulted in the deaths of three innocent people and ultimately provided a sensation which set the countryside talking.

Mr Harrison, who was turned seventy, lived with his wife and son. He was hale and hearty and made a practice of going on foot to collect the rents for his mistress's property. On this particular occasion the steward was expected home early in the evening with a large sum of money. At a late hour there was no sign of him. His wife grew anxious and as the hours went by she became more perturbed and eventually sent out John Perry, the family servant, to make enquiries abroad. He also failed to return.

When early morning dawned without news of either of the two missing men, young Harrison himself started out to see what was wrong. Not far from the front door he met John Perry, who told a long story of how he had traced his master's movements from one house to another until suddenly all signs of him had disappeared. Acting on information, the local magistrate ordered the constable to scour the district, but they were completely baffled. There was no sign of William Harrison.

The magistrates had questioned John Perry, and they considered his answers to be vague and unsatisfactory. In the belief that a taste of prison would induce him to be more frank, he was arrested. Then a woman working in a field found a hat and comb, cut and hacked out as though with a sword, and a band covered with blood. They were identified as belonging to the missing man. Confronted with these things, John Perry began to invent wild stories concerning the fate of his master, first that Harrison had been killed by a travelling tinker, then by a neighbour's servant. Then in a confession, full of detail which carried conviction, he told a harrowing story of how William Harrison had been waylaid at a quiet spot by his own mother, Joan Perry, and his brother Richard, and brutally murdered, all of which was later proved to be totally false but so convincing as to warrant the arrest of the Perrys.

Every day John invented fresh tales and the magistrates put the three members of the Perry family on trial. Mother and brother strongly denied any knowledge of Harrison's disappearance, but all three were found guilty of murder and sentenced to death. As the mother was reputed to be a witch, and it was believed would suffer her sons to confess nothing while she was alive, she was executed first. Then Richard's turn came and when he mounted the ladder he begged his brother to confess that the charges were a pack of lies, but to no avail. The triple execution on Broadway Hill was carried out.

The sequel to this amazing drama came two years later when one fine afternoon William Harrison walked back into his home at Campden as mysteriously as he had disappeared. The story he told was as bewildering as the tales told by Perry. He had collected £23 but on his way round had been set upon by two horsemen who hit him on the head with swords and carried him to the south coast and onto a ship. The ship was captured by Turkish pirates who sold him as a slave, but at his master's death he had been freed and given a beautiful bowl and, by selling it, had managed to get to Portugal and eventually back to England.

Is there an explanation for the mystery? The inference is that Harrison's presence was inconvenient to somebody. He had lived through troubled times, probably knew some secret and was a witness better out of the way. The coincidence is that his servant Perry went more or less mad on the same evening that Harrison disappeared and accused himself and his family. Harrison was probably never far away from Campden during the years of his disappearance. But whatever the explanation the case certainly exemplifies the saying that truth is stranger than fiction.

The Oddingley murders

Of all the murders perpetrated in Worcestershire none were as remarkable as the Oddingley murders. Turberville, in 1850, introduced the murders in true Victorian fashion as follows:

> The annals of crime record few tragedies so fearful in their reactment, so mysterious in their present concealment, so singular in their ultimate discovery as the Oddingley murders. A clergyman is shot at noonday, while walking in his own fields — the assassin and the motive are perfectly known, yet he eludes justice, and suddenly and forever disappears . . . at last, when twenty-four years have elapsed, the body of the murderer is strangely discovered . . . .

At Oddingley, a few miles south-east of Droitwich, a bitter dispute about tithes had arisen between the Rev George Parker and the farmers in his parish, led by a local magistrate, Captain Evans. On the morning of midsummer day 1806 the parson was walking in his fields when he was shot in the side from behind a hedge. He shouted 'Murder!' and the assassin ran forward and hit him on the head with the gun butt until he was dead. The shots and shouts brought people running to the scene, but they were threatened off with the gun. They recognised the assailant as Richard Hemming, a Droitwich carpenter, and a woman saw him emerge from a wood and

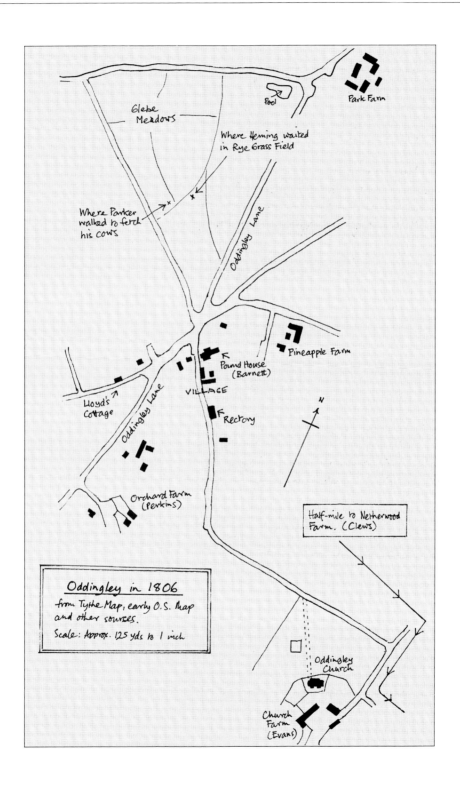

Park Farm

Pool

Glebe Meadows

Where Heming waited
in Rye Grass Field

Where Parker
walked to fetch
his cows

Oddingley Lane

Pineapple Farm

Pound House
(Barnett)

VILLAGE

Lloyd's
Cottage

Oddingley Lane

Rectory

N

Orchard Farm
(Perkins)

Half-mile to Netherwood
Farm. (Clews)

Oddingley in 1806
from Tythe Map, early O.S. map
and other sources.
Scale: Approx. 125 yds to 1 inch

Oddingley
Church

Church
Farm
(Evans)

go to the house of Captain Evans. But from there no trace of him could be found.

A report was spread that he had gone to America; but there was a lurking suspicion that he was concealed near Oddingley, and some said he had been made away with and his body hidden in a clover rick on Captain Evans' farm — put up three days after the parson's murder. Ten years later, the widow of Hemming went to the magistrates who ordered constables to search the long-standing rick, but the entire rick had been removed the night before by unknown hands.

In 1830, when taking down a barn on Netherton Farm, Charles Burton found the skeleton of a man with a carpenter's rule and knife two-and-a-half feet deep in the foundations. The skull had been beaten in. Strangely, Burton was the brother-in-law of Hemming, and he went straight to a magistrate. Thomas Clewes, the former occupier of Netherton Farm, was taken into custody under suspicion of Hemming's murder. On the third day of the inquest the prison governor sent a note that Clewes wished to make a statement that implicated four other men: Captain Evans, who had died the year before at the age of ninety-six, and his natural son, Mr George Banks, a farm bailiff of Hanbury; Mr John Barnett, a farmer; and James Taylor, the farrier, who had died a few years before. (Taylor was a very bad character who, about 1790, had stolen the communion plate at Hampton Lovett, but by a loophole in the law had managed to extricate himself, and thereafter was known as the churchwarden of Hampton Lovett!)

The gist of Clewes' statement was that the day after the parson was shot Banks came to him and said that they had Hemming at their house and were in great danger. Would he have him at his farm where there was less chance of being seen? Clewes refused, but was then told Hemming was already in his barn. They arranged to meet at night and get him safely away; but instead the Captain laid a trap, calling him out of the hay to allow Taylor to hit him from behind. Hemming was buried in the foundations of Clewes' barn. Clewes was not happy about it but they promised he would not want for anything if he co-operated. He was given money on two occasions and some years later left the farm.

The inquest continued until the fifth day when verdicts were returned implicating Clewes, Banks and Barnett on charges of aiding and abetting Hemming's murder. At the trial which followed the jury returned a verdict that Clewes was guilty of accessory after the fact, but he had not been charged with that offence and the judge would not accept the verdict. The jury then found Clewes not guilty, the prosecution withdrew the case against the other two and all three were discharged. When the unexpected news of the acquittals reached Oddingley the church bells were rung, to the great annoyance of the rector.

Three pubs were concerned in the affair. The first was the Raven at Claines (now completely modernised) where Hemming was recognised sitting on a bench waiting for the Worcester coach which had already gone. Strangely, he returned to the scene of the murder, only to be killed by those who had employed him. Then when his skeleton was discovered twenty-four years later the inquest was held at the Talbot Inn, Barbourne, Worcester. His remains were laid out on a table and covered with a sheet. When Hemming's widow was brought in the sheet was dramatically whipped away and she was asked to confirm his identity. She promptly fainted.

The third pub connected with the affair was on the canal at Dunhampstead. Thomas Clewes, freed on a legal flaw, later took over the Fir Tree and there is an amusing story told about his tenancy. In 1840, when the Birmingham and Gloucester Railway was being built, the Fir Tree, only a few yards from the line, was well patronised by railway navvies. Clewes by that time was old and confined to a chair and his daughter ran the pub. All knew of the Oddingley affair but she guarded him from inquisitive customers. One of the navvies bet that he could get a pint of ale without paying for it. The bet was on. The pint was brought to him and he straightaway drank it, then turned to old Clewes and asked, 'Was it you who knocked off Hemming?' The daughter flew at him and he moved out quickly to avoid her wrath – without paying.

THE LEGEND OF THE BESFORD JACKBOOTS

In 1930, when digging in a sandpit at Besford, a farmer found a nearly complete skeleton not more than fourteen inches below the surface. It was the skeleton of a fully grown man, obviously young from the teeth which were completely sound, and in a wonderful state of preservation – except for the fact that the feet were missing. There were no bones whatever from just below the knee joint. Who was the man? How did he die?

The gruesome find was obviously linked to a well-known but unusual story which had been told at Besford for at least two centuries. The sandpit was on a patch of land known as Dog Kennel Piece, which had once been the site of the Besford Kennels. Old inhabitants told how folk were terrified to go out after dark into Dog Kennel Lane (which leads to the sandpit) for fear of meeting a ghostly pair of jackboots which were said to walk there at night.

The legend centred on Besford Court, owned by the Sebright family who kept a pack of fierce hounds in the kennels nearby, on ground which came to be known as Dog Kennel Piece. One night a terrible noise was heard from the hounds and the kennel man was sent down from the Court to stop the quarrelling and fighting. He did not return and in the morning no trace of him could be found until the searchers were horrified to discover in the kennels his jackboots containing his feet and the gnawed stumps of his legs. They concluded that he must have been knocked down and eaten by the hounds, and the awful tale soon gave rise to the legend that his ghostly jackboots were to be seen walking the lonely Dog Kennel Lane at night.

But after a couple of centuries the discovery of the skeleton in the sandpit, minus his legs, changed the picture. There seems no doubt that the man was murdered while trying to frustrate some nefarious activity that was going on at the kennels. His body was buried nearby and, in order to cover up the crime, his feet were cut off, leaving them in the jackboots with the hounds.

THE BODY SNATCHERS

A horrifying crime in the first part of the nineteenth century was that of body snatching. With important medical schools at Worcester and Oxford there was a demand for bodies for the purpose of dissection and up to £20 was paid for a good clean corpse.

Berrow's Worcester Journal reported on 21 January 1831: 'Graves were opened at Hanley Castle churchyard and two recently interred bodies taken away. They had been sent in packing cases from the Anchor Inn, Upton-on-Severn, to London, but parties following them found them and restored them to the church. The resurrectionists were not caught.' On 24 November 1829 Joseph Rose, sextant of St John's Church, Bromsgrove, recorded in his notebook that three bodies had been stolen from the churchyard but the robbers not found.

A particularly notorious case was that of Mrs Hannah Ward, a pastry cook, who was buried at Broadway Old Church on Wednesday, 23 February 1831 at the age of thirty-seven years.

> The resurrectionists were soon at work, and obtaining the body offered the same to the surgeons, who refused the purchase as the deceased had suffered from bad legs, and decomposition had set in. To get rid of an unsaleable body and to avoid the trouble and risk of a reinterment in the churchyard, the body snatchers perfunctorily buried the remains in a large mixen that had been made at the Long Stalls, adjoining Church Piece. On the following Sunday a terrier dog was noticed scratching on the mixen and, after eating his belly full, running up the street of Broadway, after which he was never seen again. On the Monday, the body was discovered, when it was found that the dog had eaten off all the flesh from the thick of one arm. The body was identified as that of Mrs Ward by some peculiarity of the teeth.

One of the Broadway resurrectionists was a whitesmith, an ingenious craftsman, who made a cunning apparatus with a powerful screw that could lift the lid from a coffin and a hook that was then hitched under the jaw, enabling the body to be drawn out with the minimum of excavation. Though they were never caught at their ghoulish work the identity of the gang of four body snatchers was generally known. One of them was the son of the Rev David Davies, known as 'the drunken parson', who served as curate of Broadway for forty-two years from 1777 to 1819.

THE LICKEY END MURDER, 1893

On the morning of Friday, 13 January 1893, Joseph Pearcey, aged sixty-nine, was in bed suffering from bronchitis. Below, his wife was busy in the little shop they kept at the corner of Little Heath Lane, Lickey End, Bromsgrove. Suddenly, a strange young man appeared in the doorway of the bedroom and, not noticing Pearcey in bed, began rummaging in boxes at the top of the stairs. Pearcey raised himself up, whereupon the intruder saw him and dashed downstairs. Pearcey followed as quickly as he could but the man locked the door of the shop in his face and made off with the key. Turning round to speak to his wife Charlotte, aged seventy-one, Pearcey was horrified to see her lying in a pool of blood behind the table that served for a counter. There was a gaping wound in her head and the tin in which she kept her takings had been emptied.

Pearcey placed his dying wife in a chair, forced off the lock of the door with a hammer and chisel and raised the alarm. But he had recognised the strange man as a foreigner who had called at the shop four days before, hawking cheap stationery and collecting for what proved to be a bogus charity. At the top of the stairs, in one of the boxes in which the stranger had been rifling, he found a blood-stained axe, stamped with the name 'H Daly'. When the description was published in the Birmingham papers Henry Daly of Birmingham informed the police that he had missed his axe on 12 January while working in Bellbarn Road. He too had seen a foreigner hanging around.

After the police had questioned several men the English wife of a Frenchman, Hime Holman Meunier, aged twenty-five, lodging in Colmore Street, Birmingham, described how her husband had burst into the house at 11 am on the Friday and had remained indoors for four days. He told his wife that the police were after him for robbing an officer who had employed him as a valet. His wife had bought him a ticket to Dover at New Street Station, and he had escaped to the Continent wearing stolen clothes. An extradition warrant was secured, Meunier was arrested in Brussels, brought back to England and identified by Pearcey, Daly and others.

The end of the story was as sensational as the beginning, for Meunier attempted suicide while awaiting trial, grinned and mimicked his own hanging after being sentenced to death and made a speech from the scaffold calling on witnesses to testify that he was not afraid.

CHAPTER SIX

Making Merry
Food and Drink

A Christmas feast at the priory

SIXTEENTH-CENTURY WORCESTER was a very important and fortified city. It guarded the main road to the Marches of Wales and it had the only bridge over the Severn between Gloucester and Bridgnorth; so that many distinguished travellers passed the night in the city. It was a popular place for pilgrims too for here came people from all quarters to pay tribute to two great saints, Oswald and Wulstan.

The cathedral priory was the centre of hospitality. The last of the priors, William More, reigned over a community whose strict rules of life had relaxed over the centuries, and the jovial monks understood very well the good things of life: they kept a small army of cooks and kitchen menials and no expense was spared to garnish their tables with the richest food. They were grand landlords and most of their county tenants paid rent in game, venison or rabbits by the hundred.

The priory was decorated from Christmas Eve to New Year with holly and ivy (but no mistletoe, for that was associated with heathenism). On Christmas night after evensong the city bailiff and his corporation 'in skarlet gowns' came to dine with the prior and his brethren in the Guesten Hall. They all partook of a tremendous feast, including a boar's head, game, venison, dumplings and peacock pie. Oranges, a costly imported delicacy, were provided and everything was highly spiced and flavoured. The feast was accompanied by eight or nine varieties of sticky ales or wines, so thick that the guests filtered them through their teeth. Should any great lady be staying at the priory — a not uncommon event in a town on the only road into Wales — a special dish of wafers or sweetmeats was prepared by the prior's cook; and it is satisfying to note 'a dish of mince pyes for ye boyes', evidently the cathedral choristers. Broken meats and culinary failures were quietly conveyed to the prison which adjoined the priory — until a time came when the prior found the prisoners were receiving more than their share, and he put a stop to this excessive generosity.

The festivities continued right merrily until the New Year. Noble visitors were persuaded to stay on, for their visits did honour to the prior; and on New Year's Eve the bailiffs and chief citizens were once again bidden to an elaborate feast at the Guesten Hall, the prior's gifts from his tenants being so prodigious in quantity that it was necessary to consume them forthwith. In the first year of his office he received capons and 'pecocke and a pehenne, lampreys, a hampurn of wafurnes (sweetmeats), a dysshe of trowtes and grey lynges, a pygge, a lamb, a cheese, two desen and halfe of larkes, a goose and six suytes and teles'. (Noake translates these last two as 'suets' and 'tails'.) Game and venison came from various manors and rents paid in kind: a hundred couples of rabbit from Henwick, deer from Battenhall, herons and peacocks from Hallow, pigeons from Crowle and rooks from 'Master Pakyngton and his Wyfe from his manor at Hampton' (Hampton Lovett).

Perhaps it was not to be wondered at that the days of monastic feasting were drawing to a close. The great religious houses were falling into decadence and the purifying but very severe storm of the Dissolution was on its way. But old Prior More had the good sense to retire to his manor at Crowle in 1535 when he saw the storm approaching.

Drawing of the interior of the Guesten Hall, Worcester, by G E Street, c1859.

Civic celebrations

For three-and-a-half centuries the mayors of Worcester have followed — and improved on — the ancient tradition of official feasting: any and every occasion has been a cause for making merry — a coronation, the death of a king or the discussion of bye-laws about the size of quart pots. The mayor used to be given a grant for the 'keeping of a more splendid table'. In 1722 it was £40, a great sum then, and roistering steadily grew until in 1832 the corporation spent £265 out of

their total revenue of £2,000. They kept their own cook and regaled themselves
with exquisite delicacies from tripe to oysters. They also kept their own wine cellar
which was renowned for its quality, for they believed in potations long and deep.
And it was only rarely that they denied themselves, and then only in the event
of great misfortune – like the plague or the falling down of the city walls.

By the mid-nineteenth century the entertainment had reached such proportions that
despite the official allowance only a rich man could accept the office of mayor. When
Joseph Wood, responsible for so many of Worcestershire's great Victorian buildings,
became mayor of Worcester in November 1860, his inaugural breakfast for the
members of the corporation and guests was on the grandest scale. The Assembly Room
of the Guildhall proved insufficient for the accommodation of upwards of 400 guests
and tables were laid in the Council Chamber and in other apartments. Compared with
today's sparse civic meals the variety of dishes was remarkable:

2 peacocks and 3 boars' heads	12 hams and 18 tongues
1 large raised pie	12 pigeon pies
6 small raised pies	6 gelatine of veal
6 pieces of roast beef	6 roast turkeys
6 ditto braised and spiced	30 couple of fowls
2 couple of ducks	4 ditto sauce bechamel
6 potted meats in shapes	4 ditto pheasants
12 potted lampernes	6 aspic jellies
6 dishes of lobster	4 hares boned and forced
6 dishes of prawns	6 collared eels in jelly
12 lobster salads	Dishes of partridges
20 jellies and 8 blancmanges	14 dishes of mixed pastry
8 open tourtes meringues	4 open cheese cakes
18 enamelled sponge cakes	6 madeline gateaux
6 genoise gateaux	8 meringues gateaux
20 dishes of mince pies	Dishes of hot kidneys
Hot broiled ham	Hot Wiltshire sausages
20 dishes of grapes	12 dishes of oranges
12 dishes of apples and pears	2 pineapples
Charlottes à la rose	Creams, jellies, etc

Fat bacon

At the other end of the scale Mrs Roberts of Hanbury recalled that in the 1850s
her father brought up ten children on 10s a week. How he did it was beyond her
comprehension, for though she was always hungry, she never went without a meal.
Working in the field one day, the squire asked her where she lived. 'You should
have told him that we don't live – we just linger!', her father said. Gleaning after
harvest supplied the cottagers with bread for a time; and for some there was the
family pig, every part used 'except the squeal', they said with some humour.

But it was difficult even to feed the pig: 'When I be feeding the pig he keeps me as poor as a crow; but I must spake for the pig, he went on wonderful, though, fer certain, I waited on 'im well.' Except for pork, cottagers rarely tasted meat, which perhaps accounts for the taste ascribed to a typical Worcestershire lad: 'Ef oi wor a king, oi'd set on a gayte and yeat fat bacon ahl day long.'

Christmas celebrations at Himley Hall, 1819

A good squire exercised a powerful influence over the minds and manners of tenants and servants, ruling with a benevolent despotism which would be unacceptable today but loved and respected by tenants and workers alike. At Christmas he made his house the centre of that old-fashioned hospitality that formed part of English country life.

Staff of a Worcestershire country house, c1900.

The Christmas of 1819 was kept at Himley Hall in regal style. Viscount Dudley and Ward held open house for twelve days. The 'rich man's model and the poor man's friend', for thus was the noble earl styled, had enlarged and greatly added to the stately grandeur of the Hall. In one wing was a large music room with a beautiful organ. The spacious salons, with their parqueted floors, were ready for the dance. Massive chandeliers, capable of holding a hundred candles, hung from the ceiling of the enormous dining room . . . .

The boar's head was receiving final touches in the enormous vaulted kitchen, with ovens large enough to bake the enormous quantities of bread made from ten sacks of flour weekly, and given away to the poor nailers of Sedgley and Himley. Huge turkeys were revolving upon the smoke jacks. The long passages, with curious beams and boarded ceilings, were lighted only by deep circular holes, covered with thick glass, but originally with horn.

At the far distant end was a slaughter-house, a very necessary apartment when a home farm was an adjunct of every nobleman's establishment. At no great distance was the brewery, with enormous vats and ladling jars; one beer barrel so large, it was named 'Big Ben'. Vaulted and cloistered passages led to the wine cellars and muniment room, where were kept the deeds and the hatchments in use at funerals. Still rooms, in which her ladyship's elderwater, perfumes and salves were prepared, were close to the servants' hall, above the fireplace of which was the axiom 'Waste not, want not; repeat no idle tales'. Ancient retainers, in picturesque garb, waited at the festive board. Large branches of yew adorned the high mantelpiece carved with the family arms. On the completion of the feast the company adjourned to the music room, where songs and dances were played on the earl's new organ.

And at this stage it is the turn of the waits (the servants):

Supper is all ready for the waits, good old Black Country groaty pudding and mulled ale. The waits are ushered in and supper starts with:

> The cock sot up in the yew tree,
> And the hen come chatterin' by,
> I wish you a Merry Christmas,
> And a good fat pig in the sty.

(The crowing of a cock was believed to drive away evil spirits.)

Lamperns – Worcester's oldest industry

There is no river like the Severn and there was once no place like Worcester for lamperns, according to gastronomic experts. Lamperns, wrote a contributor to *Berrow's Worcester Journal* in 1936, were peculiar to a few Severnside towns and lampern catching was said to be Worcester's oldest industry. The lampern is really a river lamprey, but those who have ever tasted both will argue there is no comparison. The lampern looks like a cross between an eel and a grass snake, about as thick as a man's thumb and a foot in length when fully grown. The season started in October when the lamperns were carried up on the flood tides, and lasted until February or March when they disappeared again until the autumn. They were caught in much the same way as eels, in tall wicker baskets called putcheons, embedded in the mud where the river runs deepest.

Worcester-potted lampreys and lamperns were once delicacies known all over the world and scores of fishermen in the city gained their livelihood in this way. But by 1936 there were only two or three left (all of the Joe Jenkins' family of Severn Street). 'Lamperns', Joe said, 'are still popular with those who know about them, but the majority of Worcester people seem to have forgotten what tasty fish they are. Yet they are cheap. For a shilling you can buy one-and-a-half pound. They don't know what they are missing!'

Wines and drinks of the county

The land by the Severn and the Teme has an atmosphere of sleepy richness that every region exhales which is at once the grower of fine fruit and fine hops and other produce that makes good drinks. Besides good ale, fine cider and the lesser known perry, there was once the almost legendary lambswool and the exotic but powerful plum jerkum.

In his travels of 1763 Baskerville compared the drinks on offer at Worcester and Gloucester. The crown went to Worcester for the quality and variety of its wines – 'excellent canary, sherry and claret', sherry 1s 8d and claret 1s, 'as good as in London'; but 'for cyder and ale, Gloucester doth surpass Worcester'.

Hop kilns in the Teme Valley, c1930.

CIDER FOR LONGEVITY

Cider is a very old beverage. St Augustine described it as more delicious than any kind of wine; which would seem to betoken a considerable degree of art and care in its preparation. In this country it has been made for centuries, though what exactly is meant by cider is not always certain, for the name was occasionally applied to fermented drinks produced by fruits other than apples. But apart from this wider use of the term, cider as we know it, the fermented juice of apples, has been made and drunk in England for centuries.

It figures in chronicle and story, in history and fiction. King John is said to have hastened his miserable end by surfeiting himself with peaches and drinking new cider when he was already suffering from fever. Mature cider, however, taken for breakfast and supper with toast, produced longevity. So maintained Dr Griffin, who had an extensive practice in Ledbury about 1880. When consulted, he said that half-a-crown spent on cider was the best prescription for a long life.

In the late eighteenth century drinkers were not content with cider neat but liked to increase its power by the addition of spirits – a mixture known colloquially as 'cider-and' and to be found in *Joseph Andrews* by Henry Fielding. Dr Nash, writing about the same time, describes Mathon cider being matured in the barrel for three years and distilled, and being 'nearly equal to the best French brandy', many thousands of hogsheads exported to the East and West Indies. Cider was made in many parts of England, but chiefly in the western counties; and of the various cider-making districts Worcestershire and Herefordshire bore the palm. Farm labourers by custom were supplied with three quarts a day in a miniature barrel and a horn drinking cup; but cider as part of a man's wages eventually became illegal and this discouraged the replacing of decayed trees.

PERRY

The varieties of pears which are excellent for producing the pleasant winey beverage known as perry are wholly unfit for the table or the palate, being too tart and harsh. As John Evelyn remarked: ''tis so wicked a fruit upon the tree as needs no Priapus for protector, since (as beautiful as 'tis to the eye) it has so cursed a taste in the mouth till it be converted to perry'.

When perry was first made in Worcestershire is uncertain but the pear has been associated with the county and the city since the time of Henry V, when at the battle of Agincourt the banner of the Worcestershire men was a pear tree laden with fruit. Perry was certainly made in the fourteenth century for Langland's *Piers Plowman* alludes to it. Camden, in the reign of Elizabeth I, described the county as abounding in pears, yielding a kind of wine from the juice called 'pyrry'. Perry was the favourite drink of the farmers and of the connoisseurs, and with the right pears and skilful manipulation it was, in the estimation of many, comparable with champagne.

That perry needs greater care in the making than does cider is shown in the story of Judge Berkeley:

> Sir Robert Berkeley, who was on circuit as Judge of Assize, called unexpectedly at his house at Spetchley and, going to see some repairs being done to the roof of the perry mill, heard a workman, who was unaware of his presence, talking to his mate: 'Well, Thomas, for a wise man, my Lord Judge talked the most like an oaf I ever heard in my life.' 'Why so, John?', asked his mate from below, and the tiler explained that Sir Robert had given orders that his pears should be first ground in the new mill, and anyone should know that the new wood would spoil the perry. The Judge made his presence known and the tiler was taken aback. 'Well, John,' said the Judge,

Benjamin Williams Leader: The Smooth Severn Stream (River Severn from the Bishop's Palace), 1886. Oil on canvas. Reproduced by permission of the City Museum & Art Gallery, Worcester

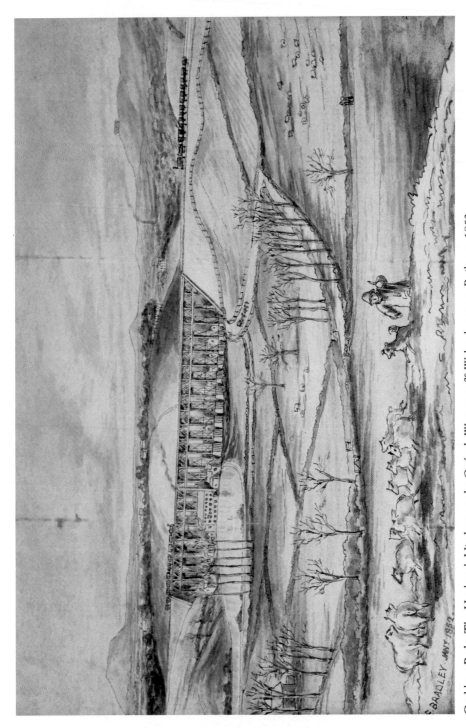

Cuthbert Bede: The Hoobrook Viaduct on the Oxford, Worcester & Wolverhampton Railway, 1852
Ink and watercolour. Reproduced by permission of the Wyre Forest Museum Service

Henry Harris Lines: The British Camp and Herefordshire Beacon, 1872. Oil on canvas. Reproduced by permission of the City Museum & Art Gallery, Worcester

The River Severn at Blackstone, below Bewdley, 1991. Photograph by M. A. Banes

'I own you understand the making of perry better than I do, and I will follow your advice, but remember that you must not call your neighbour a fool. I know the law better than you do. If you should ever want advice come to me, and I will give you mine in return for yours.'

LAMBSWOOL

A drink much appreciated in olden days was lambswool. In 1849 Noake wrote about the practice in many places on Christmas Eve of toasting apples on a string until they dropped into a large bowl of spiced ale which was called lambswool and was always acceptable in cold weather. Although Noake treats lambswool as a local speciality, it was much too good to be monopolised by a single county and there are a number of references to it in literature. Pepys recorded on 9 November 1666: 'We to cards to two in the morning and drinking lamb's wool'. Earlier, Bishop Percy of Worcester origin, who lived in the Severn Valley, described in *Reliques of Ancient English Poetry* the hospitality given to Richard Lionheart by the miller and his wife who drank to their unknown guest in a 'cupp of Lamb's Wool'.

That it could be powerful stuff is shown by a seventeenth-century complaint from Inkberrow concerning Edward Pearce, the parson, who became riotous. At Christmas he played 'Fox Mine Host', drank beer which had been warmed in kettles with apples bobbing in it and behaved to the landlady 'not quite like a clergyman'.

The essential ingredient was roasted apples and, locally, crab apples were always considered the best for the purpose. It was necessary that the pulp of the apple should be worked up in the ale until the mixture formed a smooth beverage; but the actual 'wool' is the bubbling froth which rises to the surface of the whipped ale and clings to the lips of those who drink it.

WOBBLE

In the industrial north of the county it was not unusual in the nineteenth century to see a primitive sign over a cottage door bearing the inspiring words: 'Wobble Sold Here'. Wobble was obtained from the Black Country small brewer and was the last 'shut' of the brew. The first shut was ale, the second shut was beer and the third shut was wobble. It was sold to the retailer at 1½d a bucket, or 2d a pail, with enough barm to 'work it' at the cottage. There was no licence needed for the sale of wobble and it was sold mainly to colliers, ironworkers, nailers and others in hot dusty work. In the centre of a foundry it was the practice to have a barrel of water with barley in it, for the loss of body moisture through perspiration was great. But the men despised the water and sent out for a pail of wobble.

PLUM JERKUM

In the Vale of Evesham people make a delicious wine from plums, but it is a very potent drink especially if, during the making of it, the plum stones have been crushed, for then the drink has a narcotic quality. *Berrow's Worcester Journal* in 1901 carried this advice and warning:

The other day a Wyre gardener was found wandering about Allesboro' Hill with his bicycle, and the impression was firmly fixed in his mind that he was on his way home. The bicycle appeared to be 'bossing the show', and it might have led the man a long way from home if it had not been for a policeman. There was another one, a Pershore labourer, who was found at Defford walking about on his hands and knees, and when put on his legs he promptly fell down. But these men told the Pershore magistrate the same old story. It was Plum Jerkum which had done the mischief. Plum Jerkum is so terribly dangerous that one wonders why people are bold enough to drink it, unless they take the precaution to go to bed and strap themselves in first. After the first small glass, if the consumer is determined to proceed, he should submit himself to some good and reliable test. For instance, let him try and say 'Six thick thistle sticks'.

VIPER BROTH

Mrs Berkeley of Cotheridge Court, speaking in 1932, told of a very popular dish in country districts in eighteenth-century Worcestershire: viper broth. Her recipe, dated 1738, went as follows:

> Take a dried viper, skinned, put into a saucepan with a quart of water and boil gently to a pint and a half. Let stand till cold and if there is any fatt on the top take it off. Then take a chicken, strip it of its skin and fatt, put it into the viper liquor and keep it on the fire till it boils, then take it out and cutt it to pieces, put it again on the fire, let it boil a few minutes, take off the scum and pour it off.

Worcestershire inns

In the eighteenth and the first half of the nineteenth centuries the great centres of social life for many people were the inns, to each of which was attached its own set of regular customers who gathered to smoke and to get or give the news of the day — sometimes with such regularity that each man's chair was reserved for his special use. In every town and village the hotels and pubs provided — and still do — the opportunity for a kind of social intercourse not obtainable elsewhere, places which offered amenities, good fellowship and a sense of freedom. It was not the excessive amount of alcohol consumed, for a drunken man is the reverse of companionable. It is not possible, however, without alcohol, for ginger beer will never be a factor in promoting geniality.

Inns served as clubs for tradesmen and professional men, most having a standing chairman who called for order and for songs. The Golden Lion in High Street, Worcester, was a prime example of such an inn. John Calvin, a venerable corporation officer, gravely presided in the smokeroom while Mr McMillan, the editor of the *Worcester Herald*, was the 'lion' of the nightly gatherings, filling the role of a local Dr Johnson. Though the Golden Lion was a local Radical inn, Mr McMillan was politically neutral, restrained in comment, but with a fine gift of Johnsonian phraseology. After office hours he was 'Sir Oracle', and it was a feature to hear 'Old Mac' lay down the law. He had a way of whetting the public appetite for news while ostentatiously declining to reveal secrets. There was no heavy drinking, only home-brewed ale and long churchwarden pipes, the latter playing an important part in the life of the inn, endowing the smokeroom with dignity. The length of the pipe exercised a potent influence upon conversation; quick repartee was impossible, the necessary deliberate pull afforded time for reflection and for formulating the fine phrase which delighted the customers of the buxom landlady, widow Price.

In the days when brewing was done on the premises: the Eagle & Spur Inn, Cookley, 1904.

READING ALOUD THE NEWSPAPERS

On the night when the weekly newspaper appeared, in some inns it was the custom for someone to read the news aloud for the benefit of the assembled company, with intervals for the service of liquid refreshments. Before 1850 newspapers were expensive and the percentage of educated people was small. In 1830 the only newspaper that came into Wribbenhall (the east bank of Bewdley) was the weekly *London Standard*, taken by the resident lawyer and read aloud on the following night by the parish clerk in the parlour of the Black Boy. At Kidderminster there was a reader who, whenever he came to a word he could not manage, always said 'sleeve-board'! At Worcester, the newspaper was read at the Golden Lion and the Bull's Head. At the Union Inn in Lowesmoor, Worcester, it was said that the news was read there by a child — but the child was an adult, Mr J Child. After 1855 the heavy tax on newspapers was removed, but the practice of public readings at inns continued for some time wherever serious tradesmen and artisans gathered.

THE 'HUB OF THE WHEEL'

There were ancient and famous hostelries in the county of special importance. To a wide district they were the 'hub of the wheel' of social activity. There, county justice was dispensed and meetings, dances and sporting events took place. The Hundred House at Great Witley served a large area between the Severn and Teme and is mentioned in the parish register as early as 22 September, 1653. The petty sessional court was held there and, until 1880, all parish meetings including the vestry meetings.

The Chequers in Cutnall Green, in the parish of Elmley Lovett, was the counterpart of the Hundred House, the 'hub' of a large district between Droitwich, Bromsgrove and Kidderminster. At Shipston-on-Stour, formerly in Worcestershire, the George served the same social purpose. The large market room was used as a corn exchange where corn growers and corn dealers from a wide surrounding district met and bargained over flagons of home-brewed ale and churchwarden pipes. The petty sessional court was held in what later became the billiard room and some of the high-backed court pews were long in use in the inn. Part of the house is certainly sixteenth-century and in coaching days stabling was provided for sixty to eighty horses.

AND OLD-WORLD HOSTELRY

The story of any old hotel, especially if it is the chief in an ancient town, is the story of the town itself. In 1938 T H Gough, publisher of the *Stourbridge County Express*, wrote a memoir of the old Talbot Inn, Stourbridge, one of the most famous inns in Worcestershire. It dates at least from Tudor times and behind a disappointing Georgian facade the building steps back through the centuries. Its large assembly room was used for town functions until the town hall was built; the coffee room is panelled with a fine Jacobean overmantle, the dining room has a beautifully moulded ceiling and is adorned with old programmes, playbills and sporting prints. Until comparatively recent times the ostler's bell hung in the passage in the old coach gateway along with joints of meat; and 'boots' was summoned by the primitive method of pulling a dangling leather strap outside the coffee room door.

Until the outbreak of the 1914 War market day, Friday, was the busiest day of the week. The town was bustling with farmers and corn dealers and farmers' wives who drove to market to dispose of their eggs, butter and poultry; and in the late afternoon the town's auctioneers held their property sales, business premises and private residences coming under the hammer in the room set aside for that purpose. As the afternoon merged into evening, all adjourned to the chief smokeroom of the Talbot to clinch their bargains over a drink. They sat in little knots assembled around small tables, joining up with the leading townsmen, most of them manufacturers of glass and clay goods for which Stourbridge was famous. The conversation grew louder and louder and, as the evening advanced, verged on pandemonium.

By the time the farmers joined their anxious spouses in the 'Market Room', set apart for the female sex, the husbands were more than 'market peart', and the women

Making Merry 141

officiated and drove home. If the farmer was alone the horse would be set on its way and in most cases land him at his back door without mishap.

A BLACK COUNTRY ROUGHHOUSE

Samuel Millichamp of Stourbridge kept a number of pubs in the north of the county. In 1928 he gave this account of the roughhouses of the Black Country in the last decades of the nineteenth century:

All the drink was home-brewed. I was open from six in the morning and did not close my doors until eleven at night, and sometimes later than that. In comparison, the publican of today almost has a gentleman's life . . . .

There was not the necessary number of glasses or mugs to supply all with a drink. I have had 30 to 40 men in my taproom at one time, and one would order a pint and pass it round for his friends to drink. If any refused, it was looked upon as an insult, and I have seen many a fight develop from such a refusal. Things are different now. You don't hear of rat pits at pubs now. Years ago, rat pits were one of the greatest assets of a Black Country publican. I had one when I was at the Golden Lion at Daisy Bank. It was in the clubroom, and at times there were as many as 30 rats in the pit when the dogs were put in. A lot of money changed hands in bets and there was often a ratting competition for which the stake was a good supper.

Dog fights were also staged in the taproom at many houses, and I have seen lots of them end with their owners stripped to the waist and fighting each other in the same room when a dispute arose. Those were the days when taprooms often resembled a slaughterhouse insofar as blood was concerned.

The Black Country was a harsh, rough place, and the publican had to be prepared for sudden violence. One night in the Burntree Tavern, not long after I had acquired it, two men, one probably weighing eight stone and the other at least twenty stone, were playing cards in the taproom, when, for some reason or other, a dispute arose. The little man was sitting in the corner and the other man, leaning across the table, started punching him in the face. He got the little man in such a position that he could not fall, and in a short time he was practically unrecognisable. The tops of his eyebrows were hanging down over each eye and his nose was almost knocked out of shape. My wife and I were terrified. The big man seemed to have gone mad and was threatening to kill everyone in the house. Another customer, a man who is now a minister of religion in another part of the world, came upon the scene and thought that the man had really carried out his threat. Noticing what was called a tally board — a piece of oak about eighteen inches long, five inches wide and one inch thick — on the table, he picked it up and rushed into a passage a few seconds before the big man approached. Jumping onto a stool by the door, he waited for the man and dealt him a terrific blow on the head which laid him out. His life was despaired of for some time, but he gradually recovered, as did the little man, but many years elapsed before the 'giant' learned who was responsible for putting him out of action. This happened about 1880.

Pubs and pleasure gardens

In the eighteenth and nineteenth centuries, when public gardens were in fashion and every town had its 'Vauxhall' or 'Portobello', inns with river-front gardens were very popular. There were a number overlooking the river Severn.

THE KETCH AT KEMPSEY

The Ketch Inn is a very ancient inn where Cromwell's troopers drank their ale and where Samuel Butler wrote *Hudibras*. The name comes from a type of sailing vessel which was once common on the Severn. The inn's gardens were laid out with alcoves, fountains and dancing greens, and pleasure boats carried passengers from Worcester Bridge to the riverside inn. Edward Corbett knew the inn in mid-Victorian times and wrote of it:

> The Ketch Inn was a favourite summer resort of Worcester citizens . . . a stroll along the river beneath the shades of 'Pylgrove', or a dip in the river at Teme's Mouth, and then to enjoy a drink and a game of skittles in the Ketch alley . . . was usually followed by a frugal supper of ham and eggs in the pleasant parlour, whose seated bay windows overlooked the long and lovely stretch of the river, where Samuel Butler wrote poetry in his schoolboy days. The kitchen was spotless, and the company of the kindly hostess, Mrs Clarke, and her jovial son, Ned, who was brewer, ostler and tapster, completed evenings of delight. Skittles became unacceptable to Victorian morality for some strange reason, and the alleys closed, and country inns lost much of their fun and entertainment.

HOLT FLEET INN

The Holt Fleet Inn certainly existed in 1607 and was probably older. After the Severn improvements of the 1840s it became north Worcestershire's principal pleasure resort. Set among hanging woods and flowers and some of the finest scenery on the Severn, its large pleasure gardens were a halting place between two enjoyable journeys by water.

Combined rail and river tickets from Wolverhampton and Kinver brought thousands of Black Country day-trippers to the inn. In a leaflet issued by the Kidderminster and Stourport Electric Tramways Company in 1910 the inn was said to have 'accommodation for 500 for dinners, luncheons and teas, and has a spacious coffee room. The pleasure gardens and grounds extend for 1½ miles, and have a motor car and cycle store which keeps Pratt's Motor Spirit.'

In Victorian times it was run very successfully by Mrs Pratt who 'mothered' her many visitors, and it was always a halt too for the hordes of Black Country hop-pickers who picked in the Teme valley. It was bought in the 1930s by a Birmingham brewery and the old Georgian building was destroyed. In its place was erected a monstrous building lacking the picturesque charm of its predecessor.

Ale by weight and the yard

Mr Dibble was formerly a licensed victualler at Kempsey and at Astwood Bank, and some quaint verses found their way into the London press concerning his houses and the startling information that he sold his ale by weight and the yard.

> Of this there's no quibble,
> That once friend Dan Dibble
> Sold drinks of all kinds by the pound.
> But now it's quite true,
> And I tell it to you,
> (To believe it you may find it hard)
> That by selling by weight,
> (A phrase not quite 'straight')
> He now sells his ale by the yard.

This doggerel was a statement of fact, for the quoted words 'pound and yard' had nothing to do with measurement. The parish pound was situated by the Severn Trow, his ale house at Kempsey; and opposite his Astwood Bank public house, the Red Lion, was a stone yard.

Feats of drinking

England was known on the Continent as a drunken nation and certainly for centuries the capacity for drinking has been proudly recorded. In a book of rhymes published about 1660, in a 'catch made before the king's coming to Worcester with the Scottish army', is the following:

> Each man upon his back
> Shall swallow his sack,
> This health will endure no shrinking;
> The rest shall dance round
> Him that lies on the ground:
> 'Fore me this is excellent drinking!

Some of the amazing feats recorded locally are not without humour. In the seventeenth century Roger Tandy of Tibberton was a notable drinker and a very strong man. It was said he could take a hogshead full of beer and, having drunk out of the bung, put it down again on the ground with the mere movement of his arm, without resting it on his knee or elsewhere.

Berrow's Worcester Journal of 28 October 1750 reported:

> Yesterday a woman who lived without Sidbury Gate and goes by the name of Thirsty Martha being at the Wheatsheaf Publick House in that neighbourhood, a man offered to pay for as much Ale as she could drink while he smoked a pipe of tobacco; she accordingly drank eight pints in the Time (which was less than a quarter-of-an-hour) and went off not at all disordered, excepting that she complained that she was still dry!

There were many convictions for being drunk and disorderly at Evesham and two men of the same name came before the Board of Guardians. One of these being mentioned by name, a lady guardian asked hesitantly: 'Is this the one they call — er — er — 'Born Drunk'?' 'No, madam,' replied the relieving officer, 'this is 'Forty Quarts'.'

In 1833 His Majesty's Commissioners reported that at Kidderminster prisoners were supplied with ale through a piece of straw and were in a worse state of drunkenness by the time they appeared before the magistrate the next morning. In earlier days the prisoners would have spent a time in the stocks: at Cotheridge Court, near Worcester, there was a 'sot's hole', where drunks could sleep it off.

The nineteenth-century solicitor, Edward Corbett, knew a Hartlebury farmer who for a wager drank twenty-four glasses of brandy at one sitting at the Lion Hotel in Kidderminster. When asked by a neighbour if it was true, he answered, 'Aye, Master John, but they were but three-pennuths'.

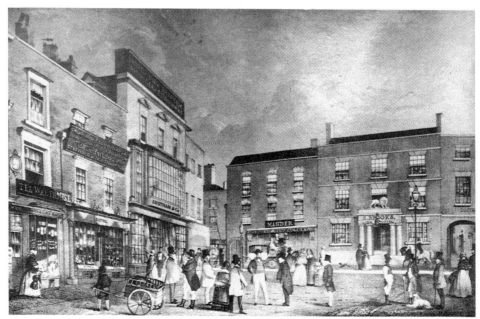

The Lion Hotel, Kidderminster. Print by J Thomas, 1845–1850.

The teetotal fightback

Inevitably a movement grew to counteract the dangers of drink. Throughout the diocese of Worcester the clergy organised groups dedicated to teetotalism. In 1855 the Clerical Association met at Tardebigge and decided actively to foster cricket, singing, boxing and other games as a possible way of preventing the problem. Temperance societies and Rechabite organisations flourished in almost every parish. At Bewdley the temperance society was so strong that William Turton of

Wribbenhall announced his intention to reduce the inns on that side of the Severn by revoking an old charter. It is said that this was the reason why Wribbenhall, on the east bank of the river, was known as the 'Christian Shore' in contrast to the Bewdley side.

In 1879 the Worcester City and County Coffee Tavern Company was formed with the avowed object of establishing houses and shops and 'other places of refreshment and entertainment in the City and County of Worcester and places adjacent' to counter the attractions of the public houses. It opened two places in Worcester and one in Bromsgrove and for a time did well. The most prominent of these was the Central Coffee Tavern on the Cross at Worcester, but in about 1925 the premises were handed over to a professional catering firm.

Later, in 1896, the People's Refreshment House Association was formed, with the Bishop of Chester as chairman. Its aims were to discourage excessive drinking and to encourage pubs to sell food and non-intoxicating liquors and provide recreation. Its watchwords were 'good order, cleanliness, reasonable refreshments of all kinds, and comfort for all classes of customer'. In 1897 it purchased its first inn (near Yeovil), and by the mid-1920s owned over one hundred and seventy, one of them, the Golden Fleece Temperance Hotel in Broad Street, Worcester, three others at Cakemoor, Mamble and Broadway.

More direct methods were sometimes used to take over an inn and close it. At Stoulton, on the road between Worcester and Pershore, the Somers Arms disappeared in mid-Victorian days, during the parish reign of Lady Henry Somerset, an ardent temperance advocate. Chesterton could well have had somebody similar in mind when he wrote:

> The Saracens Head looks down the lane
> Where we shall never drink wine again,
> For the wicked old women who fell well-bred,
> Have turned to a tea-shop the Saracens Head.

At Chaddesley Corbett the Throckmorton Arms was bought by churchgoers who closed it in the 1860s. They objected to the locals enjoying the sun and ale outside while they went past on their way to church. The licence was allowed to lapse and it became a private house.

Drunkenness at the turn of the century

At the turn of this century there was still concern about drunkenness, though whether it had increased or not is not easy to assess. The activities of the temperance societies had publicised the problem, linking it with the number of licensed houses in a district. But Mr Willis Bund, chairman of the county magistrates, had no time for any argument which sought to restrict or interfere with the lives of others. At a meeting of the justices in February 1906 he effectively demonstrated that the number of licensed houses in a district had nothing to do with intemperance in that area. Throughout the county, he pointed out, the average number of licences per population was 1:217, and the average convictions 1:206. There were several places where the licences were much above the average – Bewdley, 1:106; Blockley, 1:164; Pershore, 1:175; Stourport, 1:161; Tenbury, 1:144; Upton, 1:180 – yet the convictions were remarkably below the average.

The borough of Droitwich had a greater proportion of public houses per head of population than any other area in the county – 1:100 of its people. Yet its convictions for drunkenness were very low, averaging only 1:300. Evesham *county* district had just the same proportion of convictions though its licences were only one-third as many, *i.e.* 1:272 of the population. Evesham *borough* had more licensed houses (1:173) and twice as many convictions (1:151); but then that proved nothing, because Yardley had the same proportion of convictions and only one-third as many public houses (1:471). And Bromsgrove had the highest proportion of convictions of all – 1:137, yet fewer than average licences – 1:240. Northfield people had less pubs to choose from than anyone else in the county, only 1:511 of its people.

Not only did Willis Bund appear to demolish the link between drunkenness and the number of drinking places, he proved that very often the contrary was the case: where licences were fewest drunkenness was most frequent, where licences were most in number drunkenness was rarest.

Worcestershire pub rhymes

At the foot of Bridge Street, Evesham, was a very old inn called the Fleece. Its sign was an iron sheep and over the door was the following rhyme:

> A fleece it will keep out the wind and the storm.
> This Fleece has a fire which will keep you all warm,
> But the outside being warm, why it is not enough,
> But to warm the inside here's some downright good stuff.

The Beehive Inn at Bishampton had a sign which few thirsty travellers could have resisted:

> Within this Hive, we are alive,
> The liquor makes us funny.
> Be not in haste, step in and taste
> The flavour of our Honey.

Sadly, the Beehive lost its licence and became four cottages. One wonders if this was due to the parody composed by the parson. It went:

> Within this hive drunkards contrive
> To spend their hard earned money.
> Be not in haste to go and taste,
> There is anything but honey.

At Queen's Cross in Dudley in the 1840s Five Alls Inn had a sign with five panels:

On the first was the king with the words − *I rule all*
On the second, the parson − *I pray for all*
On the third, a wily-looking lawyer − *I plead for all*
On the fourth, a swashbuckling soldier − *I fyte for all*
On the fifth, an unhappy burdened taxpayer − *I pay for all*

The Red Man Inn in Blackwell Street, Kidderminster, was also known as the Fortunes of War. On one side of its old sign it had a soldier dressed in the red uniform of the Crimean War period − but with only one leg. On the other side was a soldier with a gold chain and medals and with both legs. The motto ran thus:

The fortunes of War − I'll tell you plain
Is a wooden leg − or a golden chain.

Near Evesham there was a village with five pubs: the Bear, the Angel, the Three Cups, the Three Tuns, and the White Horse. There was some rivalry between them, especially when the landlord of the White Horse put up the following rhyme:

My White Horse shall bite the Bear,
And make the Angel fly;
It will turn the Three Cups upside down,
And drink the Three Tuns dry.

Much more ironic was the sign of the George and Dragon in Hall Street, Dudley, which in 1855 carried this verse:

To save a mayde St George the dragon slayed,
A pretty tale if all is told be true,
Most say there are no dragons, and 'tis said
There was no George, pray God, there was a mayde.

In the bar of the Blue Bell at Upton-on-Severn this inscription once occupied a prominent place:

My furnace is deep and brewing a danger,
Friends ought to pay as well as a stranger,
Friends did come and I did trust 'em,
They left my house, so I lost their custom.
Chalk is all very well, say what you will,
But chalk never did pay my bill.
So I resolved, to my sorrow,
You pay today, and I trust tomorrow.

Nothing more on the slate there.

Parsons, Pastors and Pupils

God bless me and mar wife,
Ower Jack an' 'is wife,
Us fower, no moer.
(A Black Country prayer)

Hermits and anchorites

IN MEDIEVAL TIMES the tinkle of a hermitage bell, or the faint light from the tiny window of horn or oiled cloth, would be a welcome relief to the benighted traveller who had missed his way. Gladly would he give remuneration for shelter, however humble the dwelling, or for guidance on his road.

St Ann's Well, the turn of the century.

THE HERMITAGE AT ST ANN'S WELL, MALVERN

Tradition has it that St Werstern (or Werstan), a monk at Deerhurst, built himself a cell upon a ledge of rock on the Malvern Hills, in a ravine leading to the position of St Ann's Well. H S Brassington in *Historic Worcestershire* records that when the Danes destroyed the monastery at Deerhurst Werstern fled through the marshes and forests to the solitude of the Malvern Hills where he lived a holy and solitary life. As recently as 1825, he adds, portions of the hermitage incorporated into a little cottage were still standing. Many encaustic tiles and carved stones adorned the building, and in the orchard rude cists containing human bones were constantly found. The ancient deeds belonging to the house prove without a doubt that this was the site of a recluse's cell, referring to the place as 'The Hermitage'. The cottage and all visible relics of the anchorage have disappeared, however, the pumphouse and its Italian-style villa now occupying the site.

REDSTONE HERMITAGE, NEAR STOURPORT

Redstone Hermitage in the parish of Areley Kings is of great antiquity and is associated with Layamon, a famous monk and poet, whose memorial stone can be found in the parish church. During the restoration of the church in 1885 fragments of stone were discovered under the Norman portion of the building which when put together were found to read: 'Tempore Layamanni: Santi'. They now form the base of the font.

Layamon lived at the turn of the thirteenth century and wrote *A Chronicle of British History*, a history of Britain in alliterative verse including the earliest account in English of King Arthur and his times. All we know of him is contained in the introduction to his own poems:

> There was a priest in the land who was named Layamon; he was the son of Leovenath — may the Lord be gracious to him! He dwelt at Erneley (Areley), at a noble church upon Severn's bank — good it there seemed to him — near Radestone, where he books read. It came to him in mind and in his chief thoughts, that he would tell the noble deeds of the English, what they were named, and whence they came, who first possessed the English land after the flood that came from the Lord. Layamon began to journey wide over this land and procure the books which he took for pattern. Layamon laid before him these books and turned over the leaves; lovingly he beheld them — pen he took with fingers and wrote on the book skin and the true words set together. Now prayeth Layamon for the love of the Almighty God each good man that shall read this book and learn this counsel, that he say together these soothfast words, for his father's soul, who brought him forth, and for his mother's soul, who bore him to be a man; and for his own soul that it may be the better. Amen.

The hermitage is cut in a great orange-red sandstone cliff and contains the remains of a rock-hewn chapel and a gallery of dormitories. In 1431 the Bishop of Worcester licensed Richard Spetchley to be a hermit here, and there is no doubt that during papal times the caves were the resort of the highest in the land, for over the entrance to the chapel were carvings of the royal arms between those of Beauchamp, Earl of Warwick, and of Mortimer, lords of the manor of Bewdley.

At the time of the dissolution of the monasteries Bishop Latimer, resident at Hartlebury Castle, about half-a-mile across the Severn, wrote to Thomas Cromwell: 'Hereby is an Hermitage in a rock by the Severn, able to lodge 500 men and as ready for thieves or traitors as true men. I would not have hermits masters of such dens, but rather that some faithful man had it.'

In the seventeenth century Thomas Habington, the Worcestershire historian, described the chapel as having an altar over which was painted an archbishop saying Mass, and lines declaring an indulgence for those frequenting the place with devotion. He also mentioned that some of the hermits' income in medieval times came from navigators of barges who were accustomed to make offerings at the shrine. The custom continued long afterwards, for watermen on barges that had grounded on the dangerous rock bar when the river was low never failed, through sheer superstition, to give alms or goods in exchange for a blessing.

The hermitage is entered through the chapel, to the left of which is a long passage, with openings at the side forming a gallery along the face of the rock. Over the entrance doorway and under the remains of carving is an opening which formed the access to an outdoor pulpit, from which over the centuries preachers would address the people and pray for the safety of passengers crossing the ford. In the caves remains of huge fireplaces are still visible, with chimneys bored through the rock to the heights above, and cupboards and niches cut in the rocks. In 1736 the bodies of seven or eight hermits were found buried below the caves.

The Redstone crossing was the most famous natural crossing on the Severn. It was here that the magnificent procession escorting the body of Prince Arthur, the elder brother of the future King Henry VIII, crossed on its way to Worcester Cathedral. But the building of Lincomb Weir altered the appearance of the river here and obliterated the crossing. The great bar of sandstone which stretched across the river was very dangerous to vessels at low water and attempts had been made with gunpowder to blow a runnel or passage through; but this made navigation even more hazardous when the stream was running fast and many vessels were damaged.

In the eighteenth century Dr Nash says the caves were used as a cider house and a school. They were also used as an iron store for the Shelsey forge, and by smugglers; and many were simple cottages, the one nearest the river occupied by the Glover family who were ferrymen and lived in the rock house for generations. In 1773 they were paid compensation when Stourport Bridge was opened a short distance upstream. Later the caves were used by pea-pickers and other wanderers; and in 1919 a funfair was set up there. But the greatest damage to the hermitage came with the building of a large housing estate nearby and, inevitably, the damage will accelerate.

The Rev J L Molliott of Abberley records a curious tradition that the hermits used to rescue unwanted infants who had been set adrift on the river in baskets (coracles) from Bewdley Bridge. The hermits baptised these children and brought them up within the community, always christening them Severne; and in the Abberley church register of 1741 there appears the curious name Delarivere Severne.

BLACKSTONE HERMITAGE

Unlike the Redstone caves, spoilt by ruthless hands, Blackstone Hermitage, upstream near Bewdley, is in good condition and was until recently used as a storehouse. During the 1939—45 War valuable dyes from a local porcelain firm were kept there for safety.

The great rock of Blackstone dominates the famous crossing of the Severn and the caves have long been occupied. The most important one has a single entrance high on the face of the cliff, giving access to the three-roomed hermitage. The most memorable occupant was Sir Harry Wade who, tradition has it, became a recluse after his bride was snatched from him at his wedding. Sir Harry followed on a horse and a furious struggle took place on a bridge over the River Rea at Deritend, which resulted in the girl, Alice Clopton of Stratford, being thrown into the swollen river. When Wade reached her she was dead. Sir Harry vowed vengeance but the abductor had sought sanctuary at Bewdley (then a sanctuary town). So Sir Harry left his home and lived in rags in the caves at Blackstone for ten years until the murderer came to consult him and confess his crime. Wade seized him and drowned him in the Severn.

Blackstone Hermitage, near Bewdley

An array of bishops

The see of Worcester has been held by an array of great and, mostly, good men — one hundred and ten bishops in the thirteen hundred years from AD 680 to 1980.

Among those whose names have become part of church history are Julius de Medici (1521–22), later Pope Clement VII; and two martyrs, Hugh Latimer (1535–39) and John Hooper (1532–33), both burnt at the stake. Six became Archbishop of Canterbury, including St Dunstan, and a seventh, Cobham, was elected Primate but rejected by the Pope; eight became Archbishop of York; and several held high offices of state. Some were notorious pluralists and worldly wise; others, more saintly, gained the reputation for working miracles before and after death; while a few were men of scholarship who translated the Bible and revised the Testament and the Book of Common Prayer.

BISHOP THOMAS AND JAMES II

Dr William Thomas was the only Dean of Worcester ever to become Bishop of Worcester. He was also Bishop of St David's, holding the three offices at the same time from 1665 to 1683.

When James II visited Worcester in 1687 Bishop Thomas entertained the king with great hospitality, laying in welcome a great white broadcloth of Worcester make, all strewn with flowers, reaching to the stairs leading to the great hall. 'My lord, this looks like Whitehall', James remarked. But the occasion was marred by the king's snub for when the bishop rose to say grace before the banquet he had provided, he was brusquely stopped and waved down by James who announced he had his own chaplain, a Romanist, to do that. It brought the amiable old man to tears so that he had to be helped out of the room. To add to the insult, James' attendants rolled up the white broadcloth, worth £300, and took it away with them.

The king's curtness however did not go unnoticed by those citizens present. In the following year the city was markedly in favour of the Glorious Revolution which resulted in James being driven from the throne. Yet Bishop Thomas, so badly treated by James, refused to sign the oath of allegiance to the new king while James lived. 'If my heart do not deceive me,' said Dr Thomas, 'and God's grace do not fail me, I think I could suffer at the stake rather than take this oath.' Mercifully, he died before he was called upon to do either. Writing his own epitaph, he humbly described himself as the unworthy Dean of Worcester, the more unworthy Bishop of St David's and the most unworthy Bishop of Worcester.

BISHOP HENRY PEPYS

Bishop Pepys (1841–1860) was a marked contrast to his two immediate predecessors. He devoted himself to the simple life, becoming more of a farmer than a bishop. He had powerful connections however, being the younger brother of a lord chancellor to whose influence he was indebted for his bishopric.

The change of lifestyle at the bishop's palace was not always appreciated, and the following rhyme is said to have been attached to the gates of Hartlebury Castle:

> A park without deer, a cellar without beer,
> A house without cheer, the Bishop of Worcester lives here.

The rhyme refers to Hartlebury's ancient deer park. On his arrival Bishop Pepys presented the herd to Queen Victoria and had the park stocked with sheep.

In the 1840s the old coach road from Kidderminster to Worcester ran through the village of Hartlebury, the home of the Bishop of Worcester, and the steep hill from the centre of the village was always difficult to climb for a heavily laden coach. Coachmen, to a man, were renowned for a wide command of strong oaths and expletives, for those were considered as essential as the crack of the whip to stimulate a team of horses to special efforts.

One summer evening Bishop Pepys, who often dressed like a gentleman farmer, stood at the roadside and was shocked by the torrent of adjectives mingled with whip-cracks which announced the approach of the Kidderminster coach. So much so, that he shouted a reprimand to the driver. The coachman, Jacob Gardner, as autocratic as the captain of a ship, naturally resented interference and threatened to 'come down with his whip and skin him and teach him to mind his own business'.

Now the bishop in those days was a powerful man and when a passenger disclosed who it was Jacob had threatened 'to skin', the coachman was appalled. The next day, anxious to make amends and seeing the bishop again, the coachman brought his vehicle to a halt and jumped down, whip in hand, to apologise. The bishop, recalling the threat, retreated hurriedly towards his park gates. The coachman followed, trying to catch up, but the bishop accelerated, causing the driver to do likewise — and it ended in 'a smart sprint'. The bishop was in no state to continue; so he turned to make the best of it. To his surprise the coachman dropped on his knees and begged his lordship's pardon. With relief the bishop accepted the apology — but advised the coachman, when next seeking an interview, not to carry a whip.

THE 'COW-TAIL BISHOP'

Dr George Murray, Dean of Worcester (1828–1845), was a cadet of the Atholl family, grandson of one duke and nephew of another. In his day, the Duke of Atholl was King of the Isle of Man — hence Murray, as a young man of twenty-four without ministerial experience, was installed Archdeacon of Man; and when barely thirty was consecrated Bishop of Sodor and Man. Thirteen years later he was translated to Rochester, then a huge diocese, but with a small income which it had been customary to supplement with some more lucrative preferment.

Thus Murray, almost simultaneously with his transfer to Rochester, was made Dean of Worcester, then an excellent position. As dean he presented himself to the chapter vicarage of Bromsgrove and then, as vicar, to the curacy and dependencies of Bromsgrove. At the same time as he held the aforesaid appointments he was vicar of Kings Norton and held the livings of three chapels, those of Christchurch, Oxford, Moseley and Wythall. When Dr Murray took over the living of Bromsgrove the town had not had a resident vicar for over fifty years, the work being done by curates receiving less than £50, though the living was worth £1,200. It was customary for bishops to begin as curates and gradually rise to the episcopacy but 150 years ago Murray's exceptional growth downwards instead of upwards won him the nickname of the 'Cow-tail Bishop'.

Ministers conforming, ministers dissenting

From the early eighteenth century there had been a strong movement away from the religious fervour which had led to so much strife in the previous hundred years. The Established Church was richly endowed and privileged and appointments were often preceded by much political intrigue, with preferment going to those who had friends in high places. Some of its loftier servants were openly atheistic and the church generally reflected the cynicism of the age, most people of standing paying only lip-service to religion. Absentee bishops and clergy were common; some hardly ever went to their diocese or parish.

ABSENTEE PARSONS

The gentleman-parson had no wish to be tied to parochial duties and it was widely accepted that such a parson would be 'an absentee' who would take the stipend but put in a curate to do the work. It was commonplace for the influential absentee to obtain the livings of two or three parishes and then pay the curates a miserable pittance.

Dr Treadwell Nash, the historian, was a good example of this practice. Though he had inherited an ample fortune he acquired the livings of St Peter's, Droitwich, and of Warndon, then the livings of Leigh and Strensham. His greed for clerical preferments provoked sharp verses from an unfriendly critic. It is doubtful if he ever went to Warndon – unless it was to gather historical information. His duties elsewhere seem to have been confined to the one visit a year when he preached a sermon on the eve of the rectorial tithe audit, his text being: 'Owe no man anything'. A contemporary report of one of these occasions recalled that Nash drove over from his house in Bevere in a coach and four 'with servants afore and servants behind him, giving the tithe payers a show for their money'.

After the resident rector of 1615 no parson dwelt at Warndon for three hundred years. In nineteenth-century Noake's day the parson was the Rev George St John who was also the non-resident rector of St Michael in Bedwardine, Worcester; and over the competing claims of the two parishes of Warndon and St Michael he showed his impartiality by living in a third, Powick.

In the nineteenth century the Rev Oswald Knapp recorded a note on his predecessor at Church Honeybourne which shows well the attitude of the old-style absentee parson, even at a time when the new bishop was determined to change the old ways.

> The vicar, the Rev William Baldwin Bonaker, had held the living since 1817. He was an absentee who lived at Prussia House, Evesham, riding over to take the morning or evening services, or funerals and weddings, and would sit on his horse in the churchyard to give the (funeral) procession ten minutes 'law'. If it appeared in that time he would dismount and put on a surplice, if not, he would ride home, and 'leave the dead to bury the dead'. There was a great scandal and Bishop Philpott put pressure on him, but he was a born fighter and had a good knowledge of ecclesiastical law. At last, the

bishop issued an ultimatum: either reside, resign, or put a curate in charge. He did the latter for £95 and pocketed the balance of the endowment (of between £200 and £300 a year).

When the curate got the new post Bonaker paid only one visit to his parish, the first Sunday after the curate's appointment. He enquired of the curate what congregation he had had. 'Very good and very attentive.' 'They never were for me! I'll go next Sunday and see what they mean by it.' As usual he found the village parliament, the men propping up the tombstones, waiting for the last bell to join the women in church, but many more than he was used to. 'Well, my men, and what may you all be doing here?' There was a pause, and at last the oldest gaffer said in his slow Worcestershire drawl: 'Well, Mayster, we wor a gwine to chyurch, but now thee bist come, we be a gwine whoame.'

The clash between the two men went on and on one occasion the bishop was invited to lunch by the vicar who wanted to get a crack at him. 'The vicar enquired: "Would you like to know what my evening prayer is?". "I am sure we would, Mr Bonaker", and the guests held their breath as the vicar chanted: "From Lawyers and Doctors, Bishops and Proctors, Good Lord deliver us."'

A 'WARMING-PAN' PARSON

At Tardebigge the church living became the sinecure for the Clive family (Lord Windsor). In 1845 Lady Windsor presented the living to the Rev John Mackarness, a relative who was not then twenty-five and who had been ordained a deacon only a few months before. Having influential relations he quickly obtained preferment and in 1870 became Bishop of Oxford. Following Mackarness the eighteen-year-old younger son of Lady Windsor was marked for the living of Tardebigge, but it was necessary to find a 'warming-pan' curate until the lad was old enough to be ordained a priest. In 1855 the Rev Dickins, a Kidderminster curate, was put in to hold it for six years until the son took priest's orders. But on 24 September 1857 the young man was killed in a railway accident and Dickins was presented with the living. Having expected to be at Tardebigge for six years he remained for sixty-two.

PARSON HEADMASTERS

Church livings which were linked to the headship of a school were common; but they were often to the detriment of both school and parish. Hanley Castle Grammar School suffered for generations from clergy-headmasters who were either relatives of the local squires, the Lechmeres, or his nominees.

The curacy of Stone, near Kidderminster, usually went with the headship of Kidderminster Grammar School. It was a curious set-up, for Stone was a plurality for the Dean of Worcester who of course put in a curate, who simultaneously held Rushock but discharged no duty there beyond drawing his income. The Rev Thomas Morgan, who died in 1845 aged seventy-eight, served as a curate at Stone for thirty-five years and, according to his epitaph, 'faithfully discharged his duties in all relations in life'. But George Griffiths, reporting on the state of Kidderminster

Grammar School, found otherwise. The scholars had dwindled to two or three for whom the headmaster did not always think it worthwhile attending.

Richard Baxter's Monument, Bull Ring, Kidderminster, c1900.

Wichenford was a living often linked with the headship of the King's School, Worcester. It was a gift of the cathedral chapter and many prebendaries had held it in plurality. The Rev Maurice Day, who held the livings of Wichenford and of St Swithun's, Worcester, was appointed head of the King's School but found it in decline. For five years before, the school had not sent a single scholar to either university and the numbers attending were small. The chapter, not content with prebendal stalls and plural livings, was withholding from the school much of its share of endowments provided under the charter of Henry VIII. In late-Victorian times the livings of Spetchley and Warndon were held by the Rev F J Eld, headmaster of Worcester Grammar School.

THE MAGISTRATE PARSON

The combination of parson and magistrate was particularly unpopular for in the troubles following the Napoleonic wars those combining the roles often proved to be both intolerant and vicious. The most notorious in Worcestershire was the arch-Tory vicar of Dudley, the Rev Dr Luke Booker, who filled Worcester county gaol with so many Chartists from Dudley during the 1840s that criminals had to be moved out to make room. As chief magistrate of that town he was particularly biased and vindictive. Though he was well-known for his good living he seems to have had a callous disregard for the poverty and suffering of those trapped in dreadful conditions in the town and preached that they were a punishment for sin and a trial for a better life to come. The terrible cholera outbreak in 1832 he blamed not on the conditions, which were the worst of any town in England, but on the people who had brought on this affliction by living in sin.

A POOR PARSON'S EPITAPH

Mathon, the only Worcestershire parish on the west side of the Malvern Hills, is a delightful place, but like many another had a poor parson in olden times. Tychichus Whiting, who flourished on a miserable stipend in the eighteenth century, is said to have given orders that his body should be buried under the church porch, observing that 'as he had been trod upon all his lifetime, he might as well be trod upon in death'.

Eccentrics and reprobates

Among the clergy there have always been those individuals who have never allowed the cloth to inhibit their behaviour. Worcestershire has had its full share. It is not easy however to look back and assess the reasonableness of behaviour in times when passions ran high.

The Puritans of Alvechurch in 1637 did not take kindly to the royalist vicar being presented to the living by Charles I and accused him of 'frequenting alehouses on Sabbath and weekdays, of excessive drinking and procuring. His morals were as bad as his predecessors'. He was a curser, swearer, and notorious liar, a quarreller and fighter.' In the same year a complaint was made against the Puritan Henry Hunt, vicar of Defford, who 'broke out into violent swearing before he came forth from the pulpit. He called his parishioners by names most unfit to be used by a man of his calling. He threw stones at them, and said one of them was a devil.' At Severn Stoke, about the same time, the Rev Arthur Salwaye (a bitter Puritan) was shot at in the pulpit by a member of the Somers family. The bullet hole in the pulpit was to be seen until the nineteenth century.

Noake records a scandal involving the minister of Broughton Hackett:

> There is a tradition that the parish registers were destroyed because of a church scandal in them to the effect that the clergyman (a long time ago) had an intrigue with the wife of a farmer, who with him conspired to murder the husband and bury him under the stairs of the old parsonage; that some time after the farmer's brother came from a distance to see his brother, of whom he had heard nothing for a long time; that he arrived on a Sunday during the service and walked into the church; that the clergyman was so taken aback at the sight of him (he was the very image of his brother) that he fainted, and the whole thing came out.

Noake goes on to what is surely a most fantastic end to a strange story: 'How the woman was punished I know not, but the parson was shut up in a cage and hung up in Churchill's 'big oak' with a leg of mutton and 'trimmings' within his sight, but out of his reach, and thus he starved to death!'

At Elmley Lovett a great and notorious quarrel arose at the end of the eighteenth century between the parson and the squire. The Elmley estate was held in moiety by these two 'pillars of society'. The squire bought the parson's share and later the parson alleged that he had been duped and sought to cancel it. It led to protracted litigation which ruined both and both were consigned to the debtors' prison. 'For a long time', wrote John Noake in 1851, 'it was "neck and neck"' on the road to ruin. 'But eventually "the Squire" won it by half a length. He got into gaol six months before "the Parson".' In the process tenants were ejected, some being driven to bankruptcy, beggary, the workhouse and suicide.

In the same parish the parson and the churchwarden compelled a poor girl to do public penance by walking to church in a white sheet and sitting in the seat where her seducer should have sat in order that he should be put to shame. He avoided his part of the disgrace by staying away; and the girl lived to be a highly respected and zealous Methodist, while the churchwarden and the parson continued to quarrel. In 1809 the churchwarden was tried at Worcester Assizes for posting libels against the rector on the walls of the church. He was fined and sent to prison for a year but the sting lay in the libels' obvious truth.

In Broadway Old Church there is a monument to the Rev David Davies, with lines proclaiming his worth to the parish. In his day, however, he was known as the 'drunken parson'. During his forty-two-year curacy (1777–1819) he is said to have charged for reading the prayers for the visitation of the sick that were then regarded as a passport to a better land. On being sent for on one occasion to perform the last service for a dying parishioner he said, 'Have you got the shilling?' and, the answer being in the negative, replied, 'Let the old devil go to hell, then!'.

The Rev John Pearson was parson of Suckley and a magistrate. As a parson he preached, as a magistrate he passed sentence. A parishioner who had been prevented by incessant rain from carrying the stooks from his small patch of wheat into his barn took advantage of a fine Sunday and, reckless of both rector and magistrate, he housed the crop. The rector was outraged and as magistrate at the petty sessions he sent his offending parishioner to the county gaol. James Knight, editor of the *Worcester Chronicle* and a severe critic of clerical magistrates, promoted a protest far more widely than the parish of Suckley, and long before the end of the farmer's sentence the prison gate was set ajar and a crowd of sympathisers met him with a cheer, presented him with a pig (provided by public subscription) adorned in blue ribbon, and an escort to drive him home.

Parish clerks and nobblers

With an absentee parson the church was greatly dependent on the parish clerk. In 1856 John Tustin of Broadway had been parish clerk for fifty-two years and his father and grandfather had held office before him. Not all clerks were worthy men. When Richard Bradshaw was vicar at Tardebigge his son, also Richard, was parish clerk (from 1793 to 1814). In the 1850s he was remembered as 'Old Dickie Bradshaw', who had boasted that he had committed every crime except murder.

Country parish churches were often very badly neglected. At Warndon and Rushock the churchyards are close to farm buildings and were at times overrun by poultry. Noake tells the story of the old parish clerk of Rushock named Jackson who was solely responsible for the responses and gave out in a sing-song voice the first verse of each hymn. The vacant space above the ceiled roof of the church had become a hen roost and the fleas which fell through the cracks in the ceiling had long plagued the clerk. One Sunday morning he vented his disapproval, intoning, to the amazement and amusement of the congregation, the following as the opening verse:

> They used to come by twos and threes,
> But now, God Lord, they swarms!

Some parishes had another official called a 'nobbler' who walked softly during the service and tapped unwary bad boys on the head with his long wand of office, or poked those who had fallen asleep. At St George's, Kidderminster, the nobbler even sported a blue uniform. But church officials appear generally to have been critical of the intentions and behaviour of the whole congregation. At Broadway it was said:

> Some go there the time to spend,
> Some go there to meet a friend,
> Some go there to wink and nod,
> But very few to worship God.

Church officials were not confined to assisting with the service. At Kingswinford in 1828 five special constables were appointed at two shillings weekly. Their duties were:

1   To learn the names of those whom they shall see fishing, shooting or following their trade on the Lord's Day.
2   To see that the public houses be not kept open during the hours of Divine Service on the Lord's Day, nor for the purpose of tippling on any part of that day.

In 1735 the churchwardens of the parish of Longdon compiled a list of fourteen girls of over sixteen years of age, who were 'lazy idle girls, troublesome, etc, and want to be forced to service'.

Church services

A glimpse of a typical country church service was given by Dr A T Schofield during a lecture in 1919:

Some time ago, I was staying at the seat of the Berkeley family in Worcestershire, and in the grounds is the old chapel, full of monuments of the family; and one Sunday evening I went with my friends to listen to an old clergyman who came once a fortnight to the chapel; each of us had a tallow candle in front of us, and during the sermon I sat in a corner of the pew and was almost asleep. You must not blame me, for the clergyman was very old, and his sermon very dry; but suddenly, he uttered a sentence which galvanised me into life with a shock, and I never closed my eyes again. I have written a number of books on the words and they are my subject this afternoon: *'The mind casts a shadow just like the body, for good or for evil, on everyone that passes by.'*

In the 1930s Stanley Baldwin, born in Bewdley, recalled churchgoing in the 1880s:

The parish church which only opened on Sunday in the days of my childhood became in fact the meeting place of the neighbourhood on that day, and I can see once again the pony trap and the landau on the road, people in knots of two or three coming down the lanes, and the little crowd gathered in the churchyard, discussing the events of the past week, while the peal of bells, whose music had been the companion of the last half-hour of our walk, yielded to the urgent, shriller note of the five-minute bell. Then the smell of freshly-baked loaves in the porch, waiting for distribution after the service, the baize door, and we passed into the church in which I spent so much time counting the ten torteaux in the episcopal arms in the east window, and trying to catch the eye of one of our servants in the gallery. Most of the men in the congregation came in top hats, and the older labourers still wore their smocks. More than fifty years have passed, and this picture of a vanished England comes before my eyes more vividly each year I live.

In 1898 John Jones made enquiries about having heating put in Eckington Chapel. Edward Cross of Pershore Chapel replied on a postcard: 'Dear John, this is a degenerate age, for when it becomes requisite to have recourse to artificial heat in a place of worship it proves that the inward fires are cooling. Stoves and the like are quite modern, and such things were never used of old. The chapel here (at Pershore) was filled and people walked — note that — they walked from all parts of the surrounding districts in snow and freezing weather, without any of the modern aids to keep them warm — no furs or furbelows, and when they reached their destination — no stove! The chapel was ice-bound. But what happened; did they take cold? Nothing of the kind. On the contrary, they were on fire — the fire of love, the fervour of intense devotions. Now, alas, these mighty heat producers have been lost, and we resort to a stove — and a miserable substitute it is.'

The Rev W C Leadbetter of the Catshill Primitive Methodist Church remembered the old-fashioned Victorian Sunday: 'We neither worked nor whistled on the Sabbath. Nobody shaved, nor cleaned his boots that day. If one appeared at service unshaven at one end and unshining at the other he was admired rather than blamed. The mere suggestion of Sunday gardening would have shocked the wole community. It was certain proof of backsliding to read a newspaper on the Sabbath.'

Church music

Music of a sort had long been used in religious services, but it was not until the late eighteenth century that Church of England congregations actually took part. It is astonishing to realise that the singing of hymns did not become an accepted part of the Anglican service until 1820.

Nonconformists had used hymns since the late sixteenth century but it was Isaac Watts, a Congregationalist, and later Charles Wesley, who so popularised the idea of congregational singing that hymns became part of English life. And in those early days what gluttons the singers were. Hymns of fifteen and sixteen verses were common; there were far fewer, and so they were repeated over and over again; and as there were no hymnbooks the words were known by heart. Only with the rise of literacy was it possible for hymnbooks to be issued to the whole congregation.

Up until the mid-nineteenth century church music usually featured three instruments: fiddle, flute and double bass, sometimes helped by a 'serpent' (a wind instrument shaped like a snake). Generally the band knew only three or four tunes. Upton Warren, near Droitwich, was typical of the smaller Worcestershire churches: 'The church was aisleless and the middle passage, with high pews on each side, led to the chancel arch in which was a fifteen-foot, three-decker pulpit. The clerk wore a wig and immense horn spectacles. He was a shoemaker, dressed in black with a white tie. In the gallery sat the 'music', but it did not always play, and the clerk would sing the psalms in a majestic tone, all alone. The melody was likened unto the braying of an ass.'

At St Nicholas' Church in Worcester in the mid-nineteenth century church music was to achieve more than local fame. There the Rev W H Havergal and his daughter, Frances, both in delicate health, found solace in composing chants and sacred songs. The Rev Havergal, as often happened in the days before national hymnbooks, published his own book of hymns with his daughter's help. He wrote the tune for the popular Victorian hymn 'From Greenland's icy mountains'. At his death Frances completed his *New Psalmody* and continued to write sacred songs, among her most well-known, 'Take my life and let it be', 'How lovely are Thy dwellings fair' and 'Who is on the Lord's side?'. Her hymns and tunes are still sung all over the world and on the fiftieth anniversary of her death 'Havergal Sunday' was celebrated throughout the British Empire and the U S A.

A more intimate view of church music comes from the Rev O G Knapp's account of his parents' attempt to get a choir going in Church Honeybourne in the 1860s.

> The village orchestra was dying out and no-one came forward to take their places. When it was reduced to one violin and the ''oss's leg' (otherwise the bassoon) my father disbanded the music and bought a £5 Alexandre harmonium. My mother played it and began to train men and girls for a choir. Boys were out of the question, their voices having been ruined by bird-scaring. These she taught to sing in parts, a thing hitherto unheard of. It was uphill work at first as none of them knew a note of music, and a separate practice was necessary for each part until they were note perfect.

At the first combined rehearsal they stopped short, confounded by hearing themselves singing what appeared to be different tunes, but presently they tumbled to it, and worked so hard that in time they could achieve a simple anthem, 'How beautiful upon the mountains', or 'Behold, I bring you glad tidings' for Christmas Day. The singing may not have been very refined but they put their hearts into it. After one arduous but successful practice the leading tenor, a red-faced carter by the name of James Fry, remarked to my mother, as he wiped the sweat from his brow with the back of his hand, 'Lor, Marm, it be unkind 'ard work surely; but there, when us do get into 'im, a team of 'osses 'ouldn't pull we out'.

One hundred years ago 'Corney Grain' described a Sunday service in Cotheridge Church just before Christmas 1840. The church was decorated very simply. 'A gimlet hole was bored in the top edge of the pews, and small pieces of evergreens were stuck in, and generally declined to stand upright . . . but the crowning glory of the service was the music. The clerk left his desk and went into the little gallery where sat three gentlemen. Two played on clarionets and one on the violoncello. As a trio the combination of instruments is odd, but not so odd as the sounds produced by the executants. There was no attempt at harmony, or even at melody in unison. Each individual went his own way, or rather the way his instrument chose to take him. The clarionets were particularly erratic in their ways, and produced alarms and excursions at the most unexpected moments. The clerk gave out the tune of the hymn, and then proceeded to sing it as a solo, while the clarionets and violoncello gambolled round the melody − not quite there, but thereabouts.'

For music and fervour one had to go to the Methodist chapels. In the 1850s the Mill Street Chapel in Kidderminster (more often known as the Black Horse Chapel because it was next door to the old Black Horse Inn) was renowned for good music. Here with fiddles, brass and serpent the chapel choir would lead to inspired heights.

Isaac Wedley, organist at Stourport Chapel for some fifty years, recorded how hymns sometimes produced curious repeats with quite humorous results, much enjoyed by the less serious in the congregation. One New Year's hymn contained the line '. . . and catch the fleeting year', which when repeated spun out to '. . . and catch the flee, and catch the flee, and catch the fleeting year'. Another, sung at meetings of mothers and maids, until the minister's wife realised the hilarity it was causing, went: '. . . Oh for a man, Oh for a man, Oh for a mansion in the sky'.

The Wesleyans

At Oxford in 1714 John and Charles Wesley and George Whitefield formed a society which met for regular devotion, and led a life of methodical self-sacrifice and worship. Derisively, they were nicknamed 'Methodists', a name which they gradually adopted. The three young men made a wonderful team, the combination of John Wesley's organisation, Whitefield's preaching and Charles Wesley's hymns leading to a great spiritual revival.

Wesley's preaching was extraordinary and many who came to scoff remained to pray. It touched every phase of English life and caused the conscience of the nation to be awakened. Methodism, it was said, changed the morals of England from filth to righteousness and saved the country from a revolution like that in France.

JOHN WESLEY IN WORCESTERSHIRE

Some of the worst times Wesley experienced were in that wild area of North Worcestershire and South Staffordshire where colliers and ironworkers appear to have been made almost subhuman by the dreadful impact of the Industrial Revolution. It was an area noted for its violence, squalor and depravity; but after Wesley's visits there arose chapels in districts where the people were referred to as heathens and where preachers had not before ventured.

Wesley's first visit was in 1749 and his diary records: 'In the market place, Dudley, to a huge unwieldy and noisy multitude, till some of Satan's servants pressed in ... blaspheming and throwing whatever came to hand. I retired to the house from which I came, the multitude poured after and covered over with dirt many that were near me, but I had only a few specks.'

Wesley's meetings were timed not to coincide with ordinary services in church, yet he met hostility from clergy and squire alike, reinforced by the violence of the mob. Methodist preachers were stoned, beaten, ducked in ponds, attacked by dogs, lynched by town mobs and pelted with filth. They were unable to obtain justice from magistrates who sympathised with their assailants and even at times egged them on. In 1770 Wesley preached in Cradley and met again the violence of the organised mob. A song from that district sums up his reception:

> John Wesley had a boney hoss,
> As lean as any sin (seen).
> We took 'im down to Hayseech Brook,
> And shoved 'im yead fust in.

THE FIRST WESLEYAN MARTYR

It was not in the 'heathen' north of the county however that the first Wesleyan martyr died, but he *was* a Worcestershire man. William Seward, a young married man of Badsey, near Evesham, was a convert to Methodism. He travelled with George Whitefield to Georgia and on his return to this country went out on his own 'to preach the gospel'. He got as far as Hay in Breconshire, but there encountered fierce opposition when he preached close to where the railway station is now. He held his ground, though sorely abused, but the enemy was too strong for him. Like St Stephen, he was stoned to death. It was said that he was refused burial at Hay, his mangled body carried over the border by friendly hands to Cusop churchyard. Under two mighty trees he lies and a stone recalls: 'To the memory of William Seward, gentleman' and then the line 'If earth was all ...'.

PREACHING THROUGH THE CEILING

It was in 1770 that John Wesley preached in a private house at Stourbridge. The host was Jeremiah Skidmore of Stamford House, Amblecote, and to enable the faithful to hear Skidmore had an aperture cut through the ceiling of the room so that Wesley, by standing on a stool, was able to hold his head halfway through the opening and preach to his hearers packed in the bedroom above as well as to those in the kitchen below. Later, a lifting door was made and Wesley used it on more than one occasion.

John Wesley visited Dudley again in 1788 and wrote thankfully: 'What a den of lions was this town for many years, but now it seems that the last will be first.' He preached finally at Dudley in 1790 at the age of eighty-five.

'Restoring' zeal

The Reformation of the sixteenth century and Puritanism in the seventeenth had swept away much that was beautiful and ancient in the move against 'idolatry'. During the eighteenth century the structure of churches was often neglected and buildings allowed to fall into decay or to be used for non-religious purposes.

CHURCHES AS CHARNEL HOUSES

Many town churches were used as charnel houses, with coffins lying about the crypt unburied. Noake was continually commenting on this and reported: 'In mid-Victorian times the smell of bodies in St Swithun's Church, Worcester, was intolerable. Below one of the pews was a whole family, parents and ten children, and only the floorboards separated the congregation from their predecessors.' St Swithun's was not exceptional among Worcester churches for with shallow graves and only rarely ventilated buildings the atmosphere in most old churches was vile. The crypt of St Peter's, Sidbury, was full of bodies and had long been a charnel house, and the great crypt of St Nicholas on the Cross was full of rotting coffins and unburied corpses.

St Martin's in the Corn Market was in such a state of disrepair at the beginning of the nineteenth century that part of the floor gave way during a service and a woman fell into a vault among the coffins. No-one could remember any repairs having been done; yet the parish had considerable properties bequeathed for that purpose. Unfortunately these had been used to supplement the parson's income.

ANIMALS IN CHURCH

At Ripple there is a room over the porch once used by the medieval custodian of the church as living quarters, but in the eighteenth century used as a game store for the parson. There is a story told at Broughton Hackett about the curate, a Mr Grice, who was in the habit of dining on Sundays at a farmhouse at Tibberton. One Sunday the farmer waited for the clergyman till his goose was nearly spoilt; then, thinking he would not come, set to without him. At length his reverence appeared, puffing and blowing and explaining that he had lost a great deal of time that morning through having to turn the pigs out of church!

CHURCHES IN RUINS

At Broome in 1773 the churchwarden wrote: 'We know nothing presentable.' But this is crossed out and the second line reads: 'We present that our church is entirely fallen down.'

A lot depended on whether someone in the parish was rich or powerful enough to rebuild. The church at Huddington has survived almost completely as it was in medieval times because there was no-one with money to spare, yet in the mid-nineteenth century it was in a dreadful state. *The Antiquary* wrote:

> One of the most tumble-down, ruinous churches in the country is that of Huddington, a tiny village in Worcestershire. It has long been neglected and is in a miserable state. The walls are mostly out of upright, the flooring is much decayed, and in some places quite gone, while in the south nave wall, at the present time, is actually a rabbit-warren. It is said that many generations of rabbits have been reared in the church walls.

'RESTORATION'

It was the nineteenth century which proved the most destructive – and that in the name of restoration.

In the 1840s there were two types of restorers: the hack builder who was prepared to demolish anything that showed signs of age and decay; and the academic enthusiast who could see merit only in the 'decorated' style of Gothic architecture. On all sides there was a demand that churches be restored, and with some reason, for many had been shamefully neglected or botched up during the eighteenth century. In consequence it is difficult now to find a church that doesn't show the marks of the restorer.

Some major structural alterations were badly conceived, resulting in the destruction of architectural features. At Halesowen, one of our finest parish churches, the chancel arch was Norman and circular. Someone considered it would be better if the arch was raised, regardless of the church's architectural features. At Holt, a gilded mosaic of the Good Shepherd was placed over the Norman arch, completely out of keeping with the fine Norman church. At Pershore, the abbey church was a fragment of its former glory, the nave long demolished, the early twelfth-century Lady Chapel in ruins; but it was a beautiful relic of the grandeur of the old building. In 1846 these ruins were cleared away and a memorial apse, harsh and incongruous, was erected to a deceased vicar.

THE DESTRUCTION OF THE GUESTEN HALLS

In 1849, in an act of official vandalism, the church authorities destroyed the fine fifteenth-century Guesten Hall at Great Malvern. It was half-timbered and though it had been used for some time as a barn it was an ancient building of character and fine proportions. The Abbey Hotel was built on the site.

The Guesten Hall in Worcester, dating from 1320, had outstanding features and was the last of the cathedral guest halls. The window tracery was the best in the cathedral and the roof was quite exceptional. The hall had been used to entertain travellers and since the Reformation had become the audit hall where cathedral dignitaries entertained tenants and members of the city corporation. Despite appeals from local antiquaries and the condemnation of the national newspapers, the dean and chapter, rather than spending a trifling sum from the chapter funds to restore one of its walls, went ahead with its destruction in 1860. The roof, after some alterations, was taken to the new Holy Trinity Church, Shrub Hill. That building has now gone, but the great roof has now been raised over a newly opened building at Avoncroft Museum of Buildings, near Bromsgrove.

Watermen's floating chapel at Worcester, formerly and old Severn barge.

The Gypsies' Church on Hartlebury Common

The Gypsies' Church on Hartlebury Common, a small wooden building like an army hut, was the only gypsy church in the country. It had arched and leaded windows and a tiny cross on one of the gables; and a little bell used to hang in a tree to call the gypsies to worship.

Hartlebury Common had long been the base for gypsies and sometime before 1910 a tent mission had been set up by Gypsy Rueben Smith and had been greatly appreciated by the Romany community. About 1910 the Worcestershire County Council evicted them from the Common and their chief, John Loveridge, bought a piece of land alongside the Common for an encampment. John and his son-in-law, Will Webb, decided at their own expense to build a permanent church on the land and for nearly twenty years it was the focus of the community — sometimes with a congregation of seventy gypsies.

The church services had been conducted on Sunday evenings by laymen, among them Mr Wilson, the head gardener to the Earl of Coventry, and Sir Sidney Lea of Kidderminster; but in April 1927 the vicar of Stourport closed the church. There is no doubt that the Rev F A Murray was unsympathetic towards the gypsies and acted in a very high-handed manner. In Mr Loveridge's words: 'We were very upset. The vicar of Stourport, who is a newcomer, doesn't understand us. There was an organ in the church, for instance, it was given to us by Mr Worth, the Stourport carpet manufacturer; the vicar had it scrapped while I was away. I'm very sorry he did it, and more sorry the church is closed.' The Rev Murray, when approached, said: 'I have not been able to find suitable successors (to the lay readers). When the gypsies return from the hop fields I shall reopen the church with my curate in charge.' But the church was never reopened, for the lay readers who would have conducted the services were regarded by the vicar as unsuitable. The church building eventually became the dwelling of John Loveridge's daughter who lived there well into her eighties.

Customs and curiosities

The church was involved in all the major dramas of life and in much else besides.

BIRTHS AND CHRISTENINGS

Superstitions and beliefs surrounding the birth of a child were widespread throughout England. Among those collected in Worcestershire, several relate to the first year during which a baby

- should not be weighed (otherwise he will surely die)
- should not have his nails cut (if too long, they should be bitten off)
- should not have his hair cut (or something unlucky will happen to him)
- should not see himself in a mirror.

Others grew up around baptism:

If a girl is baptised before a boy she will grow a beard in mature age
Attending in black forebodes evil to the baby
If a child cries at baptism he will be a good singer; if he neither cries nor moves he will die early.

To ensure the newborn baby's rise in society he had to be carried a storey higher before being carried downstairs. If there was no higher storey then the nurse had to climb on a chair or up a stepladder with the child in her arms. At Wilden in 1974 an old lady, whose grandmother was nurse to the Baldwin family at Bewdley, said that when Stanley Baldwin was born she got up on a chair and lifted the child gently up until his head touched the beams of the ceiling. She couldn't say it worked every time, she said, but it did very well for him — three times Prime Minister and a peer!

WHAT'S IN A NAME?

In no part of Britain does one find a greater variety of names than in the Black Country area of North Worcestershire and South Staffordshire. In the church register at Stourbridge, dated 1676, is a registration that surely beats all others:

Dancell Dallphebo Mark Anthony Dallery Gallery Caesar Williams
son of
Dancell Dallphebo Mark Anthony Dallery Gallery Caesar Williams

In 1925 the *Stourbridge County Express* reported a scuffle at Pensnett where a young man in a fight was arrested. When asked his name the policeman was unable to write it down and the man wrote it himself. In court his father announced he had not written it down correctly. His name was Chusan Rishathaim Dodo Mahershalal Hazbaz Maximilian Manders. He was known as Cushy Manders.

Among the baptismal names in the church register at Holy Cross, near Redditch, there is one of outstanding absurdity. How an educated clergyman was ever persuaded to register it is incredible. The fact is that on 22 November 1758 a certain John Money with his wife Mary presented their baby at the font and required the priest to christen him *Ready*. Their *Ready Money*, alas, was soon gone, for they buried him the following February.

It was not only working people who chose unusual names. A gentleman in the north of the county called Rose had a daughter and, thinking of a pretty combination of names called her Wild. Unfortunately, she married a man called Bull.

In urgent cases where a child's life was in doubt baptism was performed by the midwife and was the source of all sorts of complications when names came to be entered in the church registers. In one case the record is supplemented with the words, 'Ebrietas Dementat', which, as the girl was named Robert, supplied what the clergyman thought was the least offensive explanation – that the midwife was 'blind drunk' and did not recognise the sex of the child. At Elmley Lovett two of nine children christened by the midwife, all of whom died almost immediately, were named simply 'Creature'. The christening of illegitimate children was sometimes recorded bluntly as 'Bastard' (or, worse, 'Spurious'); but at other times as 'Filius Populi' (a son of the people) or 'Creatura Christi' (a child of Christ).

Wives and widows

SELLING AND LEASING

The practice of wife-selling was by no means uncommon just over a century ago especially in the north of the county. The clergy and editors of newspapers roundly denounced the custom, the latter at the same time making quite a feature of the event. In 1859 for example:

The disgraceful exhibition of selling a wife took place at Dudley on Tuesday night. Hundreds of people were congregated in Hall Street, where the shocking spectacle was seen. The first bid was 1½d and ultimately reached 6d (at which price the woman was sold). Her husband in his ignorance thinks this repeated three times (means) she has actually no claim on him.

The formalities of the custom were very strict, gaining some sort of legal force. In the first case, the husband had to buy a new halter which, on the morning of the sale, was tied around the wife's neck. Holding the end of the rope, he would drive her through the nearest tollgate, where he paid a toll for her at the usual rate for a cow, a horse or a pig. Sometimes she was driven through three tollgates to make the proceedings more binding. With a crowd of admirers and acquaintances usually following, it was necessary to keep strictly to time, arriving at the market place as the church clock was striking the hour.

The husband acted as his own auctioneer and 'knocked down' his wife in public (as he had probably done so often in private). He related her good points and bad, and the reasons which induced him to part with her. 'Her's as sound as a roach in wind an' limb, her con baake, an' wash, an' brew.' ('Ah, thee bist reet,' shouts a voice, 'an' 'er con drink a sup, yo bet.') 'Her con mak' a suit o' clo's good's any snip.' ('An' con weear the breeches!') 'Her con swear like a trooper, an' fight like a game cock,' continues the husband. 'Now, what shan I say for 'er, who'll bid?'

Usually, someone bid a penny, then the intending purchaser offered five shillings and the woman was 'knocked down'. The way was cleared to the pub and the finalities settled over a glass of ale. The end of the halter was transferred from husband to purchaser, a paper drawn up by 'a learned clerk' and the transfer duly signed. The halter was removed and the purchase money spent in spirits and beer, the parties drinking together good-humouredly to mark the end of the 'divorce'.

Such scenes shocked many people, but most poor folk believed that over the years the practice had acquired legality, providing all the formalities were observed; and it is worth remembering that before 1857, when the Divorce Court was set up, legal dissolution of a marriage was denied to all except those wealthy enough to obtain a special Act of Parliament.

Though it was illegal to marry a deceased wife's sister, or a deceased brother's widow, there was an old Worcestershire custom which accepted that he could 'lease' her, or 'take a lease of her for life'; and there were a number of such arrangements made, the children of such 'marriages' never regarded as illegitimate.

WIDOWS

It was the practice in some parts to require widows, on remarrying, to pay a fine to the Crown, although by the mid-nineteenth century it had become a thing of the past. Such practices over the years acquired some degree of legality. *Berrow's Worcester Journal* reported a remarriage at St Swithun's Church, Worcester, in 1775 which points to the acceptance of another 'legal' practice:

> A widow, being married again, to exempt her future husband from payment of any debts she might have contracted, went into one of the pews and stript

herself of all her clothes except her shift, in which only she went to the Altar, and was married, much to the astonishment of the Parson, Clerk, etc.

But this was not such an unusual event. The *Staffordshire Mirror* for January 1798 refers to a case at St Martin's, Birmingham, when '*a woman came to the church in a large cloak* and when the priest was ready at the Altar, she threw off the cloak and, *in an exact state of Eve in Paradise*, walked deliberately to the spot and remained in that state until the end of the ceremony'.

Young and attractive widows have rarely found it difficult to find new partners. General Sir Neville Lyttleton, the third son of the fourth Lord Lyttleton, told how 'a woman, who had a proposal from a colour-sergeant on the way back from her husband's burial, burst into tears; and the non-commissioned officer, thinking that he had been too hasty, said he would see her again later. She replied: "It isn't that, but I have already accepted the corporal of the firing party!"'

John Morris wrote of a similar occurrence at Broadway:

> At the beginning of the nineteenth century there reigned as hostess of the Old Crown Inn, Broadway, a comely dame who, on account of her plumpness and dignity, was styled 'Queen Anne'. The Crown was then one of the leading posting inns of the village, and its parlour was furnished with choice china and Chippendale furniture. Happy did those then consider themselves who were privileged to sit therein and drink the good liquor and share the sweet smiles dispensed by the hostess.
>
> 'Queen Anne' had, however, her share of vicissitudes; thrice was she wedded and thrice did she with tears running down her fair face follow a deceased husband to his grave. On the last of these melancholy occasions a gentleman . . . realising the truth that in some cases delays are dangerous, ventured on the return journey to offer to do his best to fill the place in her heart and home vacated by the departed landlord. 'Queen Anne' very graciously thanked her sympathetic fellow mourner for the compliment and said that she had unfortunately accepted a similar offer from a Mr Brown the previous evening, but that she would not forget his kind offer should she ever again be free.

In fact she died before her fourth husband.

A riotous penance

In a collection of Stourbridge newspaper cuttings of about 1950 were items from 'A Century-Old Diary' kept by a Mr B Leadbetter. Benjamin Leadbetter of Dudley was the son of John and Sarah Leadbetter, baptised at St Thomas's Church, Dudley, in June 1784. His diary was found on a bookstall. The newspaper is thought to have been the *County Express* and the diary entry for 5 May 1849 revealed the fact that the custom of doing penance was still in vogue — but the ceremony of penance could be more like a circus!

The church was crowded on Sunday morning to see a man doing penance in consequence of a sentence passed on him. It was performed in the presence of a large congregation, assembled from all parts of the district — the majority of whom were of the lower order. Some persons of more respectable positions had evinced great anxiety to secure pews and seats, and on the opening of the church doors a rush took place, and every part of the church was instantly filled. The screen was occupied by bargees, who sat astride; the capitals of the column had human occupants; and in other parts struggling and fighting arose for a good view of the penitent, a man named Smith, a gardener and fiddler, whose offence was having slandered Mrs James. The Minister on coming to the service was saluted with the shout, 'Speak up, old boy', accompanied by a chorus of laughter.

The sermon was interrupted by the breaking of windows by the mob outside the church, by cat-calls, whistling, and other unseemly noises, and a dog fight in the building later divided the attention of the congregation with the ceremony of penance. The arrival of Smith the fiddler was at length announced by a tremendous uproar, which put an end to the sermon. He was received with three hearty cheers and the most discordant applause of his friends, many of whom were smoking tobacco. The crush was so bad that Smith had to be put in the churchwarden's pew. He waved over his head the paper containing his recantation, and was welcomed with one cheer more, after which a broom, hassock, pieces of pews, etc were thrown in all directions, aimed at the head of the clergyman. Smith, at the conclusion, was carried on the shoulders of several of the mob to the Plough Inn.

Funerals

THE COST OF MOURNING

Funerals were elaborate and expensive affairs for the well-to-do. The hearse was a large, heavy-looking, carved ebony carriage, surmounted with ostrich feathers as black as jet. (Eight cost over £80 in the mid-nineteenth century.) Even for an ordinary middle-class family the funeral expenses were considerable. E A B Barnard discovered the full expenses of the funeral arrangements of Sarah Charlet of Abberley, who died there in 1780 and whose body was taken to Fladbury to be interred near others of her family:

> The deceased lady died on Sunday 16th January, and the news was taken to Fladbury that same day by a messenger on horseback, who paid 3s 6d for the hire of the horse and 2s 1d for turnpikes. This was for the journey from Abberley to Fladbury and return, a total distance of 52 miles, and the messenger stayed the night at Fladbury.
>
> Forthwith that Sunday evening, the church bell was tolled at a cost of 1s. Again it tolled, morning and night, on Monday at the cost of 2s; and the same observance was continued on Tuesday and Wednesday at the same expense. The burial took place on Thursday morning when the bell was

tolled again, and also from 10 to 2 in the evening it was 'minuited', the total expense on this day being 3s. The bell was also tolled at Abberley at a cost of 10s 6d.

The parish clerk of Fladbury was one William Davis, and he and John Drinkwater, acting under the orders of Mr Welch, the Evesham solicitor who had charge of the deceased's affairs, opened the grave and made a vault at a total cost of £1.5s. of which sum Drinkwater and his man shared £1 for four days' work. A certain Thomas Garmston was the undertaker, and he charged for 'a hearse to Abberley and Fladbury, two days, 4 guineas; for a Mourning Coach to Fladbury 2 guineas; and the turnpikes between these two places cost 5s. 6d; the Sidbury turnpike requiring a dole of 2s'.

A shroud and sheet of 'fine London crepe' cost 2 guineas; a 'sett of compleat black furniture' half a guinea; a 'best Velvet Pall' one guinea; a silver inscription 2s 6d and three cloaks 2s each. Two hat bands requiring four yards of 'Alamode' at 3s 6d a yard, and seven better-class hat bands (presumably for members of the family) were made with 14 yards of 'Armzine' at 4s 9d a yard. There were also items of 10½ yards of 'ruho' (whatever that may have been) at 7s a yard; and 10 yards of ribbon at 6d a yard. One Joseph Broadhurst made a 'Wainscut oak Cofin' for 3 guineas.

Horsemen accompanied the hearse from Abberley to Fladbury on the day of the funeral. Their turnpikes cost 4s; breakfast on the way, for they all started very early that winter morning, 6s; wine 2s 6d; dinner and beer 8s 6d; and corn and hay for the horses 6s 2d. The total expense in connection with the funeral amounted to £35.16s.1d.

MUTES AND MOURNING

Mutes were employed by people of good position almost to the twentieth century. Isaac Wedley described them at Bewdley: 'I was coming over the Bridge, when I caught sight of two tall, sombre-looking figures, standing motionless on the pavement in front of the house. They were dressed in long black cloaks, reaching nearly to their feet, with tall staffs in their hands, surmounted with black bosses, huge top hats, called "High Shiners", with huge crepe bands hanging down their backs . . . . They neither spoke nor moved, utterly oblivious of everything around them, producing an effect most weird and thrilling.'

AN ALARMING FUNERAL

In less expensive funerals the coffin was simply placed across the front of the mourning coach which, at Broadway, on the raod to the old church, led to a very strange happening, as related by John Morris:

In the mid-nineteenth century, the turn round the bottom of the green to the Old Church was then much sharper than it is now, and . . . the driver drove too near the corner, and . . . shot the coffin off the coach on the reverse side. The fall burst the coffin open and awakened the supposed corpse, who as the event proved had only been in a trance.

Several years later death overtook the poor woman

> and for the second time her funeral procession came down the village street. The mourning husband, who had been that way before, was evidently uneasy, and as they approached the fateful turn, could no longer repress himself, but hastily opened the window of the mourning coach and in a beseeching tone, whispered to the driver, 'gently round the corner'!

STRANGE FUNERAL CUSTOMS

County funerals were generally simple but dignified affairs. Noake reported the ancient practice at Broadwas of halting the funeral procession, whatever the weather, and depositing the coffin in the middle of the road (Church Walk), forming a circle round it and paying the dead the homage of a ceremonial bow.

Similarly F E Morgan, when librarian at Malvern, was told by an old undertaker how the bearers back in the nineteenth century would halt at the crossroads at Malvern Link, just below the station, put the coffin on the ground and change places. The undertaker tried to stop this practice, even getting them to change places before reaching this point, but to no avail; they still stopped at the crossroads and changed places.

There was a popular belief that, if a corpse was carried on its way to burial over a private road belonging to another owner, such a road became for ever afterwards a public right of way. It was of course a mistaken belief, but there were many instances of long purposeful detours. One of these 'corpse ways' as they were called is the Burial Way from Ham Green to Feckenham Church. It is an extremely primitive track, in most parts overgrown and impassable for vehicles. It has twists and turns and makes a final wide curve to reach its destination by the side of Feckenham Church.

Stranger still was the very ancient belief in 'sin eating', common on the Hereford-Worcester border and mentioned in Aubrey's *Remaines* of 1696. He described how a visitor stood beside the corpse and was given a loaf, a bowl of beer, and a sixpence over the coffin, so that he 'took on' the sins of the deceased person, thus preventing him from 'walking or haunting'. In the nineteenth century it was still the custom to place in the room where the body lay a small table with a white cloth, glasses and a bottle of wine and biscuits. There is a record of a funeral where the visitor, unaccustomed to the tradition, refused the wine, but the old farmer insisted: 'You must drink, sir, it is like a sacrament. It is to kill the sins of my sister!'

At Feckenham, when a young single woman died, it was the custom to carry a garland of flowers before her corpse to church and there suspend it until it decayed of old age. At Holt, in the 1930s, the practice was still going strong. Less depressing is the belief that the rare flower that grows on Broadway Hill, believed to be the blue *Anemone Pulsatilla*, grows only on land where a Cavalier's blood has been spilt.

Epitaphs

The literature of epitaphs can be both philosophical and humorous. The following epitaph to Thomas Quick, who died in Stone Asylum in 1906, aged 91, is a clever play on words:

> Quick while living, slow in dying,
> At ninety-one he lays his head
> Upon Earth's breast, yet tho' here lying
> He now appears both Quick and dead.

But what story lies behind these lines written two hundred and fifty years ago of Sarah Yeates of Hadzor who died in 1733:

> Although false scandals have been rose on her,
> Since life was spent,
> God will these persons judge,
> And clear the innocent.

In the Black Country humour abounds whatever the situation and the two epitaphs below (both from the first half of the nineteenth century) come from Dudley and Oldswinford:

> Below lies for sarten
> Honest old Hartling
> And snug behind 'un
> His fat wife, a wide 'un.
> If another you lack,
> Look down and see Jack,
> And further, a yard,
> Lies Charles, who drank hard,
> And near that 'un is Moggy
> Who never got groggy
> Like Charles and her father,
> Too abstemious that rather,
> And therefore popped off
> In a tissicky cough.

> Here lies Joe all alone,
> He lies under this stone;
> His life and his death was a venture.
> He was a plague to his wife
> All the days of his life,
> And to his neighbours, a daily tormentor.

Gravediggers are supposed to have a good sense of humour. The gravedigger at Oldswinford certainly had for, having dug a grave for a Mr Button, he sent the following bill to his wife: 'To making one Buttonhole, two shillings.'

It is, however, Worcestershire's occupational epitaphs that have the widest range of interest. At Ribbesford on the Severn there are a number of men who sailed the Severn trows (flat-bottomed boats, unique to the river), mostly with the popular ending:

> My anchor's cast —
> My rope's on shore —
> And here I lie
> 'Til time's no more.

On the banks of the Severn at Shrawley is a charming epitaph to Thomas Cooke, a gamekeeper who died in 1814:

> He sleeps, no more at early morn
> To wake the woods with mellow horn,
> No more with willing dog and gun
> To rise before the sluggard sun.
> No more before the social can
> Tomorrow's sport with joy to plan.
> Death took his aim,
> Discharged his piece,
> And bade his sporting season cease.

At Belbroughton there is an epitaph to Philpotts, the publican who died in 1765. What a name for an innkeeper!

> To tell a merry and wondrous tale,
> Over a cheerful glass of nappy ale,
> In harmless mirth was his supreme delight,
> To please his guests or friends, by day or night.
> But no fine tale, how wellsoever told,
> Could make the tyrant Death his stroke withhold,
> The fatal stroke has laid him here in dust,
> To rise again once more with joy we trust.

An epitaph to another publican, who kept the Lion at Upton-on-Severn, was something of an advertisement:

> Beneath this stone, in hope of Zion,
> Doth lie the landlord of The Lion;
> His son keeps on the business still,
> Resigned unto the heavenly will.

Probably the most famous of Worcestershire occupational epitaphs is at Bromsgrove. It is to Wiliam Scaife, aged 26, a railway engine driver who, with his engineer, was killed in 1840 when the boiler of his engine burst in Bromsgrove station. The engineers lie side by side in Bromsgrove churchyard under two large stones engraved with pictures of early locomotives. Scaife was a single man and the stone was provided by his friends who went the whole hog when it came to the epitaph:

My engine now is cold and still,
No water does my boiler fill;
My coke affords its flame no more,
My days of usefulness are o'er.
My wheels deny their noted speed,
No more my guiding hands they heed.
My whistle, too, has lost its tone,
Its shrill and thrilling sounds are gone.
My valves are now thrown open wide,
My flanges all refuse to guide.
My clacks also, though once so strong,
Refuse to aid the busy throng.
No more I feel each urging breath,
My steam is now condensed in death.
Life's railway's o'er, each station's past,
In death I'm stopp'd and rest at last.
Farewell, dear friends, and cease to weep,
In Christ I'm SAFE, in Him I sleep.

From Ripple comes a warning which commmemorates Robert Reeve, the Ripple Grant, who died in 1626. He was seven foot four inches and pitted himself against two others in a mowing match. He won the wager but died of heart strain as a result.

As you pass by behold my length,
But never glory in your strength.

One of the most pathetic gravestones in the country can be found in the cloisters of Worcester Cathedral. It marks a nameless grave and has but one word on it: *Miserrimus*, a prayer for the unfortunate whose bones lie below. Wordsworth saw the stone and was greatly moved to write:

Miserrimus! And neither name nor date,
Prayer, text, or symbol, graven on the stone;
Naught but that word — assigned to the unknown,
That solitary word to separate
From all, and cast a cloud around the fate
Of him who lies beneath. Most wretched one! . . . .

Who was the wretched one? He was, in fact, the Rev Thomas Morris, a minor canon of the cathedral and curate of Claines, a man of great charm and eloquence, handsome, kindly and cheerful. His story touches on the problem of loyalty which caused so much heart-searching in the seventeenth century. He believed in the divine right of hereditary sovereigns and when James II was driven from the throne his conscience forbade him transfer his allegiance to William and Mary. Eventually he was ejected from the church, but only after the new dean and chapter had shown extraordinary forbearance, doing what they had to do only because it was law.

Thomas Morris withdrew from his offices in the church but lingered under the shadow of the cathedral, attending daily services, kind and gentle to all, leading a quiet life till in great age the Treaty of Aix-la-Chapelle extinguished the last hope that the exiled family would return, and the old man's heart was broken. He was carried to the grave in the cloister, close to the cathedral he loved, but buried outside it as he had been ejected. His coffin was borne by six maidens dressed in white; and by his desire one word, 'Miserrimus', was engraved on the stone.

The 'Miserrimus Stone'

Schools and scholars

SAINTS AND APOSTLES

In the ancient monastic refectory, which the King's School in Worcester uses as a school hall, there used to be a board giving the list of headmasters, headed by St Wulstan. It is not every school that can claim a saint as its first headmaster; but on the banks of the Severn, among the slums of Dolday in Worcester, was a very different school which claimed as its founder an apostle! It was the Watermen's Ragged School, originally an old Severn barge, transformed into a school by the Rev John Davies who, because of his work and devotion to the watermen on the Severn, was known along the length of the river as the 'Apostle of the Watermen'.

SCHOOL FOR A DOUBLE MURDER

Of all the curious foundations, surely no school can claim a more bizarre reason for its establishment than the Bishop Lloyd's Charity School, Worcester, for it began in 1714 as the result of a double murder in a village a few miles away. An account of the affair was given in *Berrow's Worcester Journal* in 1831:

> In the night of the 7th November, 1707, Mrs Palmer of Upton Snodsbury and her maidservant were murdered, and the house burnt down by a gang of desperate villains, at the head of whom was Mr Palmer, her only son, and Mr Symonds, whose sister Palmer had married. These two wretches were tried and executed. By Palmer's death, an estate of his at White Ladies Aston

was forfeited to Dr Lloyd, the Bishop of Worcester, who, unwilling to receive the price of blood, appropriated it to a school at Worcester.

Bishop Lloyd endowed two schools, one for sixteen boys, the other for eight girls, both on the same premises in the old Trinity Hall. But at the death of the bishop the charity declined and for a time 'the whole was sunk in oblivion'. The school moved from the Trinity Hall to the master's dwellinghouse, and he, Mr Greenbank Sheldon, remained undisturbed for twenty-four years during which time the school went from bad to worse. Eventually, the trustees reprimanded him, but to no avail. Then in 1779 he was found to have pawned the school books; and it was agreed that his morals were such that he should not continue as schoolmaster. The school continued with difficulty until 1896 when the endowments were merged with those of the grammar school.

Schoolmaster and scholars at the village school, Cradley, c1890.

THE WILLIAM NORRIS ENDOWED SCHOOL AT CUTNALL GREEN

The old endowed schools reached their lowest ebb in the first half of the nineteenth century. George Griffiths, a keen educational reformer, visited most of these schools in Worcestershire around the middle of the century and wrote the following:

One of the worst managed of the smaller endowed schools I found at Cutnall Green ... a quiet road-side place, remarkable only for breeding geese, for a very badly managed school, and very bad annual races. On visiting this place I had some difficulty in finding the school. The road runs through a green as the name denotes, and the school lies off the road, between which a very broken-up part of the green intervenes, so broken as to make approach difficult.

The school was such an obscure looking place surrounded by mud and dirt, and ornamented with broken windows and time-eaten doors and walls, that the passers-by knew not that an endowed school for the education of the English youth was there. Of all the free schools that I have visited this was the worst. As I approached it, my mind suddenly had a vision of Goldsmith's *Deserted Village*. Here was the green, but no 'playful children just let loose from school', here was the school itself and the schoolmaster's mansion, but not even skirted with 'blossomed furze, and profitably gay'.

John Evans was the master and his income was only £10.18s.10d per annum . . . he also lived rent free and had some ground; the total being £25 per annum. The boys paid for books and ink, and 1s a year for coals. There were in the school a few labourers' sons, who were taught spelling, reading, writing and arithmetic, but they rarely got beyond 'practice'. The master complained of the irregularity of their attendance, and their parents' indifference in sending them.

He had held the situation for 20 years (his father had held it for 37) and his health was so bad that he had occasionally to teach the boys in the kitchen of his house, which adjoined the school. This accounted for the wretched state of the schoolroom; the grate could scarcely hold a fire; the writing desks were actually falling to pieces from decay; the boys' ink bottles were suspended from bacon hooks in the ceiling; and the windows were glazed with wood. The master had three boys that paid him 4d a week each. John Evans' health precluded him from attending to his duties, and he was so illiterate, although his father had been master of the school so long, that he could not spell words of two syllables.

Cutnall Green may have been the worst but there were many other bad schools as Griffiths found. So often endowments meant to benefit the sons of local poor families were being used for quite different purposes. One day Griffiths got on his horse and rode to Shelsey Beauchamp since there was no railway or coach to that beautiful but rather out of the way place: 'When I reached the School-house I found that the Master, Mr Mapp, was absent. I had an interview with his eldest son, who told me there were from twelve to eighteen boys, who attended the school, and that his father was ninety years old.' Further enquiry established the familiar picture that the funds were being used for other purposes and that, in fact, on many occasions no more than one or two boys were to be found in the school.

AN INFANT SCHOLAR IN THE MID-NINETEENTH CENTURY

Not every village had an endowed school and the alternative was usually a dame school. Life for a child was hard, especially for one who did not take readily to book learning. Mr G Gibbs of Bengeworth, Evesham, recalled vividly the methods used to deal with the reluctant scholar.

My father died when I was just over four years old, and our home was consequently broken up, and as there were three young children dependent on my mother's earnings, the eldest child, who was eleven years of age, was sent out to service. My other sister, who was two years older than I was, went to live with my aunt at Peopleton, and I went with her. Our mother went out as a nurse in order to get a living.

Whilst I was with my aunt I was sent to a dame school to learn spelling and reading, and when I tell you how we were treated, you will not wonder that, young as I was, I often 'played away'. At last the inevitable happened, I was found out! First of all I had what was called 'Custard' which was a stroke of the cane across the open hand. Well, that did not stop me, so stronger measures were adopted. I was now given so many 'words of meaning', that is to say, words with their meanings to learn. I could not do the task in time, and so I was placed outside the door and a large black badge like a turned-up peak of a cap was tied round my forehead bearing the word 'Dunce' in large letters. After a time I was called in for the mistress to see how I was getting on, but what with grief and shame, I could not learn my task.

It being midday, I was sent home to dinner, but first of all my hands were tied behind me, and on my head was placed a large black hat of the beadle kind, and painted on it in large yellow letters were the words 'Blockhead', and so I started off for home, the laughing stock of all who saw me. The news of my trouble had reached my small sister, and she came to help me, crying bitterly, and helped to drag me over the stiles as well as she could, considering the helpless condition in which I found myself. When I arrived home, my aunt pretended to be afraid to untie my hands, but at last she said she would risk it. After a very spare dinner she fastened my hands behind me again, put on my 'fancy' hat once more and sent me back to school.

THE SCHOOL INSPECTOR CAME

Before the 1870 Education Act made it compulsory for all children to be educated, many a child was brought up unable to read and write. The *Worcester Herald* of 3 December 1904 had a piece about an old man, living companionably with his wife, who had only 'a vague idea that there is a world outside' but who got on with his farming jobs, did what his master told him and was regarded by everybody as a useful member of society. 'When he was a youngster, living was hard and food was scarce. Instead of receiving a schooling he had to be a farmer's boy, rise painfully early in the morning, live on rough bread, skimmed cheese and fat bacon, and submit to his master's tyranny. The better times came, and his parents sent him to school for a while. He was put with boys of his own age, in a class too advanced for him. Soon after his instalment there was a learned and terrible inspector came to examine the school. He pounced on Tom and began to probe the depths of his knowledge. "Spell *Beast*" said the inspector. Tom, in relating that experience said, "I burst into tears, for I could no more spell *beast* than a beast could spell me. In those days I didn't know a big 'A' from a bull's foot." Thenceforth, he abandoned 'schoolin'.'

Children of St Hilda's Orphanage, Malvern Link, 1915. Both girls and boys are wearing dresses.

SUNDAY SCHOOL IN THE 1860s

Schools were hard places in the mid-nineteenth century and Sunday Schools were almost as harsh as the day schools. In the country there was no choice: attendance was compulsory and the power of the parson was very great indeed. Jessie Shervington of Evesham described Sunday School at Peopleton in the 1860s:

Our Sunday School was held in the church. We had a very strict master who came from Worcester to teach us on Sundays. But the Rev G Dineley ws most 'bitter severe' though, perhaps, all for our good. We had to learn and say the collect for the day, one of Dr Watts' little hymns, the Church Catechism, the articles of Religion, etc. It was not all thrown away for I can repeat most of it at this present time. The treatment seemed so harsh then in comparison with today. First, the boys all had to wear white smock-frocks, the gift of the parson. These smock-frocks were made round, with frippets on the shoulders, and a hole through which to put one's head, and the smocks must be scrupulously clean for Sundays, or the lad was sent home and his mother censured in the week.

The girls had to wear straw bonnets (coal-hod shape) with a strip of blue ribbon over the top put through the sides, with just enough left to tie under the chin. In this attire we had to say our lessons, and learn to sing. There was no music in those days except on Feast Days, when the old carpenter brought what was called the 'father fiddle'. Well, if there was any misbehaviour or lessons not properly said, the scholar had to stand in the aisle of the church while the parson preached his sermon, and if it was a bad case, the boy was locked in the church during the dinner time. I have seen some go up into the tower, get out through the holes, clamber down the roof onto the porch and away. This was only adding punishment to themselves, as well as to their parents, for the parson held the whole parish in the palm of his hand. I was locked in only once. Then my elder brother brought and gave me an apple dumpling through the window. It was more than my father and mother dare do for, if found out, father would have been discharged from his clerkship and mother would have lost her flannel at Christmas.

CHAPTER EIGHT

Worcestershire at Play

I

Wakes and fairs

'WAKE' IS THE NAME given to a holiday festival once celebrated in all the country parishes in England. Established to commemorate the birthday of the saint to whom the church was dedicated, a night of religious devotions in the church (hence the name 'wake') was followed by a day of merrymaking.

Often wakes coincided with fruit picking: at Hartlebury it was known as the Cherry Wake; at Dodford there was a Strawberry Wake, where for a small fee visitors could pick what they could eat; on the Lickey Hills there was a Bilberry Wake attracting great numbers of Black Country workers who, once the fruit was picked, drank huge quantities of beer. For Shrawley Wake a special cold cake was made (like a Banbury cake) and after the feast there followed dancing on the green to the music of two brothers, blind Abel Spragg on the fiddle and his brother on the flute. The wake gradually lost its religious significance and became an excuse for drunkenness, rowdyism and immoral behaviour. Claines Wake, held on Trinity Sunday, was notorious in the early nineteenth century. Extraordinary scenes were witnessed in the churchyard where travelling showmen and vagabonds plied their professions on the graves; and such scenes were not uncommon at other Sunday wakes until the mid-nineteenth century when they brought down the wrath of zealous Sabbatarians.

CROPTHORNE WAKE

> Whitsuntide early, Whitsuntide late,
> The week after Whitsuntide's Eckington Wake.

Not all wakes were riotous. Some were well run and organised more as village sports, with showmen and outsiders not welcome. Such were Eckington and Cropthorne wakes in the mid-nineteenth century. C F Stratton, the landlord of the New Inn, Cropthorne, organised the wake on a field adjoining the inn for over forty years. His son recalled the sporting rivalry between the surrounding villages in the traditional sports and games which were eagerly looked forward to by young and old:

First, the game of back-sword or single-stick, with which the combatants would strike at each other, and the first to draw blood was adjudged the victor. This battle was a favourite pastime with the country folk. Some few men would put off their differences until Cropthorne Wakes. There they would settle them in a determined contest with bare fists, afterwards toasting each other in a jug of old barleycorn. (In) shin-kicking with hob-nailed boots, each combatant would take hold of the other's shoulder and would kick his bare legs below the knee until one or the other cried enough . . . .

For children there was the challenge of fishing oranges out of a tub of water with their teeth, hands tied behind their backs, or coins out of a shallow tub of flour; and there was bobbing for buns or rolls which were hung from string between two posts and covered with treacle. There were all sorts of races — a wheelbarrow race for men and boys, each competitor blindfolded, a sack race, an old men's race, an old women's race, boys' and girls' races and even a pig race in which a small pig, preferably without a tail, was greased all over and let loose and whoever caught him and held on was ajudged the owner. For the young and carefree there was a chance to climb a greasy pole and win a leg of mutton; older men and women would dance for prizes of tea, tobacco, hats or gown pieces; and there would be high and wide jumping, hornpipe and country jigs, blind man's buff, kiss in the ring, scrambling for nuts and hot coppers, and quoit-pitching contests, skittles or nine pins. It was a good family day.

The hurdy-gurdy man in South Worcestershire, c1900.

BROMSGROVE FAIR

There is an account of Bromsgrove Fair in 1876 describing the many attractions: 'Towards two o'clock the town looked as of yore on similar occasions. The bells of St John's Church rang a merry peal. Watt Close was well filled with the usual motley assemblage of shows etc, including Bennett and Patch's Theatre, Mander's Waxwork Models, a circus, Godfrey's Curiosities of Nature ... a 'Correct Model of the Blackburn Child Murder', the monster whale, etc. Shooting galleries were numerous and swingboats and roundabouts were also plentiful. There were the usual 'bazaars', several photographic galleries, where a correct likeness could be obtained for sixpence and a great number of stalls for the sale of toys, cakes, etc.'

THE QUACK DOCTOR

With the fairs came the odds and ends: the fire-eaters, sword-swallowers, cheap-jacks and quack doctors. One of the latter was Sequah, known throughout the country, whose speciality was drawing teeth and curing rheumatism. He was the prince of quacks, the most colourful showman since Barnum, and toured the fairs in the 1880s and 1890s dressed as a Sioux Indian chief, surrounded by his 'Indian braves' and a brass band. He harangued the crowds and held them spellbound with his tales of miraculous cures. One of his best sellers was a potion called *Prairie Flower*, which he claimed would cure anything from rheumatism to 'flu.

He must have been one of the pioneers of autosuggestion: at Kidderminster a well known grocer went on to the platform with crutches and walked off without them. He once extracted seventy-four molars in fifty-seven minutes and when teeth were being drawn the conductor, receiving a nod from Sequah, roused the band to a terrific pitch to drown the yells of the patients. The 'great healer' was known later as Dr Hannaway Rose, presenting a most dignified and cultured appearance; but he died in poverty in 1934.

ELEPHANT COUNTRY

'I had to come to Alfrick, deep in the Teme Valley, when the cherry orchards shone like snow, but not to see the blossom. I had come to see Bridges Stone Mill. Bill Costello, who owned the mill, led the way through the mill yard to a barn and said, "Look at that wall". It was an extremely solid stone wall but it had a bulge in it, and the middle part had obviously been rebuilt. "What do you think caused that?" he asked. I shook my head, for I had no idea. "Elephants!", he said ....

'Before us were two magnificent cherry trees and between them was a dip in the ground. Bill Costello in a matter-of-fact way said, "There's an elephant buried here". He saw my obvious disbelief. "Oh yes, it's here all right. And that's not all. Do you see that cage?" pointing to iron railings leaning against a wall. "Lions! We had all sorts of things here. There were lions in cages around the orchard, monkeys swinging from the trees, and we even had part of the millrace blocked off with sea lions swimming in it."

'Bill obviously enjoyed surprising his visitors, and then told me how elephants came to be here in this far corner of Worcestershire. During the Second World War a famous circus was in Birmingham when the bombing started, and to avert the danger of wild animals running amok in the city the whole outfit was moved to the country and eventually finished up in Alfrick at Bridges Stone Mill. "The elephants were kept in that barn", said Bill, pointing to the one with the bulge, "but one night there was a bad thunderstorm and one of the elephants got frightened, so he put his head down and charged right through the wall." I looked at the wall again. It was two feet thick. "And it killed him?" "Oh, no", replied Bill, "it's the other elephant that died later and is buried here in the orchard."

The circus comes to Malvern — a parade to bring in the crowds, 1904.

'Then I recalled that Alfrick was not the only place in Worcestershire to be troubled with elephants. I remembered being told that the old bridge at Evesham, and the Town Gate at Bewdley, were destroyed by elephants. It happened this way: a century ago travelling circuses and menageries moved whenever possible by night. Elephants especially were kept out of sight. Mr Stratton, who kept the New Inn at Cropthorne in the 1860s, told how he was brought downstairs in the middle of the night by a loud knocking (this was the time when inns could keep open all night) and opening the door was confronted by an elephant and its keeper. The keeper ordered half-a-gallon of best old ale and gave it to the elephant.

'When travelling by day the elephants were compelled to walk in an elephant wagon. This was a large bottomless caravan, drawn by several horses, and was very difficult to manoeuvre. The trouble at Evesham happened when a circus was crossing the old bridge there and the elephant wagon sank into deep mire. The bridge was very narrow, similar to the old bridge still existing at Pershore. When extricating the wagon from the mud the bridge was damaged and cracked and left in a dangerous state, and when a little time later in 1854 an old woman was crushed to death by a passing wagon it was decided to build a new bridge.

'At Bewdley in about 1805 the old Town Gate was removed after Wombwell's Menagerie got into trouble when departing up the Cleobury road. The elephant van would not go under the archway. The road had to be excavated several feet to allow its passage and the gate was later removed as an obstruction to traffic.

'But it was at Pershore that elephants came into their own. Pershore Fair had for centuries been held in the abbey churchyard, for in the days of Henry III the Abbot of Pershore had obtained a patent to hold a fair on the feast day of St Eadburga, the patroness of the abbey. Like many another fair, it had by the early nineteenth century become a very rowdy and lusty affair.

'It was the time of religious revival and in 1836 Henry Sherwin, editor of the one and only issue of the *Worcestershire Mirror* which was printed and published in Pershore, denounced the fair and described the scene in the churchyard: "Scarcely was the Sabbath worship concluded when the sacred gates were thrown open and the churchyard was presently filled with the very scum of society ... who began erecting booths, stalls, and stages for the ensuing fair. On the following day, instead of the awe-inspiring appearance of a Burying Ground, I was greeted with all the noise and bustle of a country fair; a large caravan of Wild Beasts in one part, Giants and Dwarfs in another, stages of Dancing Girls, all resting upon the scattered graves, endeavouring to outbawl each other ... mocking the inscriptions which said 'Sacred to the Memory'." Sherwin went on to ask, "Can the many respectable inhabitants of Pershore look upon such a scene without disgust, suffering it year after year to take place, and not strenuously endeavour to prevent it?"

'Henry Sherwin's words brought the churchgoers to action, for after the service they barricaded and locked the gates of the churchyard and formed up in a solid phalanx in front to stop the showmen entering. Though the battle was a sharp one they held their ground against the stallholders, but the showmen brought up the elephants and the defenders were routed, the gatepillars were broken down and the gates forced open. The showmen had won, but for the last time. From that year Pershore Fair ceased to be held in the churchyard. Perhaps it should have been at Pershore that Bill Costello's elephant was buried, with the inscription 'Sacred to the Memory'.'

STREET ENTERTAINMENT

Before the coming of the motor car there was entertainment in the streets almost every day. An old Bromsgrove resident recalled the 'good old days' in that town and bemoaned the loss of the strange characters that brought the streets alive in the days of his youth:

> The dancing bears in the charge of Frenchmen or Spaniards ... are not
> the only sights of half a century ago that have disappeared from our streets.
> There were other amusement caterers who no longer appear from time to

time to divert us and shake their collecting boxes in our faces. Gone are the German bands, and the Italians with their queer bagpipes and concertinas. Street shows are no longer encouraged and we now rarely or never see Punch and Judy, the necromancer who swallowed fire and swords, the Samson who broke chains or the Hardyman who lay down in the market place and permitted his partner to crack with a sledgehammer the big sandstones which had been placed on his chest. Itinerant traders who seem to be no longer with us include Italians who carried on their heads boards loaded with plaster statuettes which they peddled from door to door, the cheap-jack with his amusing patter, and the Breton sailors with strings of onions.

Performing bears in the Tything, Worcester, outside the Saracen's Head, c1910.

II

The theatre in Worcester

EARLY DAYS

In medieval times plays were a feature of all cathedral cities and certainly Worcester would have seen many companies of players and mummers performing for the great number of pilgrims visiting the shrines of Oswald and Wulstan. The first recorded evidence appears to be from the reign of Henry VII, when the Worcester guilds had five pageant-plays performed on Corpus Christi Day and on the following Sunday the guilds went in procession to do worship 'to God and the Citie'.

In addition to the travelling groups of players each parish seems to have had its own drama group. The diary of William More, Prior of Worcester, begun about 1518, refers to 'ye players of St Mychell's', and 'c(er)ten younge men of Seynt Eleyn's', who performed at the Christmas festivities in the Guesten Hall. There is also an item of money given to the players of 'Seynt Petur's', when the monks were feasting at their manor house at Battenhall. The favourite play seems to have been 'Robert Wode' (Robin Hood).

Play acting was very popular in Elizabethan days and travelling companies were paid, surprisingly, from municipal funds. In Worcester municipal records of theatrical performances exist as far back as 1572, when the 'Low Baylie', a civic functionary equivalent to the city sheriff, was reimbursed out of the corporate funds for a sum of 3s 4d expended upon the 'last players'. When Queen Elizabeth visited the city in 1575 a company of strolling players was engaged, again at a cost of 3s 4d out of the corporate funds.

Payments, on the other hand, were sometimes made to keep the players *away*. In 1631, 1632 and 1634 the King's Players were paid 13s 4d 'to prevent their playinge in this city for feare of infeccon' for plague was causing problems. In the years which followed few if any plays were performed. A growing spirit of puritanism abroad also kept the players away. In the words of one contemporary, 'No true Puritan will endure to be present at plays'. Before long English drama was ruthlessly trampled on and the players ceased to play. It even became a penal offence to witness a stage performance.

By the mid-eighteenth century Worcester had become the centre of social life for a wide area; country gentlemen came to the city for the season of the races and the Assizes, many owning or renting houses in the Foregate or the Tything. This, and the flourishing cultural activity of the coffee-house intellectuals, led to a demand for high quality performances like those available in the capital and in Bath. Worcester was never amongst the most important on the theatre circuit. London, Bath and York were the more brilliant; but if the circuit is judged by the genius it has produced then Worcester deserves pre-eminence, for it was the home and nursery of the Kembles and the Siddons.

SARAH KEMBLE – THE GREATEST TRAGIC ACTRESS

The King's Head Theatre is traditionally celebrated as the theatre where the greatest tragic actress of the British stage made her first appearance. Sarah Kemble, later Mrs Siddons, was the daughter of Roger Kemble and granddaughter of Mr Ward, both of whom managed companies at Worcester. She was the eldest child in a family that produced a number of famous players.

The Kemble Company played at the King's Head in 1767 and stayed for several weeks, during which five members of the Kemble family, including the young Sarah, appeared in a historical drama called *Charles the First*. Sarah was then twelve years old and played the young Princess Elizabeth. The curious playbill was as follows:

Worcester, 12th February, 1767
Mr Kemble's Company of Comedians

At the Theatre at the King's Head, this evening
Will be Performed

A CONCERT OF MUSIC

(To begin exactly at Six O'Clock)
Tickets to be had at the usual places

Between the Parts of the Concert will be presented gratis, a celebrated historical play (never performed here) called

CHARLES THE FIRST

The Characters to be dressed in ancient habits, according to the fashion of those times.

The Part of King Charles, by Mr Jones;
Duke of Richmond, Mr Siddons;
Marquis of Lindsay, Mr Salisbury;
Bishop Juxon, Mr Fowler;
General Fairfax, Mr Kemble;
Colonel Ireton, Mr Crump;
Colonel Tomlinson, Mr Hughes;
The Part of Oliver Cromwell, Mr Vaughan;
Servant, Mr Butler;
James, Duke of York (afterwards King of England),
Master J. Kemble; Duke of Gloucester (King Charles' younger son), Miss Fanny Kemble; Sergeant Bradshaw (Judge of the pretended High Court of Justice) Mr Burton; The Young Princess Elizabeth, Miss Kemble; Lady Fairfax, Mrs Kemble; The part of the Queen, Mrs Vaughan.

Singing between the Acts by Mrs Fowler and Miss Kemble

To which will be added a comedy called

THE MINOR

Miss Kemble (Sarah), it can be seen, continued the custom of singing a comic song between the acts of a tragedy — her brother John declared her to be 'the finest comic singer in the world'.

Sarah's juvenile beauty brought her much admiration. Her affections were, however, bestowed on William Siddons, a young actor who joined the company from Birmingham. Unfortunately, her preference led to his discharge from the company and at his farewell benefit at Brecon Siddons recited some doggerel, soliciting sympathy for the discarded lover. He had his ears boxed for his pains by Mrs Kemble. Perhaps it was too near the mark for Mrs Kemble had disobeyed her father's refusal to allow her to marry an actor.

Sarah Kemble was sent away to Warwickshire to be a companion/lady's maid to a friend of the family; but she returned home still constant in her affection and married William on 26 November 1773 at Trinity Church, Coventry. The young couple had to find another company however, the Chamberlain and Crump Company at Bath, which played in various county towns.

After her marriage Sarah's marvellous talents began to blossom until her reputation reached London, the goal of every actor. Garrick, then in the zenith of his fame, heard of her and sent his manager, Mr King, to Cheltenham in 1775 to see for himself. The report was not convincing; so he sent a second emissary in the shape of Parson Bate, a notorious clergyman, who was anything but clerical but accounted a notable judge in such matters. He arrived in Worcester (his letters of report are still preserved in the British Museum) after travelling 'some of the cursedest cross-roads in the kingdom', and watched Mrs Siddons' performance whilst standing in the wings of the theatre, which he described as a sort of barn with a stage three yards wide. Parson Bate was enchanted: she would make a valuable addition to the ranks of Drury Lane, he declared. Though she had been on the stage from her cradle, he said, the young actress 'had contracted no strolling habits .... Nay, beware yourself, great little man, for she plays Hamlet to the satisfaction of the Worcestershire critics'.

At the end of 1775 Mrs Siddons made her first appearance on the London stage as Portia in *The Merchant of Venice*. It was a disastrous evening. Overcome by nerves, she made the poorest showing and was damned by the critics. She was no doubt quite overawed by the huge auditorium, with seating for 3600 people, and at the end of the season she was not engaged, returning instead to the dismal drudgery of the country circuit and the barns.

After another five years in the provinces Mrs Siddons again appeared in London, and this time she was an overwhelming sensation. Overnight she established herself as 'the first tragic actress now on the English stage'. London was infatuated, the public talked of little else. 'To have seen Mrs Siddons', Hazlitt wrote, 'was an event in everyone's life ... she was not less than a goddess ... she was Tragedy personified.' She reigned for years as the very Queen of Tragedy.

THE GEORGIAN THEATRE IN ANGEL STREET

By the 1770s the old wooden theatre at the back of the King's Head was almost at the end of its life. A barn theatre in an inn yard was not worthy of the fashionable county capital that Worcester had become. The city changed rapidly during the eighteenth century and many improvements were made. The Guildhall and almost all the churches were rebuilt; the streets were paved and lighted; the old medieval Foregate was removed to make way for a fine wide street, lined with new town houses for the country gentry. And theatre productions changed as well. The building used by Garrick, Sarah Siddons, the Kembles and generations of players was no longer suitable for the more dramatic, built-up stage settings, nor was the auditorium convenient or large enough.

After the Kembles had moved to the London stage a Mr Whiteley from Manchester became the manager of the King's Head Theatre. He was mean and brutal in his business dealings but so financially successful that in 1779 he left the yard of the King's Head and erected a theatre at a cost of £1,000 in Angel Street. It lasted for just a hundred years and during that time all the greatest British actors and actresses — including Edmund Kean and William Charles Macready — played on its stage. It was demolished in 1874 and a more lavish Theatre Royal was built on the site.

SPECTACLE AND PAGEANTRY

When the great names were not available other attractions enticed audiences into the theatre. In April 1798 Macready (not yet famous) played in *A cure for Heart-Ache* but the bills prominently announced that after the play there would be 'a series of favourite songs, a hornpipe, and a leap through a brilliant Sun of Fireworks, by Mr Fox'. Three days later *The School for Scandal* ended with a 'Grand Engagement between the British Fleet and the Spanish Armada, in which the latter is entirely defeated, many of their ships being Sunk, Blown-up and Burnt to the Water's Edge, ending with Rule Britannia by the Whole Company in Full Chorus'. Both the gentry and the riffraff responded with surprise and delight to such pageantry and spectacle, applauding the grand climax.

The inns sometimes rivalled the theatre in providing special entertainment. At the Bell Inn Assembly Rooms in Broad Street in June 1815, among other things, the enigmatic Mr Moon decapitated chickens and then, to spare the ladies' finer feelings, stuck the severed heads back on again. Mr Moon was no common-or-garden conjurer. He professed the ancient art of thaumaturgics which the Oxford dictionary defines as the knack of working miracles. *Berrow's Worcester Journal* reported that the exhibition was a great success with audiences.

RECOLLECTIONS OF THE OLD THEATRE ROYAL, WORCESTER

By the mid-nineteenth century the standard of drama in Worcester was poor, a fact reflected in the recollections of Mr W Gommersal who came to Worcester as 'second low comedian' in 1852 and returned in the 1880s as manager of the theatre.

> The scenery there was very limited, a drop scene representing Worcester Cross was only shown on special occasions, when announced on the bill; and the style in which effect was given to a piece may be imagined when a bow-legged local celebrity named Phillips, 4 foot 2 inches high, and another man 5 foot 11 inches in stockings, named Spiers, constituted 'the army', in *Richard III*. Phillips was the 'artist', and many of his landscapes were to be seen in Worcester public houses, and Spiers was carpenter, property man, wardrobe keeper and gas man, and also played small parts.

On one occasion 'a donkey was required in a performance of a favourite drama known as *Susan Hopley*. The owner of a "Jerusalem" agreed to hire it for a shilling and two "orders" and sat in the pit to witness the behaviour of "Neddy" who comported himself tolerably well till it was time for him to make his exit, when he stubbornly refused to go off. Persuasion was lost on him, and more forcible arguments were about to be tried, when the owner, jumping up in the pit, exclaimed, "Here, don't beat that donkey!" and scrambled over the orchestra (giving the double-bass player an accidental kick *en route*) and went to the rescue of his pet. The owner's persuasion, however, was as useless as the actors' and Master Neddy, proving to the audience that he was one "wot wouldn't go", had to be carried off!'

The theatre at Stourbridge

The first record of a theatre at Stourbridge comes from *Aris's Gazette* of 1752 with the announcement that the Playhouse 'would shortly be opened by Mr Ward'. This was the grandfather of Sarah Siddons of the Ward Company of Comedians that played at Worcester and on the West Midland circuit. Called simply The Theatre it stood on a site near the Bell Inn Yard in Bell Street, more substantial than the barn playhouse at Worcester but with similar accommodation. The same itinerant companies played there too.

In 1792 The New Theatre was erected by Mr Watson who had also built one at Cheltenham. It was 'as neat and handsome a playhouse for the size as any in the Kingdom'. A sale bill not much later described it as 'a substantial and lofty Theatre, with Dressing Rooms and Offices, Cellaring and Vaults under, convertible to Warehouse or Manufactury. A Dwelling House adjoins the Theatre, with Parlour, Kitchen, Cellar and Three Lodging Rooms.'

The Theatre Royal, Stourbridge, was established about the year 1840 in Barlow's Yard, off High Street, at the rear of the Coach and Horses Inn. It was let in 1841 to Mr Hayes of the Theatre Royal in Bath, who undertook to open the theatre for three months every year. Hayes daringly announced: 'The Premises now undergoing complete repairs, and when finished will be *The Most Beautiful Theatre in the Kingdom*, with a *Magnificent Entrance Hall and Grand Staircase*, with a *Splendid New Saloon*, etc, etc. Scenery and Machinery entirely new. Dresses of the most costly description. *Splendidly Illuminated with Gas*. Prices: Boxes 3s, Pit 2s, Gallery 1s. Half-price at nine o'clock. Private Boxes for eleven £1.10s. Doors open at 6.30. Start 7.0.'

The Theatre Royal's playbill of 15 September 1843 must surely be one of the most remarkable ever seen. Sankey, the manager of a company of players, being in financial straits, called them together and paid each 5s, advising them to get out of town. He himself quickly left by coach for Gloucester but the players, unable to follow his example, appealed for help to the local inhabitants. They had a bill printed, exposing the conduct of the manager in large type, and put on a melodrama, designed to appeal to the people of Stourbridge, called *The Fair Maid of Stourbridge* or *The Maniac Lover of Hagley Park*.

THEATRE ROYAL, STOURBRIDGE

Appeal to the Public. HEARTLESS CONDUCT OF THOMAS SANKEY, Manager of the Gloucester, and late of this Theatre.

THE ACTORS' APPEAL

The Members of the Company most respectfully beg to state now that Sankey, the Manager, has left them, that during the time the theatre has been open none of the Actors have been paid anything like their Salaries, many of whom came 200 miles to join him. On Wednesday morning he started per coach to Gloucester, saying to the Company, 'You may do the best you can and get out of town'. On Monday Night last, upwards of £20 was taken and out of that Sum he paid Five Shillings to each Member of the Company, etc. They beg the public to support the First and only Night of the New Drama, entitled:

THE FAIR MAID OF STOURBRIDGE or THE MANIAC LOVER OF HAGLEY PARK

Characters: Phillip d'Arville, the Lord of Hagley Hall
Miles Melville, an arrow maker of Stourbridge
Andrew Adze, an amorous carpenter of Oldswinford
Michael Earle, the Maniac Lover (played by Mr Mantz)
Dame Stapleton, of Church Street
Mary, the Fair Maid

Scenery and Incidents: Act 1. Scene 1.

The Old Market Place, Stourbridge Market Day, lots of custom, meeting of Miles and the Amorous Carpenter; 'I must have a wife — will you have one?' Treachery of D'Arville. Interview of the Fair Maid with the Seducer. The Fickleness of Woman.

Scene 2. Dame Stapleton's House. Lament of the Lovers. The Cockney arrival. London fashions and Country Hospitality. Andrew's Wooing.

Scene 3. A Wild Glen in Hagley Park at Night. The Approaching Storm. The Maniac Lover's story of his suffering, a tale of woe, the schemes of D'Arville for the ruin of the hapless maid.

THE STRUGGLE!   THE SCREAM!   THE CRIME!!!

Act 2. Scene 1. The Chamber in Dame Stapleton's House. The loss of the Maid. Where is she? The perjured vow. The Murder of the Maniac. London Manners and London Fashions.

Scene 2. Gardens of the Old Hall at Hagley. More Mystery. Remorse of the Fair Maid. Mary's interview with the Gardener. 'Is there no escape?'

Scene 3. View near Oldswinford Church. Flight of the Maniac. The meeting of the Lovers. The Dagger. The Crest. The mystery unravelling.

Scene 4. Chamber in Dame Stapleton's House. The return of the deceived, tho' not betrayed. A lover's vengeance. No friend for the distressed. Arrival of the villain D'Arville. Perilous situation of the Fair Maid of Stourbridge, who is saved from treachery by the death of the Maniac Lover.

The theatre at Kidderminster

A couple of centuries ago, when puritan opposition to the theatre was still active, a Mr Watson nailed the following lines to the door of the Summer Theatre Royal where a group of itinerant actors were being well received by the town:

> How art thou fallen, Oh! Kidderminster;
> When every spulster, spinner, spinster,
> Whose fathers lived in Baxter's prayers,
> Are now run gadding after players.
> Oh! Richard, coulds't thou take a survey
> Of this vile place, for sin so scurvy,
> Thy pious shade, enraged, would scold then
> And make the barn too hot to hold them.

('Spulsters' wound yarn onto bobbins, and 'Baxter' was Richard Baxter, the famous seventeenth-century divine of Kidderminster.)

The Summer Theatre Royal, a converted barn, was so called because it opened only in the summer months. With heating installed the 'Summer' part of the name was dropped; but by 1902 the wooden structure was regarded as unsafe. It was taken down and the parts conveyed by canal boat to Cradley Heath to be erected there; but the magistrates refused to issue a licence for the building to be used for public performances and it was brought back and sold by auction at the canal wharf, New Road. In 1903 a new theatre called The New Opera House arose on the same site. But between the two wars British theatre-going was on the decline and by 1945 The New Opera House was in a derelict condition. It was bought by the Nonentities Society and restored at a cost of £20,000. The society had created considerable interest in amateur dramatics and in theatre-going in the town when elsewhere in the county theatre was at a low ebb. The society re-opened the theatre and renamed it The Playhouse Theatre with a repertory company playing Bernard

Shaw's *Pygmalion*. The theatre on this site ended when it was the subject of a compulsory purchase order in 1968; but the Nonentities have gone from strength to strength in the splendid and attractive Rose Theatre.

The theatre at Bewdley – the troubles of an itinerant company

At Bewdley a barn theatre existed in 1778, but the site is not known for certain. It seems probable that it was in the Angel Inn Yard, but a booth or barn was also used at the rear of the George Inn. It is from Bewdley that we have one of the clearest pictures of the squalor and degradation of the life of an itinerant company of players.

Mr Phillips and his Company of Comedians had arrived in Bewdley from Ludlow in debt, having failed to receive the patronage of that town. They sought to recoup their losses at the Bewdley Theatre but the local magistrates had considered that they were likely to increase their debts to the detriment of the town and had refused them permission. The company – now much smaller and seeking drastic measures to pay their way – issued the following small quarto sheet:

ADVERTISEMENT

Bewdley, February 9th, 1778

Mr Phillips, late manager of a company of comedians, through the inflexibility of an individual, who, meritoriously avails himself upon an Act never meant to deprive an honest man of the means to discharge his just and lawful debts, begs leave to acquaint his friends and the public in general that he has taken a house in BEWDLEY, where he proposes to carry on the business of stationer in all its branches, and humbly hopes he is justifiable in following a profession he was regularly bred up to – Mr Graham and Son have also taken the front part of the Angel Inn, in order to open an academy for the education of young gentlemen – Mr Parsons a house where he intends to follow the business of a cutler – Mr Warner to carry on the profession of a painter in general – and Mrs Johnson apartments in order to instruct young ladies in all manner of netting and needlework.

The above persons willing upon all occasions to render themselves agreeable to the ladies and gentlemen of BEWDLEY (which they now look upon as their place of residence) will for a few nights only entertain their friends with several moral and instructive lectures; the subject of which will be illustrated in the bills of the day.

These 'lectures' apparently tided them over, at least until 20 March, for by then they were back in business at the theatre with a 'Concert of Vocal and Instrumental Music', and the usual plays and pantomimes on Friday nights. The problems were not over, however: another postscript declares that performances will start promptly whatever the size of the audience.

The bill for one of these performances entitled *The Suspicious Husband*, followed by a pantomime called *The Fairy Revels* or *Harlequin Statue*, gives a good idea of the type of entertainment on offer:

> The scenes, cloathes and machinery entirely new. Harlequin, Mr Warner. Pantaloon, Mr Parsons. Sir Fopling Macaroni, Mr G Graham. Soup Maigre, Mr Evans. Rush-Man, Mr Ward. Cupid, Miss Phillips. Fairy King, Master Phillips. Fairy Queen, Miss Phillips. Cuddy Softhead, Mr Graham. The rest of the fairies by the children of the town . . . .
>   Scenes: Grand Deceptions: Apothecary's Shop — from 'The Invasion'. The Table — from 'The Elopement'. The Chest — from 'Mercury Harlequin'. The Monster and the Devil — from 'The Frolic'. The Castle That Falls to Pieces — from 'Mother Shipton'. The whole to conclude with a grand representation of a Fairy Court.

The man who wrote 'It's a Long Way to Tipperary'

One morning nearly eighty years ago Jack Judge, a songwriter from Oldbury in Worcestershire, woke up to find himself famous. During the 1914—18 War everybody was singing '*It's a Long Way to Tipperary*'. The tune was composed by Henry Williams and he and Judge had sung it jointly prior to 1912. But at the beginning of that year Judge, who had a stall on Oldbury market and was always making up songs as he sold his wares, substituted 'Tipperary' for Connemara (which was in the original version) and won a £5 bet for a 'new' song which proved to be one of the best known and most sung of this century. Both Judge and Williams received royalties for the song.

III

The sporting life

DOVER'S HILL GAMES

For two hundred and fifty years a grassy plateau known as Dover's Hill, which rises above Broadway to a point where the counties of Warwick, Worcester and Gloucester met, was famous for its games. They were the successors of the 'Whitsun-ales' festivities, but in the seventeenth century Robert Dover, an attorney at Barton-on-the-Heath, Warwickshire, organised the games on a more elaborate scale, marking a revolt against the puritan attack on old English pastimes, the cessation of which, he complained, drove people to the pothouse.

By the eighteenth century the games had become a popular sporting festival for the surrounding villages. Two travellers, more accustomed to the 'sophisticated pleasures of London society', visited these sports about the year 1740 and gave the following rather condescending account:

> We now approached the place of rendezvous where the revel was held, which was a large plain on the Cotswold Hills. Our ears were saluted by a confused noise of drums, trumpets and whistle pipes: not those of martial sounds, however, which are heard in the field of battle, but such as those harmless instruments emit, with which children sometimes amuse themselves in a country fair. There was a great number of swains in their holiday clothes with their belts and silk handkerchiefs; and nymphs in straw hats and tawdry ribbons, flaunting, ogling, and coquetting in a rustic way with as much alacrity as any of the gay flutterers in the Mall. A ring was formed about the wrestlers and the cudgel-players by substantial farmers on their long-tailed steeds, and two or three forlorn coaches sauntered about with their vapourish possessors, who crept from their neighbouring seats to contemplate the humours of these awkward rustics and waste an hour of their tedious month in the country, where, as a great modern observes, 'small matters serve for amusement'.

But a programme of the Dover's Hill Games of 1818 claimed a much wider patronage: 'The high estimation in which this truly laudable Festival is held (being so famed for the celebrated Olympic Games) is fully evinced by its having been the Admiration of every true and undesigning Briton for more than two centuries, and is now patronised by the Noble Heroes of the present age, and by every well-wisher for the prosperity of the British Empire.'

The favourite sports on Dover's Hill were wrestling and back-sword play, and the 'Noble Heroes' were local men skilled in those arts. In the back-sword contests the combatants would strike each other over the head, the first to draw blood ajudged the victor. Some combatants prepared themselves by drinking a mixture of gunpowder and vinegar which is supposed to prevent a flow of blood. The wrestling contests were perhaps the most popular, for the strength and prowess of the contestants brought pride to the villages around.

In the nineteenth century, the Cotswold Games (as they came to be called) became more than a local event and by the late 1840s some thirty thousand people attended. It had become, said one historian, the resort of all the scum of the Black Country, so riotous and lawless that the neighbourhood was demoralised and decent folk feared to attend. G M Stratton recalled in 1909 a few incidents related by his mother who kept an inn at Evesham:

> One day a stranger was locked up for some trivial offence; my father, hearing the man had no money or friends, gave him food and employed legal assistance, and the man was eventually discharged. Hereby hangs a tale: my mother at that time used to go to Dover's Hill each year, taking a large tent, a good supply of ale, cider, wine, spirits and eatables to sell during the gaming week. She made a good sum of money, but the surroundings

were so alarming that as fast as her silver changed into gold she would drop the sovereigns into the large barrels of ale or cider through the bung-hole (this was her safety bank). She also had a couple of loaded revolvers under her serving table ready for use. She never left the tent day or night until the festivities were over, as no-one was safe from the lawlessness of the crowd of card-sharpers, thimble-riggers, pickpockets, thieves, confidence men, vagrants, and criminals of the deepest dye . . . .

During the daytime the turmoil was terrible, but all night long it was perfect pandemonium. Cries of murder were often heard, and disorder and rapine held full sway. If the shadow of a person showed through the sheeting of the tent at night (the occupant) would be almost sure to be struck with a heavy bludgeon from without, and the miscreant would crawl underneath and rob his victim. One year every stall and tent (except my mother's) was levelled to the ground and their contents pillaged. Scores of persons, nut-sellers and others, found a safe asylum in my mother's tent. The scenes she said were indeed terrible. Yet my mother went there each year with her serving maids and her men, and with eatables for sale, and was never molested or robbed. Neither was any pedlar or benighted person who sought shelter in her tent ever molested or injured.

The reason for this was – the man who was locked up at Evesham, and whom my father befriended and assisted, proved to be a sort of leader of the lawless band who attended Dover's Hill. It happened one day at the next Dover's Hill meeting that this man and several of his confederates entered the tent for refreshments. He at once recognised my mother. He immediately turned and addressed his companions in a slang understood by them, and every year afterwards she and all who sheltered within her tent were always safe from molestation.

Things had certainly become very bad at the Dover's Hill Games and in 1851 the authorities put an end to it. One wonders if Robert Dover would have approved of the closure. Or would he have regarded it as the work of Victorian puritans, and opposed it as he had done the Puritans of the seventeenth century?

PRIZEFIGHTING: SPRING VERSUS LANGAN, 1824

Wrestling had been a popular sport at wakes and games for centuries, strictly controlled and judged on clearly defined rules. The looser forms of the sport led to fisticuffs which became a form of pugilism very attractive to the English aggressive character. By the end of the eighteenth century it had been made illegal, but had become so popular that magistrates dare not break up fights. The champions were national heroes and a pub regarded it as a great asset to have the local boxing club at their premises.

On the walls of most sporting pubs in the nineteenth century was an engraving of the most famous of all old-time prizefights, that between the English champion, Tom Spring, and the Irish champion, Paddy Langan. It was fought with bare fists on Pitchcroft, Worcester, in 1824. The contest was illegal, of course, but many of the county's chief magistrates were officiating at the fight. There were forty thousand spectators, including peers of the realm and gentry from the surrounding counties. Worcester had never seen such crowds. The hotels and pubs were packed to overflowing and even the smallest beer shop, with the meanest accommodation, charged a guinea for a bed.

In those days prizefighters were feted like heroes, and Spring had stayed at Croome Court during the days leading up to the fight as a guest of Lord Deerhurst who, with Sir John Musgrave, acted as timekeeper. Colonel Berkeley was umpire. Paddy Langan meanwhile made the White Horse in Silver Street his headquarters.

A print of the Spring v Langan fight, 1824.

The fight started at 1.40 pm. The rounds were not of equal length, the first round lasting ten minutes. In the second, the fight was interrupted as one of the temporary stands, grossly overloaded, collapsed and over thirty people had to be taken to the infirmary with broken limbs and ribs, one of them later dying. When the fight was resumed it went first with Spring, but in the fifth to ninth rounds Langan inflicted heavy punishment. From then, there was much wrestling and in the seventeenth round the ring broke with the pressure of the crowd. Those near the ring used whips and cudgels to keep back the mob. The fight fluctuated until the eightieth round when Spring finally took control, and in the eighty-fourth Langan fell exhausted and dripping with blood. The epic battle had lasted two hours and thirty-two minutes and the winter light had almost gone. Both men were medically examined and in a few days were pronounced fit again.

The county magistrates who had officiated at the fight came under scathing attack and it became much more difficult to stage such a contest, as an 1848 report in the *Worcestershire Herald* shows:

> An immense number of horsemen and pedestrians assembled near Tibberton on Wednesday last, but no sooner had preliminaries begun than the appearance of the police obliged all parties to beat a retreat. On the following morning the meet was held at Broadheath, where the combatants (two lightweights named Crisp and Lockley) had scarcely commenced, when the 'beaks' again appeared, and the multitude once more moved off. Another county was resolved on, and at length the ring was formed on Bringsty Common, near Bromyard, but the police were here also. So finding themselves worn-out, hungry and disappointed, the pugilists gave up the fight and with their partisans returned home.

BOWLING ALLEYS AND BOWLING GREENS

Bowling was exceedingly popular in Elizabethan times and earlier, and there were many bowling alleys attached to pubs, some in the eighteenth and early nineteenth centuries becoming the focus of outdoor social gatherings. One of Worcestershire's most famous greens is at Hadley, near Ombersley, a crown or hog's-back green, dating back to 1575 at least. Membership was deemed a high privilege and in the eighteenth century included all the county families. The club was stimulated by its exclusive atmosphere, and the periodic reunions were 'prime social delights'. There was an elaborate and private code of rites and taboos, among them: 'If a member fails to pay his debts, the servant of the green shall draw him on his breeches across the green.' Swearing cost 2s per offence, the money going to the poor of the parish.

The bowling green at the Diglis Pleasure Gardens, Worcester, from an engraving c1830.

Another famous green was in Worcester, at Diglis, and was highly popular in the eighteenth century, especially at festival times; but about 1840 it came to an untimely end. After dusk members were accustomed to playing cards in the adjoining Assembly Rooms and a disagreement ended in violence — one of the members receiving a stab wound from which he died. As a result, the green was abandoned and, as was the custom in Worcester at that time, a red hand was painted on the wall as a sign that a murder had occurred there.

OLD-TIME SPORTS

The old brutal sports of the eighteenth century lingered in the Black Country long after they had gone from other parts. Harsh and brutal conditions bred hard and brutal men. 'Battles' between bulls and dogs were of a vicious and disgusting character and went on into the mid-nineteenth century. A strong stake in the ground held the bull by a chain which, being loose, permitted the animal to face an opponent from whichever side it came. The 'fancy' would assemble on their holidays with their bulldogs and pay money to let them 'have a round at the bull'. The dog, if well trained and an 'old hand' at the job, would slip under the bull's body and, passing between the front legs, would pin his nose to the ground. The infuriated beast would roar with pain. But the dogs, if inexperienced, were often maimed or killed outright. One who saw the 'sport' said: 'I've seen owners of dogs hold out their arms to catch the dogs as they came down.'

Bear-baiting, too, was popular and there was always a demand to have a 'pop at Bruin'. Although muzzled, the beast was able to inflict heavy punishment on his enemies by his claws and hugs. In 1830 an exhibition in a marl hole was being held in Brettel Lane, Stourbridge, when the stake came out and the bear was suddenly among the spectators — who beat an indecent exit. Rat-killing was another popular sport in the north of the county. The smaller the dog that could kill the greatest number of rats in the shortest time, the more highly prized he was. A tiny terrier might literally be worth his weight in gold amongst the 'fancy'. The contest took place in a rat pit constructed of thin iron bars, three to four feet in diameter and about the same height. There were many of these arenas in the Black Country towns well into this century.

COCKFIGHTING

In the early nineteenth century cock-throwing was common and practised in the schools on the day of Shrove Tuesday. At Hartlebury School and elsewhere the masters presided at the 'battle'. The cocks were tethered to stakes, or sometimes buried up to their necks, and the boys were encouraged to throw sticks at the unfortunate birds in the belief 'that he was knocking down a Frenchman!'.

Cockfighting was popular among all classes and meetings were arranged between gentlemen of adjoining counties. In 1791 Lord Plymouth of Hewell Grange, Tardebigge, in letting a farm to one, John Moore, obliged him to keep 'one dog and one cock' for his use in hunting and cockfighting. When cockfighting became illegal the methods of concealment were elaborate. A few contestants near Oldbury held their cockfight in the church; and when the Bush Hotel in Dudley was being demolished in 1929 workmen discovered at the rear of the building a secret cockfighting pit, entrance to which could could only be made via a hinged panel in the floor. The room was of good dimensions and contained pens which harboured the fighting cocks.

THE RACES

Many inns had fields or greens where regular race meetings were held. At Crowle in late Victorian times the point-to-point was based on The Chequers and became the local equivalent of the Grand National, featured in early *Punch* cartoons by Leech. At Cutnall Green race meetings were held at The Chequers where the host, Mr Trow, was blind but, it was said, could recognise a horse or dog from touch and even describe the colour. At the Camp House Inn, Grimley, the adjacent meadow was used as a racecourse and in the taproom of this fine old waterman's inn is a framed racecard of the Camp Races of 1834. The local squire, Richard Griffiths of Thorngrove, was a rich sportsman and was for years organiser and steward. When some trouble arose over the horses he ran in 1834, he withdrew his support and the races came to an end.

COUNTY CRICKET: 'FOSTERSHIRE'

In the 1840s cricket took the place of bowling as the social game and has remained the principal sport of the county. One of the earliest games recorded was between Worcestershire and Shropshire on Hartlebury Common in 1844. The home team was composed mainly of Stourbridge and Dudley club members, two of the oldest and most famous clubs in the county. In about 1850 Stourbridge boasted a team as strong as any in the Midlands, their patron being the Earl of Stamford who in 1851 was President of the MCC. Although not so strong as Stourbridge, Ombersley ranked among Worcestershire's leading clubs, with several famous players including Herbert Peel, cousin of Sir Robert. Their match with Stourbridge was looked upon as a local Derby, each side usually engaging one of the leading professionals in England for the occasion.

In 1865 the Worcestershire County Cricket Club was formed at Boughton, Worcester, an event which substantially enhanced interest in the game. Here W G Grace made his first appearance in the Midlands; though only twenty, he was already the greatest cricketer of the day. The occasion was the meeting between the twenty-two of Worcestershire and the United South of England XI. Victory went to the home team by 57 runs. W G also played for Worcestershire at Boughton in 1870 against a North of England XI when his brilliant batting was a feature of the game.

In 1896 the adaptation of three meadows off New Road, Worcester, to form the county ground — dominated by the cathedral across the Severn — gave Worcester one of the prettiest grounds in England. It had its drawbacks, however, for it was invariably flooded two or three times a year. It was quite common to go boating on it, and on one occasion a salmon (or was it a pike?) was caught from the pavilion steps. Although the ground is pretty central, there was a farm next to it (which existed until the 1960s). At the match with Derbyshire in 1899 a pig appeared and charged the umpire.

It was a time when whole families were involved in the sport. Bromsgrove School was renowned for its cricket team and the county side was often matched against them. The Hagley match of August 1867 between the school and the Lyttleton family was almost unique; eleven Lyttletons beat the Bromsgrove School XI by 41 runs:

> Collis and his crack eleven,
> Good to bat, to bowl, to fag,
> Vanquished in the strife uneven,
> Strike the ancient Bromsgrove flag.
> Sing the song of Hagley cricket,
> Come whate'er eleven may,
> Quoth the peer, 'My boys shall lick it,
> My eight boys shall win the day.'

The only other family game on record was when eleven Graces met eleven Robinsons; though later the Fosters could field a team which included a daughter.

Two of the most remarkable bowling records in this county were both made at Pershore. On 4 August 1879, in a match between Pershore Cricket Club and the Rev G Swinden's team, R T P Tearne took ten wickets for *no* runs. Dozens of men have taken all ten wickets, but none without conceding a run. On 6 July 1899 A J Coombe of Pershore Cricket Club took six wickets with consecutive balls, 'and good wickets too'.

At the turn of the century Worcestershire was aptly called 'Fostershire', for the county was enormously indebted to the sons of the Rev H Foster of Malvern College. In 1899 against Hampshire W L and R E Foster each completed two separate centuries in one match. G N and Basil Foster (the latter was on the stage) were prolific run-getters, and M K Foster only needed to get going to show that he could do as well as his elder brothers. The press of that period was well aware of the family's contribution to Worcestershire cricket and all sorts of quips and rhymes appeared:

> There was an old Foster, who lived in a Pav.,
> He had so many sons, he didn't know which to have,
> So he took 'em in turns, and from those who scored best,
> He picked his eleven, and sent home the rest.

R E Foster was the most brilliant of the brothers. He died in 1914 at the age of thirty-six of diabetes and tuberculosis. In the 1903–4 Test series in Australia – in his first Test innings – he scored 287 runs. Three times he scored two separate centuries in one match. In 1900 he scored three centuries in successive innings; and on one occasion he hit the great W G four times in succession out of the ground. He was also a highly skilled golfer and played football for England against

Scotland at Crystal Palace in 1900, playing inside-left to Fred Blackburn, the most famous footballer of the day. Before the match started the two were introduced to each other and this is Blackburn's version:

G O Smith: 'Blackburn, Mr Foster. Mr Foster, Blackburn.'
R E Foster: 'How d'y do, Blackburn.'
Blackburn: 'How d'y do, Mr Foster.'

Foster Bros cricket: R E and W L Foster leaving the field having each scored centuries in both innings against Hampshire in 1899.

After these rapid exchanges the men took their respective places and, according to Blackburn, not another word was spoken until the game was finished.

TWO GREAT ATHLETES

W G George was one of the world's greatest runners of whom more should be known. He was apprenticed to a chemist in Worcester who looked with disfavour on his involvement in any kind of sport. There were very few tracks in existence and he had to train as best he could and 'on the quiet'.

A lanky youth in his teens, W G ran his first mile race in 4 minutes 29 seconds. The world record stood then at 4 minutes 29.25 seconds and everyone wondered who the new star could be. No-one was more surprised than W G when he found himself drawing away from the rest of the competitors to win the event easily. From then on success was assured. Between 1876 and 1886 he won over a thousand prizes and his subsequent record reads like a fairytale. On two occasions he won four championships, the half-mile, mile, four-mile and the ten-mile in a single meeting! He was unbeatable.

Only one man in the world could in any way be compared with him and he was the great W Cummings who held the professional mile record for 4 minutes 16.25 seconds. Interest in these two great runners was intense, but since W G was an amateur and Cummings a professional there seemed no prospect of them ever meeting without W G losing his amateur status. So W G turned professional for no other reason than to meet Cummings. On their first meeting W G lost and Cummings beat the world record for the ten-mile. The next year they met again. Cummings was at the height of his powers. Nevertheless, it was then that W G put up his most remarkable performance and ran the mile in 4 minutes 12.75 seconds leaving Cummings in a state of collapse. It remained the world's professional record for the mile for some *forty years*.

Dudley had the world's champion standing jumper in the 1890s. *Joe Darby* held all the world records for spring jumping, only three having been beaten since they were made. Among his jumps were:

a forward spring jump of 40 foot 9 inches in 1890
a forward spring jump with weights of 12 foot 1½ inches in 1892
a backward spring jump of 12 foot 11 inches in 1891
a stand-high jump with ankles tied of 6 foot in 1892.

In 1892 he cleared a full-sized billiard table, lengthwise, at Wolverhampton for a bet of £100.

References

S OME OF THE information in this book is based on local newspaper reports, so often the only source of information about personalities and events thought in their day to be of little importance. The student of Worcestershire history is very fortunate for Worcester's newspaper publishing in the eighteenth and nineteenth centuries was unmatched by any other provincial city's. Some items have their source in the Palfrey Collection which consists of nearly 300 volumes of material dealing with local affairs, a particularly valuable collection containing cuttings from papers that have been lost or are no longer available for study. There is an identification problem, however, for some of the early volumes are undated and all are unnamed, though grouped under a general heading of, for example, *Worcesteriana, Volume 5*. The Collection is grouped under five headings — material relating to Dudley, Evesham, Kidderminster, Stourbridge and Worcester.

The following abbreviations have been used below:

Newspapers
BWJ   Berrow's Worcester Journal
CE   County Express
EJ   Evesham Journal
KS   Kidderminster Shuttle
WH   Worcester Herald

The Palfrey Collection
D   Dudliana
E   Eveshamiana
K   Kidderminsteriana
S   Stourbridgiana
W   Worcesteriana
(The number following the letter refers to the volume.)

Chapter One
Three sisters: K6 (1.8.1925); Thomas Habington *Survey of Worcestershire 1606–47*
The Forest of Wyre: Based on an article in the *Birmingham Post* 2.10.1937
The National Land Company in Worcestershire: Poem from Winifred L Bond *From Hamlet to Parish: the Story of Dodford*
The Black Country: F W Hackwood *Oldbury and Round About* (1915)
The mystery of the old county boundaries: Based on work by Professor C W Oman

Chapter Two
Augustine's Oak: WH 22.8.1903
Medieval funerals: (Prince Arthur) F T Spackman *The Ancient Monuments and Historic Buildings of Worcester* (1913)
Remember, remember, the fifth of November: WH 25.5.1909
'Tinker' Fox: K34
Captain Kidd and the Droitwich MP: W3 (4.6.1912)
The Napoleonic threat: E30
Carlyle takes the water: W28 (10.9.1927)
The elopement of the Vernon heiress: BWJ 17.1.1904
The fall of the house of Foley: WH 12.10.1907

A Victorian melodrama: *BWJ* 13.4.1901
The Gypsy Countess: The Saturday Book No 20, 1960
The MP who bought up Leicester Square: *KS* 1.11.1924
Oliver Baldwin and the gypsy: *KS* 15.9.1923

Chapter Three
The Worcestershire dialect: *BWJ* 20.2.1932; H J Massingham *Cotswold Country* (1942)
A cottage flower garden: *WH* 2.7.1904
The village water supply: Rev O G Knapp *Honeybourne 80 Years Ago*, *E25* (*EJ* 1937)
The village medical service: Rev O G Knapp *op cit*
Village trades: Rev G W Gillingham *Ombersley: An Omnibus of History and Sport* (1952); *BWJ* 26.10.1901; *EJ* 30.8.1924
The village alehouse in the seventeenth century: *E3*
The enclosures in Worcestershire: *EJ* 1.2.1913
Agricultural wages in the mid-nineteenth century: *E3*, p 113
Ploughing by oxen: *EJ* ('Notes and Queries', 1909)
Sir John Throckmorton's coat: *WH* 15.7.1911
Love haul at Chastleton: *E2*
Farmhouse fare in the 1860s: *EJ* 10.5.1924
Farm feast at Leigh: *BWJ* 1.2.1930
In the hopyards: *BWJ* 1.10.1910; *BWJ* 25.9.56
Village superstitions: *Transactions of the Worcestershire Naturalists' Club*, p 268; Rev O G Knapp *op cit*
Christmas and Twelfth-Night customs: (Ripple's holy thorn) *BWJ* 27.3.1959; (Wassailing) Edwin Lees *op cit*
Some old sayings: *EJ* 29.3.1924
Weather lore: *E3* (*EJ* 1908–9)
Herbal medicines: *E3* (E E Sutton, p 124)
Nuts and nutting: T Waldron-Bradley *BWJ* 5.11.1904

Chapter Four
Travelling the old roads: *W3* (1911)
Packhorse trails: (Bewdley) Mrs S F Parker 'Some Bewdley Recollections', *Transactions of the Worcestershire Archaeological Society*, 1944
Drovers' inns: G M Stratton *EJ* 20.6.1925
Travellers on the roads: *BWJ* 1.3.1883
Horse sense: *CE* 27.1.1934
Worcester: a railway centre: *W3* (11.6.1910)
The Birmingham and Gloucester Railway: (Big Bertha) *W61*
Railway accidents: (Hell-Fire Jack) *Worcester News & Times* 29.7.1959
Candlemaking at Evesham: *E3* (*EJ* 1913)
Old shop signs: *EJ* 22.7.1933
Three Worcester tradesmen: *WH* 25.12.1909; *BWJ* 14.6.1919; *BWJ* 11.10.1924
Victoria House: *BWJ* 3.3.1926
The Black Country in 1860: *S4* (11.9.1909)
Child labour: *KS* 17.12.1938
Butties, foggers and tommy-shops: *D27* (6.4.1953)
The lost trades of Bewdley: *K28* (16.8.1941 and 7.9.1941)
The glass trade of Stourbridge: *S14* (21.6.1919)

Chapter Five
Eighteenth-century elections: *W69* (28.1.1950)
Rival corporations and screaming women at Bewdley: *KS* 31.10.1914; *KS* 18.8.1923
County elections: 1831: *WH* 1.10.1910
Political propaganda: *The Curiosities of Dudley*, p 31
Strange election customs: J Noake *Guide to Worcestershire*; *E1* (1908–9)
A very grand jury: *WH* 6.1.1900
The last recorded 'trial by water': 'Stroller' on Redmarley D'Abitot (in the Worcester Public Library)
A Halesowen diary: *S21* (2.10.1926)
Church courts: J S Leatherbarrow, 'Churchwardens' Presentments in the Diocese of Worcester c1660–1760', *Worcestershire Historical Society Occasional Paper*
The life of a country policeman: *S1* p 43 (1905)
The old county goal: *BWJ* 24.12.1910 and *BWJ* 27.5.1911
Hangman Berry: *W56* (11.3.1939)
The Campden Wonder Case: *EJ* 4.1.1913 and 30.7.1921
The Oddingley murders: T C Turberville *Worcestershire in the Nineteenth Century* (1852)
The legend of the Besford jackboots: *EJ* 5.4.1930
The body snatchers: John Morris *EJ* 3.5.1924
The Lickey End murder 1893: *W63*

Chapter Six
A Christmas feast at the priory: Based on J Noake's transcription of the diaries of Prior More 1518–1535
Civic celebrations: *BWT* 14.11.1931
Fat bacon: *S29* (16.8.1930)
Christmas celebrations at Himley Hall 1819; *DIO* (27.12.1930)
Lamperns – Worcester's oldest industry: *BWJ* 19.12.1936
Wines and drinks of the county: *WH* 31.12.1910; *D6* (13.2.1926); *BWJ* 6.4.1901
An old-world hostelry: T H Gough *CE* 15.10.1938
A Black Country roughhouse: *Stourbridge Gazette* 30.1.1928
Feats of drinking *EJ* 11.11.1939
Worcestershire pub rhymes: Mrs Berkeley 'Some Worcestershire Inns', *BWJ* (a series from 1923–29)

Chapter Seven
A Black Country prayer: *W76* (23.10.1934)
Redstone Hermitage: *WH* 26.6.1920; *K3* (14.9.1918)
Blackstone Hermitage: Isaac Wedley *Bewdley and its Surroundings*, p 106 (1914)
Bishop Thomas and James II: *BWJ* 27.7.1935
Bishop Henry Pepys: *E26*
The 'Cow-Tail Bishop': J Randall *WH* 7.11.1908
Absentee parsons: Rev O G Knapp *op cit*
A 'Warming-Pan' parson: M Dickins *A Thousand Years of Tardebigge*
Eccentrics and reprobates: J Noake *Guide to Worcestershire*, p 316; *ibid* p 79; *ibid* p 144; 'Stroller' on Elmley Lovett; John Morris *EJ* 3.5.1924; 'Stroller' on Suckley
Parish clerks and nobblers: *Ibid*; 'Stroller' on Rushock
Church services: *K22* (19.6.1937); Rev O G Knapp *op cit*; *EJ* 24.5.1941; *Bromsgrove Messenger* 22.9.1956
Church music: 'Stroller' on Wychbold; *KS* 5.12.1936 and 19.12.1936; Rev O G Knapp *op cit*; *WH* 15.2.1896; Isaac Wedley *op cit*

Preaching through the ceiling: *SI* (8.1.1907)
Churches as charnel houses: J Noake *op cit*
Churches in ruins: J S Leatherbarrow *op cit*; *BWJ* 9.6.1900
The Gypsies' Church: *KS* 1.10.1927
What's in a name?: (Wild Rose) *BWJ* 30.6.1900
Selling and leasing: *S20*
Widows: *D5*; *WH28*: *EJ* 3.5.1924
A riotous penance: *D7* (25.6.1927)
The cost of mourning: *EJ* 28.1.1928
Mutes and mourning: Isaac Wedley *op cit*
An alarming funeral: *EJ* 3.5.1924
Strange funeral customs: J Noake *op cit*
Epitaphs: (Quick) *WH* 15.12.1906; (Hartling and Joe) *SI*; (Mr Button) *D7* (2.7.1927);
   (Miserrimus) Dr Moore Ede *Worcester Cathedral and its Monuments*
Saints and apostles: *BWJ* 15.11.1930
School for a double murder: *BWJ* 8.9.1917
The William Norris Endowed School: G Griffiths *Going to Markets and Grammar Schools*
An infant scholar: *E3*
The school inspector came: *WH* 3.12.1904
Sunday School in the 1860s: *E3*

Chapter Eight
Cropthorne Wake: G M Stratton *E3*
Bromsgrove Fair: *The Bromsgrove Messenger* 27.6.1876
Recollections of the Old Theatre Royal: *WH* 19.4.1908
The theatre at Stourbridge: The Foley scrapbooks (Worcester Record Office); *K40*
The theatre at Kidderminster: The Foley scrapbooks (Worcester Record Office)
Dover's Hill Games: G M Stratton *E3*
Spring versus Langan: *WH* 30.9.1911; *BWJ* 8.1.1924; *WH* 10.9.1910
Old-time sports: *D10*
County cricket: 'Fostershire': H E M Iceley *Bromsgrove School through Four Centuries*, p 76;
   WH 15.5.1909; *WH* 4.12.1926
Two great athletes: *BWJ* 8.9.1928

Selected Index to People and Places